FIRST EDIT
500

A
CHILD OF
ETERNITY

A CHILD OF ETERNITY

An Extraordinary Young Girl's Message from the World Beyond

ADRIANA ROCHA
and KRISTI JORDE

BALLANTINE BOOKS
New York

Copyright © 1995 by Kristi Jorde

Library of Congress Cataloging-in-Publication Data
Rocha, Adriana.
    A child of eternity : an extraordinary young girl's message from the world beyond / Adriana Rocha and Kristi Jorde.
        p.   cm.
    Includes bibliographical references.
    ISBN 0-345-38945-X
    1. Rocha, Adriana—Mental health. 2. Autistic children—United States—Biography. 3. Autistic children—Religious life—United States—Case studies. 4. Facilitated communication—Case studies.
5. Reincarnation—Biography.   I. Jorde, Kristi.   II. Title.
    RJ506.A9R627   1995
    618.92'8982'0092—dc20
    [B]   94-26633
                                                                             CIP

Book design by Ruth Kolbert

Manufactured in the United States of America

First Edition: September 1995

10 9 8 7 6 5 4 3 2 1

We Dedicate This Book to a Woman of Love,
a Spirit of Love, Coreece Fisher.

Acknowledgments

For me, this book is a manifestation of grace. There is no other explanation for how all the parts and characters could have come together how and when they did, each contributing to the unfolding drama. Personally, I feel very humbled and intensely grateful for the role in which I've been cast.

And I'm grateful, too, to so many others. Loving thanks to my parents, Jim and Joanne Jorde, and my sister and brothers, Jan, Mike, Eric, and my soul-twin, Jamie, for the lessons they've brought to me. Tender appreciation to Missy and John, my "other" children. Thank-you to Naomi and Jack, Robin, Ben, Felice, Anamika, Teddy, Virginia, Mahesh, Dr. Kitahara, Laura, Jamie W., Gloria, Julia and her family, Moo Moo, Consu, Annie, Emilce and Emmy, Ryan and Teresa, Claudia and Wei. All my love to Coreece, whose spirit lives on to inspire me, and to her family and children.

A special thank-you to Rosemary Crossley for her discovery of FC, and to Douglas Biklen and Syracuse University for their deep and tireless commitment to bringing and sustaining FC here in the United States. To Marilyn Chadwick for being Adri's first facilitator, and to Michael McSheehan, Annegret Schubert, and Renee Wilson who worked so diligently and compassionately with me in the Adriana Foundation disseminating FC.

My deep-felt appreciation to all those who shepherded this book through the publishing world: to Ned Leavitt, our talented agent, and to Ginny Faber, our editor at Ballantine, who shaped and honed this work with loving expertise. Another hug to Liz Williams and Kim Hovey, our hard-working publicity "girlfriends."

And finally, to my Colorado family, my deepest love and gratitude: to Charmaine and all the staff and parents at school, to the fifth graders, to sweet Becky, to Joan, my forever friend, to Rodrigo, my dearest husband and mirror, to Seby and Brie, the angels in my life, and to Adri, my teacher, my daughter, my love.

Not my will, but thine, be done.

Contents

Part Three

A CHILD OF ETERNITY

Foreword

Adriana Rocha is an unusually beautiful child with thick, wavy hair and enormous blue-gray eyes. Small for her age, but lithe and long-legged, she runs and climbs like an athlete. But although her body is present, her mind often seems light-years away. Because she is autistic. Adri marches to the beat of an unknown drummer attending to a world very different from our own. This book gives us a precious glimpse into that world, and into the soul of a little girl who has described herself as a "catalyst for history." When asked what she meant by that, Adri replied, "I open peoples hearts to God." And so she does. This is her story and her invitation for you to open your heart.

I first met Adri's mother and father, Kristi Jorde and Rodrigo Rocha, at a couples' week at a health spa in June of 1991. The first night of our stay we were each asked to stand up at the long, rectangular dinner table and say something about ourselves. About twenty people told a little bit of their life story, but somehow Kristi's few words remain etched on my mind like a verbal snapshot. She was standing at the far end of the table, silhouetted against a long window that overlooked the San Gabriel mountains of southern California.

Tall and thin, she stood up and pushed back her auburn hair, smiling tentatively at the assemblage of sweatsuit-clad strangers. She spoke quickly. "I am a mother of five children. Three birth children—Seby, Brie, and Adri—and two foster kids—Missy and John. I also run two foundations: the K.I.D.S. Foundation, to help birth parents develop the skills they need to bring their children out of foster care and parent successfully, and the Adriana Foundation, to educate people about autism. Our oldest child Adri, who is nine, is what they call a low-functioning autistic person. She has no language." Kristi paused to take a breath. "I'm also halfway through a master's degree in social work to help me be a more effective advocate for kids, so I really need this week just to relax."

As Kristi sat down, I thought about how challenging it had been for me raising two healthy children in the process of doctoral and postdoctoral studies at Harvard Medical School, and I felt moved by this young mother's energy and determination. Every evening after dinner we had to climb a hill and touch the "golden door" on the gate after which the spa was named. Kristi and I walked that hill together later in the week, exploring our mutual interest in healing. As a medical scientist and psychologist trained in mind-body medicine, my primary interest is in the power of the mind to heal and the nature of extraordinary human potential. I had a hunch that Kristi's long search to find healing for Adri's autism might have a lot to tell us about the nature of the human mind.

Autism is a mystery that our science still knows relatively little about. What we do know is that autistic people are not simply disabled; many are actually differently abled. While autistic people show a striking disinterest in interacting with other people, some manifest amazing mental powers. The sensitive portrayal by Dustin Hoffman of Raymond, a young autistic man in the movie *Rainman*, showed some of these remarkable abilities. Raymond, for example, was a lightning calculator. Such individuals can instantly give answers to complicated mathematical problems that would require an ordinary person hours to work out. Like Raymond, these so-called savants call upon mental pathways unavailable to most of us.

Studies conducted by Dr. Bernard Rimland of the Autism Research Institute indicate that 10 percent of autistic people are gifted savants. Some have photographic memories. After a cursory glance at a page, they have full recall of what was written. Others are musical prodigies. They can play or sing any melody perfectly after hearing it only once. Some are "calendar calculators" who can, for example, compute instantly the day of the week on which Valentine's Day will fall in 2984. Some savants show incredible athletic abilities. Like Adri, some can climb great heights without fear. Rimland cites cases of babies who were observed walking the perimeter of their cribs by balancing on the rails, or swimming proficiently at three months of age.

A small proportion of savants are reported by parents and teachers to show signs of extrasensory perception. They reliably relate incidents of which they had no knowledge, hear conversations that are definitely out of range, and respond to thoughts that have not been verbalized. Since the existence of ESP is still controversial despite excellent scientific research that proves its existence, it is quite likely that some parents simply don't notice or report their child's extrasensory capabilities. Many parents, however, have reported that their autistic children have an unusual interest in religious or spiritual matters.

Several weeks after returning to Boston, Kristi and Rodrigo invited my husband, Miron, and I to their home for dinner. When Kristi told us that Adri had some clear indications of savant skills, we were fascinated. As I mentioned earlier, Adri does not speak. But as you'll read in her story, she had begun to communicate through a process called *Facilitated Communication*, or FC, a few months before Kristi and I met. In this process, a helper (facilitator) stabilizes the autistic or otherwise talking-disabled person's arm or hand, enabling him (her) to pick out keys on a small computer. While some people need continued support, others can "be faded." In the latter case the facilitator might first need to support the person's hand, but over time can move support to the wrist, the arm, or the shoulder, until finally the person is capable of communicating unaided.

FC had been newly brought into the United States from Australia shortly before Adri was introduced to the technology and began to communicate through it. As you can imagine, parents of autistic children who neither speak nor interact in the way to which we are accustomed sometimes doubt whether anyone is "at home" inside their child's body. Kristi wept as she showed me the early communications with Adri that showed, beyond the shadow of a doubt, that a very bright little girl was present in a body she was unable to completely control.

When Adri calmly stated that her education came from past lives, Kristi, as many of us might be, was shocked and skeptical. Throughout Kristi's experience with Adri, and often in this book, she questions whether Adri's words might actually stem from her own unconscious. Since she was helping Adri type could she, or the other people who have acted as Adri's facilitators, be influencing her communications? Some experiments with FC have shown just that. These experiments, however, cannot explain how some people who at first need facilitators can eventually type on their own, communicating in the same way they did before.

Adri often looks away from the keyboard as she types. When asked how she can do that, she says that she sees the letters in her mind. While this may not be possible for a nonautistic person, it is perfectly in line with some of the unusual capacities of autistic people. If you saw the movie *Rainman*, for example, you might remember the scene in which Raymond correctly counts about two hundred matches as they fall from a box onto the floor. There are clearly modes of perception beyond what our usual five senses can provide.

Adri's story is a definite challenge to go beyond our usual perception. Whether or not the communications come from Adri, from Kristi, or are in some way a product of the unique way in which their two minds meet, they have the power to touch your heart and change the way that you look at the world.

In the three years that I have known Adri, I feel that she has certainly facilitated my own process, caused me to question what I believe, and beyond that, to press beyond belief and opinion into a more disciplined spiritual practice. Adri tells us that when we open our hearts to God, help is always available to us from the unseen world. She asks us to get in touch with our guides, what some of us might think of as guardian angels. What Adri asks is not fanciful, but practical. At times she has chastised her mother relentlessly.

We are here to love one another, she says. This same message is at the core of every religious tradition. It is also the primary message of the near-death experience (NDE)—a phenomenon that many people find deeply inspiring. I had the privilege of cofounding and then directing a mind-body clinic at one of the Harvard Medical School teaching hospitals from 1981 to 1988. During that time I saw many patients with cancer, AIDS, and other life-challenging illnesses. Many of those patients told me of their death experiences or the pre-death visions. The message was the same one that Adri so eloquently delivers. The earth is a kind of classroom in which we gain knowledge and learn how to love.

Adri's communications have an urgency about them, as do many of the messages brought back from the Other Side during NDEs. We do, indeed, seem to be poised at a threshold. For the first time in recorded history, we have the potential to destroy ourselves—not only through nuclear arms, but through the slow but sure destruction of the earth in the name of progress. And for the first time in recorded history, people seem to be undergoing a wholesale spiritual awakening. More than one in twenty Americans has had a near-death experience. A third report transcendent visions. Two-thirds report experiences of ESP, and about the same percentage reports contact with the dead. It is, as has been written, the best of times and the worst of times.

For Adri, too, this life seems a combination of the best and the worst. On the one hand, she appears to be in constant communion with a brighter, more loving, wiser world than this. On the other hand, she is locked into an autistic body. She seems a wise woman in the broken body of an autistic child, perhaps more than anything else.

Adri gives us the message that spirituality is not about perfection. Life is inevitably filled with challenges, doubts, pain, and disappointments. Perhaps without these difficulties, we would never really learn to love.

In reflecting on Adri's life, I have found much comfort in the story that one woman, "Martha," related to me about her near-death experience. She "died" during a car crash and had the typical experience of leaving her body and finding herself in the presence of a Supreme Being of Light who radiated absolute love, forgiveness, and wisdom. Many people who have NDEs report that this Being of Light gives them a choice about whether to return to life on earth or continue on in the soul's journey. Most people who choose to return do so either because they want to raise their children or because they have become aware that they have a particular mission or purpose in this life that has not yet been completed. Martha reported that the Being of Light gave her three choices. She could continue on into the Other Side, return to life with minor injuries, or return in a vegetative state. When I asked whether she might have chosen the latter, her response was an unqualified yes. Martha explained that while present in the Divine Light of the NDE, she understood that the most important thing was learning to love. If, through her returning in a vegetative state, the hearts of her family and friends might have been opened, she would gladly have taken on that mission. Since that was not to be the case (a fact that was revealed when the Being of Light showed her a life review of her loved ones run from the perspective of her remaining in a long coma), she chose to return with minor injuries.

I can only speculate that Adri's autism is a spiritual mission, a soul contract that she made, to open people's hearts to themselves, to one another, and to God. May this book be a comfort and a spiritual awakening for you. If it is, pass it along to your friends. Together, we can make a difference in this pivotal time.

—JOAN BORYSENKO, PH.D.

Part One

THE
*B*EGINNING

Chapter 1

ADRIANA ARRIVES

I first met my oldest daughter early one April morning in 1981. I was twenty-five and living in New York City. My boyfriend, Rodrigo, and I had stopped by a drugstore the night before and, with feigned nonchalance, picked up a home pregnancy test. For the previous two weeks we'd been talking around the possibility—"What if it's true?" or "What would we do?" It was light banter, not because the idea was unimportant but because, on an unacknowledged, unspoken level, it was so very important.

Within weeks of our first meeting nine months before, Rodrigo had begun talking about getting married. We'd been dating for about five months when the lease on my too-small, too-expensive efficiency apartment came up, and though I wasn't ready for marriage, I liked the idea of living together. So in January 1981 I moved into what I called Rodrigo's "brown" apartment. The sofa was brown, the walls were a lighter brown, the bedspread was brown, the table, the chairs, the carpet, even the view of East Seventy-first Street was brown. It was perfect for hibernation.

I slept fitfully that night. Rodrigo was on one side of me, the pregnancy test on the other. I wasn't sure what made me more nervous—the possibility of being pregnant or of not being pregnant. Wanting a baby was an inadmissible desire, like eating forbidden fruit. I wasn't married. I wasn't even sure I wanted to be married. And most significant of all, at twenty-five I was barely beginning a career, while Rodrigo, who was thirty-six, was already confidently manning the helm of his own insurance business.

Since graduating from Stanford University in December 1977, I'd moved to New York and become an assistant buyer at Saks Fifth Avenue. I had what I thought I wanted—a career in fashion and a fast track to the top of the corporate ladder. Still, by this fateful April morning, what I could see of the top had begun to look more bureaucratic and less appealing each day.

At dawn I slipped out of bed, kit in hand, and tiptoed to the bathroom. With painstaking care I measured, mixed, corked, and shook the test tube exactly as instructed, then placed it gently in the stand. I went into the living room and sat down on the brown sofa, thoughts drifting through my mind. My father was a successful farmer in North Dakota, a self-made man, and achievement was highly valued in our home. If I were pregnant, both he and my mother would certainly be disappointed. Of their five children I was the one who zipped to the forefront, the fearless leader, the creator of action and excitement. What if I were to settle for being "just" a mom? And what about Rodrigo's parents in Mexico? We'd visited his family there a couple of times. Although Rodrigo's father was unfailingly polite, I always came away with the strong impression that he found me an unsuitable match for his son. I had no particular wealth or lineage—an old-fashioned concept, but one that still carried weight in the Rocha patriarchy.

I glanced at my watch. It was time. I felt a moment of panic—I wasn't ready to be a mother, I didn't feel worthy. Nevertheless I resolved, if fate were to so grace me, I would rise to the occasion and graciously and gratefully accept this new responsibility. If not, then so be it. I'd swallow my disappointment and get on with my life. Like a child I closed my eyes and took a deep breath. Ready, set, look. There it was, the circle of life. The baby existed. I ran into the bedroom smiling broadly, and when Rodrigo saw me, he knew. Holding me close, he whispered, "Let's get married."

I toyed with the idea of single motherhood for a good week at least. I envisioned myself, infant in tow, proudly, confidently, courageously forging our path together. But it didn't take long for my Joan of Arc persona to begin to crumble. I was almost three months pregnant, and I realized that I really did want a mate with whom I could share both the joy and the responsibility of this new being. Finally I decided consciously what I'd probably decided deep down the first moment I suspected I was pregnant. When I finally told Rodrigo, "I think we should get married after all," he was more delighted than surprised.

From that moment things moved quickly. An obstetrician confirmed the pregnancy and gave us our due date, December 15th. Not wanting my "out of wedlock" pregnancy to be the subject of coffee-time gossip, I gave my boss two weeks' notice. Consulting Rodrigo's calendar and a map of the United States, we settled on Lake Tahoe, June 4, 1981.

I wanted to get married quickly without families or fanfare. I didn't want a church ceremony. In my Lutheran upbringing I'd considered the church relatively innocuous, a kind of stage for social gatherings. But over the years, as I was exposed to a greater range of religions, including the intimidation methods of religious conversion, I'd begun to suspect it was little more than a culturally sanctioned forum for power seekers, a trap for the weak, and a haven for hypocrites. Although I liked the idea of a personal God, I'd never found enough evidence to support the belief in my own life. Rodrigo, though still quietly loyal to the traditions, was basically a nonpracticing Catholic.

In Lake Tahoe I came upon an advertisement for a small, charming, historical chapel that billed itself as the ideal setting for weddings. Rodrigo booked a time, and on the morning of June 4th a limousine arrived to drive us to the chapel. I was wearing a blue peasant-style blouse and skirt that I'd bought in Mexico, complete with a pin to hold the waist together, as I could no longer button it. The airlines had lost Rodrigo's luggage, so he was wearing the sports jacket he'd come in and a pair of trousers we'd scavenged from the hotel gift shop.

The driver pulled up to the address, and at first glance it did seem to be idyllic. Walking along a dusty path, we passed several picturesque log buildings. But things swiftly turned from picturesque to bizarre when we came upon several horses, both live and wooden, tied to hitching posts. Men in ten-gallon hats and cowboy boots, and women in long red-and-white checked gingham dresses, greeted us along the way. Strange, yes. But it wasn't until we met the "minister," also attired in boots, hat, and kerchief, that we finally realized that this "historical chapel" was actually a leftover set from the old *Bonanza* TV show. Our wedding may have been prompted by an unplanned pregnancy, but it was not pretend. Making our excuses, we backed down the aisle and out the door.

Six tacky chapels later, at the "Chapel of Love," we finally found a justice of the peace, who drove us to a magical spot. Rodrigo and I stood beside each other against a backdrop of the setting sun blazing across Lake Tahoe. Our driver picked some flowers, presented them to me, and then served as our witness. It was a simple but beautiful ceremony. Finally, tired but happy, Rodrigo, the baby, and I became, in the words of the slightly sauced justice, "one."

After spending a quiet honeymoon week in Lake Tahoe, we flew back East and rented a house in Greenwich, Connecticut. I made a few neighborhood friends, and occasionally one of Rodrigo's business associates would come over for a cookout. But most of my time was spent at home getting ready for the baby. The nursery already had pastel baby curtains, but they looked insipid to me. I wanted my baby surrounded by bright, cheerful primary colors. Thinking that it would be easier, cheaper, and more fun than buying new curtains, Rodrigo and I bought red fabric paint. Sitting together in the evenings and on weekends, we painstakingly painted every pink petal of those all-over-floral-design curtains bright red. It took a lot of time, but to us it felt like a way to connect with this new being, an act of love.

In the fall we faithfully attended weekly Lamaze classes. At night we talked about what to name the baby. Unable to decide, we each made a list of all the names we liked, exchanged them, crossed off the names we didn't like from each other's list, and finally agreed—on a girl's name. My plan was to have the baby, stay home nursing and caring for him or her for some time, and then return to my career in fashion. But I wasn't in any hurry. I liked being pregnant. I felt content and at peace. My life was, I thought, in order.

On December 8, 1981, around six A.M. a sharp and painful contraction awakened me. I had been warned to anticipate a long labor this first time, so I stoically told Rodrigo to go ahead and take the train to work. The contractions continued throughout the morning, infrequent and irregular, but getting stronger. About ten-thirty A.M., I phoned my doctor to ask whether I should come in. I'd chosen her with great care, partly because she assured me that, barring a natural disaster, she'd be there in person to deliver the baby. I'd considered homebirthing and midwives, but both options seemed a little too daring for us.

Slowly I drove to the doctor's office. She examined me and then promptly sent me home, telling me not to expect the baby until the following day. I felt almost embarrassed. Here I was, barely in labor and already complaining. Was I one of those weak, whiny women incapable of tolerating a little discomfort? I decided to keep doing my breathing exercises and to try to ignore my contractions.

Rodrigo arrived home shortly after I did. Seeing me, wrenched over, he wasn't so convinced that this was ignorable pain. By five o'clock the pain was more powerful than my ego, so I allowed Rodrigo to take me to the hospital. There I was told to expect an overnight labor and, when I didn't want to return home, was reluctantly admitted. That night a full moon hovered overhead—infamous for heralding births. It turned out to be serendipitous that I'd arrived early, because within hours the maternity ward was full to overflowing. Women were laboring in beds lining the hallways, and nurses and doctors were in short supply.

I was feeling anxious and jittery; the contractions were centered in my lower back. Anticipating that things would get worse as the night wore on, I begged Rodrigo to find a nurse or doctor. He was told there were none available but that our own doctor was expected to check in soon. Not long after that, much to my surprise, I suddenly felt an intense urge to push. My Lamaze training had taught me not to push without a doctor's orders, so, once again, I desperately sent Rodrigo out for help. While he was gone, I experienced another sharp contraction. I heard myself hollering for help, but to no avail. My voice simply blended in with the rest of the laboring cacophony.

Finally Rodrigo laid claim to a nurse who, after examining me briefly, ran out to call a doctor. Within a few minutes she returned to tell me that the hospital had located a doctor at a nearby cocktail party and he was on his way. What about my own doctor, I asked, where was she? It turned out that she was unreachable in a nearby town, testifying, ironically enough, at a hearing on the responsibility of doctors to be present during a patient's last stage of labor. This baby was not about to wait for her conclusions. Ten minutes later the doctor rushed into my room, took a quick look at me, and threw off his jacket. They loaded me onto a gurney and wheeled me down the hall to the operating room—there I was finally allowed to push. Within minutes I heard my baby's first cry. Then someone said, "Oh, what a beautiful girl." Rodrigo grabbed my hand. We had a new baby daughter.

Adriana Noelle Rocha was tiny—five pounds fifteen ounces. But she was healthy. Her Apgar scores were normal and she looked absolutely perfect. She had fine hair covering her little head, and her face was smooth and evenly colored, not red and bruised like some newborns. The doctor laid her on my chest, and I held her close, reluctant to let go. Rodrigo stood beside me, alternately stroking my head and hers. I was exhausted, exhilarated, and completely awestruck. How could this extraordinary being have come from Rodrigo and me? How had we earned the right to such a miracle? I had occasionally wondered, during the pregnancy, if I could love anyone, even my own child, so much that I'd be willing to sacrifice my life for theirs. It wasn't until that moment, as Adri and I lay there heart to heart, that I fully understood the power of love. I knew I'd die for her in a minute.

Hospital policy dictated that they take Adri away to the nursery and, not knowing any better, I let them. She was brought into my room around eleven P.M., and then I didn't see her again till early the next morning when it was time for us to nurse. I was eager to begin breast-feeding, but from the very beginning Adri and I struggled with it. Even when I could get her into a good position, she barely sucked.

Because the nurses felt she needed more fluids, they started giving her sugar water from a bottle. After that, although we continued trying to nurse, we made even less progress. I wanted her to breast-feed, but I wanted her to get sustenance even more. So I started giving her the bottle too. But even from the bottle she nursed very little, barely an ounce at a time. It didn't seem like enough, but since neither the doctor nor the nurses seemed concerned, I figured it must be.

Hospital checkout was scheduled for December 12th. But that morning Adri woke up jaundiced. Her bilirubin count rose steadily throughout the day, and although both the pediatrician and the nurses assured me that jaundice was common in newborns, perfectly treatable and not dangerous, I was scared and upset. I longed to be at home with my new baby daughter.

When her count continued to rise the next day, the doctors recommended treatment. I watched tearfully as Adri was taken from her little bed beside me and put into the lighted nursery incubator. No longer could I pick her up at will. Now I had to wait for those appointed few minutes a day to hold her. Even now I can picture her, helpless and alone, untouchable, unreachable in that brightly lit glass cocoon. It was two long days until her bilirubin levels finally returned to normal and the doctor said I could take her home.

That morning Rodrigo and I bundled Adri into the tiny red knit suit with white fur trim that we'd bought for just this occasion some months before. Though the suit was small enough to fit a doll, Adri still swam in it. I sat in the wheelchair, Adri in my lap with only her little face peeking out, as the nurse wheeled us to freedom. It was a cold day in Greenwich, but the sun was shining brightly as we joyfully strapped our adorable new daughter into her car seat for the short ride home.

Chapter 2

SHIFTING SANDS

During those first few days at home Adri spent much of her time sleeping, and Rodrigo and I spent much of ours hovering admiringly over her, eager and willing servants of this tiny new enchantress. Trying to understand her ways, we were like most new parents, overly careful, holding her as if she might break at the slightest jostle, and clumsy in our efforts to bathe her or change her diapers. But it wasn't long before we felt as if this child in our midst had always been there, an intrinsic part of our lives.

Since I was no longer trying to nurse, Rodrigo and I took turns feeding Adri every two hours or so. We were still using the small four-ounce bottles, but even so, Adri never took more than half a bottle at a feeding. The doctors hadn't seemed concerned, so I tried not to let it worry me.

Doctors should know, I reassured myself. A few days later my mother came from Arizona to stay with us, and Rodrigo went back to work.

During the day Mom and I relaxed around the house, napping when Adri did. Nights, however, were rarely so restful. I'd usually begin to feed and rock Adri about eight o'clock. It might take an hour, but finally she would drift off to sleep. Then I would slowly and carefully rise from the rocker and begin to lift her over the side of the crib. But no matter how deeply asleep she seemed to be, the movement would wake her and we'd have to start all over again. Each time she woke up to be fed, the ritual had to be repeated. In those first months I learned to walk and even crawl across her floor with stealth, holding my breath, praying I wouldn't disturb her.

There was something else that worried me too. I'd look in on Adri often as she slept, sometimes placing my hand just inches from her mouth to make certain she was breathing, she was lying so still. Then I'd fall back into bed, relieved that she was all right. It might be moments, it might be hours later, but suddenly, out of nowhere, a shrill and piercing scream would startle us all out of sleep. Rodrigo or me or my mother—or all three of us—would leap from our beds, our hearts pounding, race to her crib, and scoop her up. We'd check her over, looking through her crib and around her room, but nothing was ever amiss.

I would pace the room holding Adri over my shoulder or cradling her in my arms as she cried. I could feel her anguish and I tried my best to console her, to communicate my love to her, to bear some of that pain. Rarely, however, could I comfort her. Most of the time she seemed oblivious of my presence, alone in her nightmare, until finally, exhausted, she would fall back to sleep. Then I'd gaze down at her face, peaceful at last, and breathe a long sigh of relief.

After a week my mother returned to Arizona to celebrate the holidays with my dad and brothers. We enjoyed our first Christmas as a family. We festively decorated a big tree and wrapped packages. Rodrigo and I bought Adri toys, clothes, and even books. On Christmas Eve we delighted in opening them all. Adri was three weeks old. Holding her in my arms, feeding her only ounces at a time, and anticipating a sleepless night, I couldn't help but feel a twinge of concern. But, intent on a merry Christmas, I brushed it aside.

Shortly after Christmas Rodrigo's mother died unexpectedly following an emergency appendectomy. Rodrigo made plans to leave for Mexico immediately. I was tired and didn't relish taking a three-week-old infant on such a long trip. But I kept my complaints to myself. Under the circumstances a whiny wife was the last thing Rodrigo needed.

At Rodrigo's father's house Adri and I mingled some with the streams of people coming through to pay their respects to Rodrigo's mother. Mostly, though, we stayed in our bedroom. Rodrigo urged me to let the maids care for Adri, but I was leery about leaving her with people I didn't know. And to tell the truth, caring for Adri gave me an excuse not to linger for hours with strangers whose language I didn't speak. After three long days, we returned home.

Our routine was soon reestablished, and Adri's appetite improved. But she also began to experience crying episodes that seemed to be related to problems with digestion. Rodrigo and I would lay her on her back and move her little knees in and out to ease the cramping. We tried all kinds of positions, hoping to make her more comfortable. As soon as she was able to hold her head up, we began putting her in a windup baby swing, supported by pillows on all sides. She loved it. The rocking motion of the swing often soothed her when all human touch failed. Eventually things improved when our pediatrician suggested that we switch her to a soy-based formula.

On Easter Sunday, giving in to tradition, we took Adri

to church for the first time. There we ran into friends of ours. They'd brought their son who, although only two months older than Adri, seemed much more advanced. He was about twice as big as she was and held his bottle confidently, swigging down its contents without pause. He also interacted with the people around him, coquettishly responding to their baby talk and actively trying to catch their attention.

This was so unlike Adri, who tended to stare fixedly into people's faces. Adults would return her gaze for a moment, then turn quickly away, uncomfortable under the scrutiny. Sometimes they would comment to me about her "obvious" intelligence. Although I liked that explanation, Rodrigo and I still couldn't help but be struck by the contrast between Adri and my friend's baby. It was hard to imagine that in just two months she could develop the kind of maturity and autonomy he seemed to have.

That summer, when Adri was about seven months old, we hired a wonderful grandmotherly woman to help clean and baby-sit. Adri was now mobile, but rather than doing a "proper" crawl, she'd sit on her rear and use her hands to push her body forward. Quite proficient at this mode of transportation, she was able to scoot around quickly.

With child care taken care of, I decided it was time to return to work. I accepted a position at Calvin Klein, Ltd., selling his designer clothes to retailers. Rodrigo and I also decided that if we were both going to be working in the city again, it would be easier to live there. In New York, we reasoned, Adri would have access to incomparable cultural advantages. We rented a place, and that fall we moved in, delighted to be back.

At twelve months, though not yet trying to walk, Adri was very active. She was a master of negotiating stairs and was able to pull herself up and stand as long as she held on to something for support. Her motor development seemed a bit on the slow side, but I wasn't nearly as concerned about that as I was about her continuing lack of interest in people and in her environment.

For her first birthday I invited several toddlers and their mothers to lunch. Wearing her party hat, Adri presided over the table, but in contrast to the other children she didn't really participate in the festivities. She didn't try, as they did, to enter into our adult conversations by gesturing or babbling, nor did she show much interest in their attention-getting antics. Instead she amused herself by picking up her food and dropping it on the floor. I'd chastise her and hold on to her hand, but as soon as I let go, she'd start right in again. When one of the other children tried the same thing and was scolded by his mother, he stopped immediately.

By fifteen months Adri was still not walking, nor was she babbling as much as other toddlers. If I said her name, in a rare instance she might turn toward me. But more often than not she simply carried on with her own activity and ignored me. We wondered if she had a hearing problem. But that didn't make sense because sometimes she turned toward sounds, and almost always she responded to music. Could she understand her own name? Did she recognize it? We weren't sure.

With toys, too, Adri was unpredictable. A new toy might interest her, or she might never even look at it. After a time we learned that if we wanted to engage her attention, we had to buy toys that made noise or, even better, ones that had spinning parts. Adri would never "drive" a toy car, she only spun its wheels over and over, enraptured and totally immersed in the experience, giggling and bouncing with excitement.

At each visit to the pediatrician I would ask about her limited sound making, her "odd" play habits, her inconsistent or nonexistent response to sounds. In my heart I suspected that something was wrong. Yet I suppressed that knowing, relieved to be told each time that I need not worry, that all children develop at their own pace. And, too, although the differences between Adri and other toddlers became more pronounced every day, just when I'd become convinced that I had to insist on some type of developmental assessment, she'd surprise me by responding to a request or by playing appropriately with a toy for a moment or two. I'd tuck my anxiety away again and wonder if I was just being an overzealous mom.

Around this time I took Adri for an "interview" at our neighborhood Montessori school. Although I felt the idea of "interviewing" toddlers was ridiculous, I was still nervous. This was partly because I knew how difficult it was to get into a New York preschool, and partly because I also knew that Adri was unlikely even to react to the interviewer's questions, much less respond appropriately. As Adri crawled around, exploring the room, I sat on the edge of my chair, crossing my fingers and trying to appear nonchalant. The director talked mostly to me, watching Adri out of the corner of her eye. Occasionally she'd address Adri directly. Luckily she didn't expect an answer.

Toward the end of the interview, just when I thought we'd made it, the director suddenly turned to Adri and said, "Adri, can you please bring me your jacket?" There was a moment of expectant silence while the interviewer waited for a response. Not surprisingly Adri ignored her completely. That's it, I thought to myself, we're out. Then the director repeated her request. After a few moments, to my complete surprise, Adri suddenly stopped playing, picked up her hat, and crawled over with it to the interviewer. It wasn't quite what she'd been asked to do, but I was still very impressed. The lady accepted the hat with a smile. I was beaming on the outside and cheering on the inside. Adri was accepted into the school for fall.

At sixteen months, almost as if she knew it was her last chance to make the charts, Adri began to walk perfectly. And as soon as she began walking, she also started dancing to all kinds of music. During the spring and summer weekends Rodrigo, Adri, and I took car trips exploring the countryside. We went to county fairs, farms, zoos, and children's concerts. If there was music, Adri would always stand as close to the performers as she could, rocking from foot to foot, swaying with the rhythm. With her short golden curls, her tiny wiry body, and her rapturous smile, she was a charming sight. People would gather to watch her, delighting in her delight. Of course, when anyone tried to talk to her, she ignored them. But she was small and adorable, so people took it in stride, laughing and commenting about how very busy she seemed to be. I laughed nervously along with them.

At a picnic when Adri was about eighteen months, I watched as a mother asked her toddler to bring her the salt. The child looked at her mother, then went over and picked up the salt shaker and brought it to her. I was dumbfounded. Was it really normal for a child of this age to understand and carry out such a complex activity? I asked the mother how old this genius was. "Fifteen months," she told me. I nearly started to cry. I looked over at Adri, wandering beside the tree, touching it, tapping on the ground, lost in a world that seemed without meaning or purpose. She was light-years away from delivering a salt shaker. I felt frightened for her. Physically she was so beautiful, so perfect. What was going on here? What was wrong with her? Or with me? Or with us?

I felt Adri knew that Rodrigo and I were her parents, or at least special people in her life. We were often treated to warm, bright smiles and outstretched, welcoming arms. Yet at the same time Adri never cried when either of us left her. From the time she was very small, she was smiling, happy to be in the arms of whoever was holding her. When Rodrigo and I left for an hour, a day, or a week, Adri smiled as we left and she was still smiling when we returned.

I was Adri's mother, but I didn't really know what that

meant. Adri never came running to me with hurts or pains. In fact she rarely seemed to have any. And although she was usually smiling and cheerful, she didn't respond much when I tried to play with her. Sometimes in an unguarded moment, as I looked at other mothers who, though tired and complaining, still basked in the love and adoration of their children, I realized that for me motherhood didn't seem as rewarding as it was for them. But whenever those feelings came up, I'd quickly shake them off. What right, I asked myself, did I have to expect more from Adri? Did I think my child had some obligation to satisfy my needs? It was easier to blame myself than to consider the possibility that something might be very wrong with Adri.

In the fall of 1983 Adri started attending the morning Montessori program. I was relieved to have her in school, comforted by the illusion that because she was going to a normal school, she must be normal. And I kept myself busy, too busy to dwell on her development—or lack of it.

Rodrigo was busy, too, working long hours and traveling. At home we talked about his business or about how beautiful and wonderful Adri was. But whenever I tried to share my concern about her with him, he'd dismiss it. He simply couldn't see what I was worried about, particularly given the pediatrician's assurances. Besides, he reminded me, we had a precedent—he hadn't talked, either, until he was almost five. She'd catch up.

Chapter 3

HELP FROM HELL

At the age of two Adri seemed to reach a plateau. Her vocabulary consisted of four words: *Mama, Dada, bye-bye,* and *all done.* On one rare occasion, when Rodrigo was reading to her from an animal book, she repeated the word *tiger.* We were elated. But our excitement was short-lived. Adri never said the word again.

In school, with much repetition and prompting, she had managed to learn the daily routine: getting out her mat, choosing an activity, returning the activity to its place, selecting something else to do. She did not, however, progress in her use of the developmentally designed Montessori materials. Still, her teacher was not yet ready to suggest there might be a problem. In November Adri tested below normal in a school-sponsored routine speech-and-language screening. Hesitant to draw conclusions, the team simply recommended that she be retested in the spring.

Adri loved to swing, so Rodrigo and I often took her to the playground near our home. As we pushed her, she would lean back as far as possible, laughing with glee. The higher she went, the happier she was. But while other children were learning how to pump to keep themselves swinging, Adri didn't, or couldn't, learn despite all our efforts. When we weren't swinging, youngsters would sometimes try to engage Adri in play, chasing her around the yard or climbing into the sandbox after her. As usual Adri ignored them.

I found myself beginning to create a subtle distance around us whenever we went to the playground, perhaps when we went anywhere. I didn't want to pretend that I couldn't see the sidelong glances of the other mothers. I didn't want to get into conversations with them and have to try to explain why she was so aloof, why she couldn't talk, or why she didn't play. How could I explain? I didn't even know myself.

For Adri's second birthday Rodrigo and I bought her a baby doll. We didn't expect her to do anything with it—after all, it didn't spin or make noise. In fact it was more for me than for her. I just wanted her to have the baby doll. My older sister, Jan, was visiting us from California, and all of us were sitting around a table at a friend's house. Feeling almost selfish that we'd gotten her a present she wouldn't like, I handed her the package and helped her take the paper off. For a moment she just stared at the doll. Then she picked it up, and instead of dropping it on the floor or twirling it around, she pulled it close to her heart. I watched, mesmerized, as she got up and walked slowly around the table, hugging her baby. My sister and I exchanged glances, tears in both our eyes. Jan felt it too, Adri was connecting with us, with our world. But then she dropped it, and never picked it up again.

The Montessori school sponsored a second speech-and-language evaluation in April 1984. Again their results were inconclusive, but this time they recommended that we have Adri's hearing tested. These tests came out normal. With nowhere else to go, I returned to Adri's pediatrician for help. Finally acknowledging that there might be a problem, he referred us to a psychologist for further evaluation.

When Adri and I went to that appointment a couple of weeks later, I didn't have the slightest idea what to expect. But the psychologist's kind smile and warm manner quickly put me at ease. She and I sat down. Adri went over to some toys in the corner of the room, picked something up, and began to bang it on the floor. I wasn't sure what to do. Was I supposed to go with Adri? Should I stop her from doing that? Or was that what the therapist wanted to see, Adri's normal style of play? I looked at her questioningly. She smiled, explaining that Adri was free to play as she wished. As we talked, she kept an eye on Adri. It was such a good visit, such a relief to be able to express my concerns about Adri. And it was such a relief to be in a place where her behavior was accepted, where I didn't have to stay on top of her.

Adri and I visited the psychologist three times. Though I would have liked her to see that with encouragement Adri was sometimes capable of more complex play, I held back, convinced that she wanted to see Adri engaged in her own natural style of play. By our last visit, although I still didn't know what conclusions she'd drawn, I'd begun to feel as if the psychologist and I shared a camaraderie, a partnership aimed at understanding and helping Adri. I was almost sorry to see it end.

As I left her office that last morning, she handed me the bill to submit to our insurance company. I casually scanned it, noticing nothing unusual, until I came to the last page. There, after the word *Diagnosis*, were the boldly typed words *PARENT-CHILD PROBLEM.* I was completely shocked. The psychologist had never even intimated that she thought I was the problem. Quickly glancing through the rest of her comments, I gathered that the supporting evidence for her diagnosis was the aloof, noninteractive style of behavior that I had exhibited toward Adri in our sessions. I felt devastated, betrayed. She hadn't been trying to help me help Adri. Instead all this time she'd been gathering evidence to indict me.

Though part of me rebelled against the diagnosis, another part felt very guilty, like a criminal finally brought to justice. Somebody had seen through me, had seen what a bad mother I really was. Bad enough to hurt, to almost destroy the person I loved most in the world. It felt like a death sentence.

I had expected to be a normal mother, to bear a normal child. I'd even considered myself an enlightened parent. Before giving birth I had resolved not to burden my child with excessive expectations. She or he would be free to follow his or her own path, whether it be Ivy League or bohemian. What I had failed to consider, however, was the possibility that I might not have the opportunity to be so magnanimous. It didn't occur to me that I might bear a child who was not only ineligible for Harvard but ineligible for kindergarten. Nor did it ever occur to me that I might be the cause of her suffering. Overnight my world turned from black and white to gray.

Unlike me Rodrigo was simply outraged by the psychologist's report. I was very relieved that he didn't agree with her, but his response wasn't much help to me as I struggled in my guilt, pain, and confusion. The psychologist recommended that I start therapy with her, but that was the farthest thing from my mind. When Rodrigo suggested that this might be a good time for us to follow his business interests to California, something we'd been talking about for several months, I quickly agreed.

So, in the summer of 1984 Rodrigo flew to Los Angeles

to rent a house. I wanted to get as far away from New York as I could. But I wasn't sure about anything else—not my own feelings, not my ability to mother, not even my marriage. Our baby-sitter was unable to move with us, so I hastily hired a new one. Although this must have been hard on Adri, she gave no indication that she knew we were moving, much less that her old friend wouldn't be going with us. I was under such pressure, such stress, that all I really wanted was to be by myself for a while. Yet how could I leave Adri? Finally, confused and desperate but still unable to justify taking time alone, I sent the new baby-sitter; Adri; Kathy, who was Rodrigo's secretary and my best friend; and her three-year-old daughter, Rae Lynn, to California while I stayed in New York for two weeks, ostensibly clearing up our personal business.

I called daily. Kathy said that Adri was doing fine, although she didn't seem her usual cheerful self. Adri was healthy, that's all I chose to hear. But when I finally saw her two weeks later, I just started to cry. I had sent a lively, almost too lively, smiling, noisy toddler to Los Angeles. The child I found was disheveled, listless, and silent. I was horrified and angry with both myself and the psychologist. I'd been away from Adri before, but at least I'd always had the sense to leave her in her own home with a familiar and beloved caretaker. Before those sessions with the psychologist I would never have sent my two-and-a-half-year-old daughter off with strangers to a new and unfamiliar place. To Adri my absence must have felt like an eternity.

Chapter 4

CALIFORNIA

Fortunately once we were together, Adri's spirits brightened, and within a few days she seemed to be back to her old self. Although I wouldn't have intentionally hurt her for the world, I did learn something invaluable from our separation. I discovered that I was important to Adri, that my daughter loved me and needed me even though she couldn't always show it. It was a hard-won lesson, but it meant a lot to me.

In Los Angeles Rodrigo had to be up each morning at four-thirty to get to his office before the bond market opened. Between his work and his traveling he was away from us much of the time. But Adri and I enjoyed being together. We spent our days swimming, playing in our new garden, and reveling in the warmth and beauty of southern

California. Not surprisingly, the baby-sitter I'd so hastily hired in New York didn't work out so after she left, my twenty-year-old cousin, Julie, came to stay with us for a while. We became an amicable house of women—Kathy, Julie, me, Adri, and Rae Lynn, sharing work, laughter, and tears.

Not long after we arrived, I discovered that Los Angeles was the home of one of the most renowned neurological diagnostic centers in the world—the Neuropsychiatric Institute (NPI). I immediately set up an appointment for the first available slot. I also found a new pediatrician and began to search for an appropriate school, one that would nurture Adri and provide the kind of individual attention she needed. I wasn't sure what to tell prospective schools. I certainly didn't want to share the New York psychologist's diagnosis. No, here in California, we'd start fresh. Let the experts at NPI draw their own conclusions.

Midsummer marked the beginning of what proved to be a two-year stint of appointments with NPI. Over the first several months Adri was sent for various speech and language evaluations. Nevertheless, while the reports I received at the end of that process described Adri's developmental difficulties quite well, they never actually came up with a diagnosis. And by this time, although we encouraged and created opportunities for Adri to use the three or four words in her vocabulary, even those had pretty much disappeared from use.

After the first round of evaluations NPI recommended speech therapy. So Adri began attending weekly sessions geared toward helping her master such developmental tasks as pointing to things or demonstrating that she understood cause and effect. Sometimes I sat in on the sessions, other times I simply observed through a one-way mirror. Adri's speech therapist was very enthusiastic, so even though Adri seemed to watch more than she participated, she still seemed to enjoy the sessions. But then, every once in a while, she'd startle us both by suddenly pointing correctly or pushing the right button. It was a mystery. We couldn't inspire or coerce her to respond. We could only appreciate those rare moments when she did.

I remember one morning at home, Adri had just gone through the living room of the house pulling magazines out of the rack and off the shelves and scattering them all over the floor. I was really tired of this routine, since she did it at least once and sometimes twice every day. I'd ask her to pick the magazines up. But she'd usually ignore me, and I'd end up doing it myself. Because the magazines belonged to the owner of the house, I couldn't throw them away. I suppose I could have put them out of reach, but I had some notion that Adri needed to learn to live in the existing environment as much as possible rather than our always having to adapt the environment to her.

On this particular morning I asked her in my most matter-of-fact voice to pick the magazines up. Nothing happened. I repeated my request in a louder voice. Without acknowledging me at all, Adri walked over to the magazines, sat down, and began to rifle through them, ripping some in the process. With mounting irritation I strode over to the mess, picked up a magazine and with exaggerated motions, put it on top of the pile, announcing that this was what I expected her to do. I then placed a few more magazines on the pile. But despite my loud voice and my deliberate movements, Adri just didn't seem to get it. So I took her hand in mine and we performed the task together. We picked up the magazine and placed it on the pile. And we did it again. And again. But the moment I took my hand away, her hand dropped away too.

This was a straightforward, uncomplicated task, and I was convinced that there had to be a way to get through to her. With enough modeling and repetition, how could she not learn? We sat there together, practicing for over an hour. I was totally frustrated—and so was Adri. The implications were really frightening. Could she possibly be so impaired that even this simplest of tasks was beyond her? What could the future possibly hold for this child if she was this limited?

I kept at our task, determined that she would pick up those magazines. I just couldn't accept the bleak future those scattered pages represented. After two hours I was ready to surrender. Adri must have been equally exhausted because suddenly, to my utter disbelief and amazement, she jumped up from the floor, stomped directly to the magazines, angrily reached down, picked one up, and slammed it onto the pile. I didn't know what startled me more—the fact that she finally performed the task, or that she seemed to be angry. Both of these behaviors were entirely new.

Now I was even more confused. Was this just a battle of wills? Was the issue really just compliance? It certainly didn't seem so. Especially since Adri appeared more withdrawn than defiant most of the time. And yet clearly she was capable of understanding and completing a task. I puzzled over this grasping for understanding, but I came no closer to unraveling the mystery of Adri.

Unfortunately this was not the beginning of a new era marked by compliance and achievement. It actually represented one of the few battles like this that I ever won. Like Adri's other moments of isolated awareness and competence, this one, too, became just another memory. After a while I wondered if it had really happened, or had I just imagined it? Could Adri choose these moments of competence, or did they somehow choose her?

Rodrigo and I often took Adri to amusement parks because she loved the spinning rides so much. There was one trip I'll never forget. From the time she was very small, one of the things we'd noticed about Adri was that she rarely hurt herself, and when she did, she never cried about it. In fact she seemed almost insensitive to pain.

That morning we were in line to buy tickets to Disneyland. Rodrigo was at the window, and Adri and I stood behind him. A metal ledge ran along the whole length of the booth. It was shaded and cool where Rodrigo stood, but the rest of the ledge was exposed to the heat of the sun. Suddenly I noticed that Adri was leaning on the ledge, her hand resting on the metal. I quickly reached out to touch it and yanked my hand back in pain. The ledge was burning hot, and my fingers were bright red. I grabbed Adri's hand and looked at her fingers, expecting the worst. However, they weren't red at all, and she showed no discomfort. Both Rodrigo and I were astonished. Was her sensory system that different from our own?

In September Adri started school. The program I had found was officially for emotionally and behaviorally disturbed children, although there were several other children who, like Adri, lacked a specific diagnosis.

Parents were encouraged to assist in the classrooms, so I began to spend one or two mornings a week with her. I soon noticed that even though other children in her class would act up or cry a lot, they still participated in activities. Adri, on the other hand, generally sat alone. And sometimes, if the teachers allowed it, she'd simply run around the room. During "morning circle" time Adri was required to sit with her class. Though she complied, she spent most of her time paging through books, holding some of them upside down, totally oblivious of the class discussion about what day it was, what month and year, and what the weather conditions might be. I didn't so much care about her lack of participation as I did the upside-down books. I'd seen children less than a year old purposefully turn books right side up. In an effort to allay my anxiety about her development, I'd quickly reach over and turn her book around. Was Adri really trying? If she was, we were in trouble. If she wasn't, why not?

I wanted to go back to work again, but not in the fashion industry and not full time. Fortunately my circumstances made it possible for me to take a volunteer position. In Los Angeles the social services system often assigns its difficult child-abuse and neglect cases to what they call a Guardian Ad Litem (GAL) office. I read that GAL was looking for volunteers, so I applied and was accepted. My job was to visit the children assigned to me weekly, interview the parents, foster parents, and other relevant parties in order to make placement recommendations to the court.

I soon discovered that I loved this work. I met some extraordinary children and some extraordinary foster parents. One of these incredible foster mothers was Coreece Fisher, who became a dear friend and a continual source of inspiration. Never have I seen anyone so lovingly and so selflessly parent one foster child after another, several of whom she adopted. And never have I seen anyone more adept at forging bonds between people regardless of race or class.

Although I was never free of my concern for Adri, this was a happy time for us all. Adri loved the ocean, and most days after school, she'd kick off her shoes and, with one of us—myself, Rodrigo, Laura, or Jamie (Adri's baby-sitters)—beside her, take long walks on the beach. Even so, these adventures weren't entirely relaxing. If you accidentally dropped Adri's hand, she'd be gone in a flash. Each of us at some time found ourselves racing fully clothed directly into the ocean to retrieve her. And she was just as passionate about the sand as she was about the sea. Handfuls of it went into her mouth. Whoever was with Adri at the time would have to reach into her mouth and try to get the sand out without getting bitten. This was daunting—and rarely successful.

And yet by this time we all knew that being bitten and

scratched were the hazards of the job. You'd be hugging Adri and suddenly feel teeth or fingernails digging into your flesh. She was also an expert at biting the arm that held her. Our shoulders and the insides of our arms were almost always black and blue. Our foreheads and necks carried telltale scratches. Laura, Jamie, and I all became adept at camouflage makeup. We tried to make light of it, laughing so that we wouldn't cry. We all knew Adri wasn't being malicious, but because we were giving so much of ourselves to her all the time, trying so hard to get through to her, it was hard not to feel hurt when she responded by biting or scratching. Still, despite the pain, strangely enough we all wanted to be with her. Somehow, in the bright light of her love, the hurt and pain receded into the shadows.

Just after she turned three, Rodrigo, Adri, and I went to my aunt's house in Mexico for Christmas. One afternoon we were swimming together in the pool. Adri was wearing her last pair of inflatable "floaties," but just as I feared, she bit right through them. We scoured the city for more, but we couldn't find any. Not wanting to keep her out of the pool, Rodrigo and I decided that if we stayed right next to her, she could go in without "floaties." Maybe we could even teach her the rudiments of swimming. I stood up in the shallow end, about a foot away from them as Rodrigo gently let go of Adri. I was poised to grab her if necessary, but much to our surprise, rather than floundering between us, she just swam away like a little fish. Again, we were perplexed. Just when, and how, had Adri taught herself to swim?

After the holidays we scheduled a new round of appointments with NPI, hoping they might eventually send us to someone who could understand and diagnose Adri. Over the next months her hearing was tested and retested. The results, again not totally conclusive, indicated what we already knew, Adri's hearing was normal.

In April I took her to see a psychiatrist who specialized

in developmental assessment. Having learned a hard lesson from my previous experience, I asked the doctor if she wanted me to interact with Adri. She told me kindly that it was all right for me to just observe, she'd let me know if she needed my assistance.

The doctor sat down on the floor across from Adri and tried, unsuccessfully, to engage her attention. Then she placed some wooden blocks in front of her, hoping Adri would stack them. Not much chance of that.

"Did Adri ever stack things?" the doctor asked. I told her, quite truthfully, that she'd occasionally done it at home. The doctor nodded, giving Adri credit for the task. Then she asked Adri to arrange the blocks like a train. Not even a little chance. Adri had never played with a real toy train, much less an imaginary one. Giving up on the blocks, the doctor tried putting a ball in front of Adri to see if she would roll it. Adri touched the ball and it rolled away. This was counted as a success. Then the doctor asked me several more questions about the kinds of things that Adri did at home, and gave Adri a few more points.

However, when it was over, despite the doctor's liberal scoring techniques, Adri scored only in the 50s. According to the charts, this meant she was moderately mentally retarded. I suppose I should have realized that this was an official IQ test, but I was stunned. I'd never thought of Adri as mentally retarded. It just didn't seem right. Her eyes were simply too alert and her movements too sharp. All the retarded children I'd met shared a rather slow and gentle quality. And unlike Adri, they seemed to be able to learn, albeit more slowly and with a lower ceiling than other children.

I also didn't understand how the assessment process we had just completed could lead to an accurate diagnosis. Certainly Adri *didn't* do the activities as requested, but did that necessarily mean she *couldn't* do them? And without knowing why she didn't or couldn't do them, how could the doctor draw a conclusion? As far as I was concerned, the test results were based on questionable assumptions.

So now I had another ill-fitting diagnosis. Clearly Adri was lagging developmentally, but did that mean she was retarded? I felt shaken, yet paradoxically, the diagnosis was a kind of absolution. I was no longer to blame for Adri's difficulties. But at the same time exonerating me seemed to close a door on her. As long as the problem was me, there was a chance she could change. If somehow I got "fixed," then miraculously so would she.

I called Rodrigo from a nearby pay phone. Once again his reaction was different from mine. Although he hadn't believed the psychologist in New York, he believed this psychiatrist immediately. For him it seemed logical that Adri would be retarded. As I listened to Rodrigo, suddenly something began to sink in. Even if Adri wasn't retarded, she could well be permanently and severely impaired in some other way. And that meant she might never get better. It was a new and sobering thought for both of us.

That August we went on a vacation that turned into a nightmare. We were renting a house and Adri had a hard time getting to sleep the first few nights, but by the second week she was resting soundly. One evening we went to bed, each of us assuming that the other had checked all the windows and doors. At about two A.M. Rodrigo suddenly bolted up out of a deep sleep. "Adri" was all he said as he jumped out of bed and raced down the hallway.

I ran to her room, she wasn't there. Alarmed, I rushed back out and found Rodrigo leaning through the open hallway window, looking up. He quietly motioned me over. Looking down, a shiver ran through my whole body. We were two very tall stories above the ground. Below us lay the brick pavings of the courtyard. No one could survive a fall like that. Thank God she wasn't there. But then I looked up, gasped, and grabbed Rodrigo's arm. There was my tiny three-year-old daughter perched on the steeply pitched tile roof, one leg dangling over in our direction. Though I was terrified, Adri looked totally content straddling the roof, smiling among the stars.

Without pause or comment Rodrigo climbed out of the window and up onto the roof. I was frightened that Adri might get excited at his approach and try to stand up and move toward him or wave her arms. But no. She waited calmly for him to approach, lift her gently from her perch, and carry her down. Perhaps she was not so totally oblivious of the danger after all. They inched back down, Rodrigo feeling for each step until they were close enough for me to reach out the window and help them back through. Once they were safely inside, I clung to them both. Rodrigo had been incredibly heroic. We took Adri into our bed and held her close. I've never been so scared in my life. But just as Adri had shown no fear or awareness of her predicament, she showed no relief when it was over. Did she know the danger she'd been in? Did she know how frightened we'd been? All I could think was she must have a guardian angel.

In the fall of 1985, back in Los Angeles, we prepared for the new school year. Adri would be returning to the same class in the same school. My goal for the year was potty training. We'd been trying to do this, unsuccessfully, since she was two. Now almost four, Adri still wasn't trained, although she was fully capable of removing her clothes and dirty diapers and indulging herself with great pleasure in "artistic" pursuits. While we never became immune to this smelly task, we all became adept at cleaning up "painted" carpets, walls, windows, doors, beds, books, clothes, and bodies.

We were still involved with NPI, still searching for answers, still hoping for a diagnosis that fit. This time NPI recommended a neurological assessment that would include a bone scan to determine if her bones were developing normally and a sleeping and a waking EEG to assess her brain wave patterns. I agreed to the tests, but I doubted that Adri would allow electrodes to be attached to her head and body and then just drift off to sleep, on command, in some strange hospital room. However, when I brought Adri in that morning, anticipating the worst, she astonished me by climbing right up onto the table and allowing the nurse to attach the electrodes to her head and chest without a single protest. The doctor easily monitored her for the waking EEG. Then the nurse dimmed the lights. Within a very short time she drifted off to sleep. The doctor must have wondered how well I knew this child. I wondered the same thing.

Both EEGs turned out normal. The following week her bone scan also came back normal. Once again there was no clear diagnosis of Adri's problem, but now that we had gone through the departments of speech and language, psychology/psychiatry, and neurology, NPI could offer us little else. Stymied, having exhausted the resources of one of the most illustrious diagnostic centers in the country, we took a temporary vacation from the world of medicine.

A short time later when the house we'd been renting was put up for sale, we had to move. Our new home had a large fenced-in yard with a pool behind, and Adri loved it. Because we could see into the yard from the kitchen window, I allowed her to play out there by herself for short periods of time. Now four years old, Adri deserved an occasional taste of freedom.

One day, after about three minutes of being on her own, I went outside to check on her and found Adri gone. I called frantically to Laura to begin searching the house for her while I ran back outside to check the yard and pool area more thoroughly. I was starting to panic when, suddenly, I heard a faint splash and a giggle. I ran back to check the pool again. She wasn't there. I looked around. The fence that separated our house from the neighbor's seemed too high and too smooth for a child to climb over. Nevertheless, as I ran toward it, the giggles grew louder. Desperate, I called Adri's name; there was no answer. Then I noticed a big tree not too far from the fence. I struggled to grab one of the lower branches and pull myself up so that I could peer over. To my utter amazement there was Adri, fully clothed, swimming in the neighbor's pool. I scrambled over the fence and ran to the pool, shouting for her to come out. When she ignored me, I waded into the water and pulled her out of the pool, hugging her and scolding her all at the same time.

Three minutes alone and we'd lost her—it terrified me. What if she hadn't gone into the swimming pool but wandered off into the street instead? Once we'd tried putting an ID bracelet on her, but she'd pulled it off, and we hadn't replaced it. Without language or knowledge of who she was and where she lived, anything might happen to her on the street. Even worse, what if she'd gone into the pool wearing heavier clothes or shoes? What if our neighbors had owned a guard dog?

Yet despite my feelings of anger and relief, I was also amazed. To escape our yard, Adri had had to notice the tree, climb it, swing from the tree to the fence, climb over the fence, and then drop down into the neighbor's yard. Was this the planning and behavior of a severely impaired child?

About this time Adri suddenly acquired another new and disruptive behavior. She started to sling dishes without warning across the room. They could be her own dishes or someone else's, empty or full, plastic, paper, china, or glass, it didn't matter. While we did our best to stop her or at least slow her down, plates and cups flying across our kitchen became a familiar sight and sound in our home that spring. One unsupervised moment was all it took, and chaos reigned. She wasn't doing it to aggravate us, she just seemed to delight in the crashing, shattering noises and all the household flurry it brought on.

When Adri "misbehaved" in this way, I tried to correct

her, even though I suspected the effort was futile. I didn't think she knew what a privilege was or if she could possibly understand the concept of deprivation, so taking something away from her didn't make sense. I didn't even know what she might consider a privilege. She had one friend, Rae Lynn, the daughter of Rodrigo's secretary, Kathy. However, Adri wouldn't have noticed if she were not allowed to see Rae Lynn. And in fact depriving her of that contact would have been counterproductive, since we were eager for her to socialize more. We tried taking away the Popsicles she loved so much, but that had no noticeable effect on her behavior either.

Other kinds of punishment seemed equally meaningless. I don't believe in spanking, and although there have been lots of times when I've lost my temper, yelled too loudly, or grabbed her arm too tightly, I've never seen any benefit to it and I've always felt ashamed afterward.

At Adri's school "time-out" was the favored discipline. But having seen certain kids "timed-out" more often than in, I wasn't a big fan of the method. Still, we cooperated with the school and dutifully set up our own official little time-out room off the kitchen. From that point on, Adri unfailingly found her way into it at least once or twice a day. I think she really liked being in there. It was a small, cozy space and no one bothered her. We usually had to ask her to come out. It wasn't exactly a major deterrent.

That March my friend Kathy announced she was getting married and I learned, to my surprise, that I was pregnant again. While the prospect intimidated me a little, Rodrigo was really delighted and excited. In the face of his enthusiasm my anxieties soon melted away. I threw myself into planning Kathy's shower.

For entertainment another friend had suggested I hire a psychic. Not knowing much about psychics, and more or less equating them with magicians, I really didn't know what to expect, but it sounded like fun.

On the day of the party about a dozen friends and the psychic gathered in the living room. He asked if anyone had photographs of friends or family members. Everyone rummaged around and found something. Without looking he accepted a photo from someone and, keeping it facedown, closed his eyes. Then he entered into a trancelike state and began to describe the personality and history of the person in the picture in an extraordinarily accurate way. We were all perplexed, amazed, and unsettled by his abilities.

When it was my turn, I gave the psychic a photograph of Adri wearing a little sailor suit and smiling brightly. I told him it was a picture of my daughter. He held the photo facedown and began to speak.

He said that the person in this picture had lived an earlier lifetime on the sea. This person, he added, had loved the sea and would never be happy in a structured, routine sort of life—she needed great freedom. Still in a trancelike state, he paused, a puzzled expression on his face. This person, he continued slowly, seemed to be coming from very far away. "From very far away," he repeated.

The reading was unlike any of the others he'd done, and even he seemed puzzled by it, uncertain of what it meant. It made sense to me, though. Coming from very far away. What better way to describe Adri? Even when she was with us, Adri always seemed to be very far away.

Suddenly the psychic's whole body jerked to attention. His face turned beet red, sweat poured off him, and his hands started to shake as he blurted out that there was a fire. She was in a fire and burning. He was very upset. He seemed to pull himself out of the trance then and he asked me if Adri had ever been in a fire. Even when I said no, he couldn't seem to shake off the image. He asked me where she was now and when I said, "Upstairs sleeping," he asked me to go check on her. I ran up and found her as I had left her, sleeping peacefully. I don't think he knew quite what to make of his impressions, but he warned me to watch her

very carefully around fire. He'd been amazing, but the fire
stuff really scared me. When he finished a short while later,
I was glad to see him go.

Not long after, Adri came down with a cold, so
Rodrigo and I took her to the doctor to check it out. Because her regular pediatrician wasn't in, we saw a new,
young substitute doctor. As we expected, the cold wasn't serious. We chatted with the doctor a bit, but it wasn't till we
were nearly out the door that he suddenly turned to me and
blurted out what must have been on his mind the whole
time: "What's wrong with her?"

I was surprised at his bluntness, but in a way pleased. At
least he'd acknowledged there was a problem. I told him we
didn't really know what was wrong with her. He asked if
we'd taken her to the Neuropsychiatric Institute for an
evaluation. I explained that we had just completed almost
two years of evaluations at NPI. The young doctor asked
me if we'd ever seen Dr. Parmalee. When I said no, he
suggested I set up an appointment for Adri as soon as
possible.

When Rodrigo and I brought her to see Dr. Parmalee
several weeks later, he greeted us warmly and invited Adri
to play freely. She sat down on the floor by a shelf of toys
and began to spin the wheels of a car. The doctor observed
Adri for a few minutes, asking us some questions about her
behaviors at home. And then, without fanfare, he told us
that she was autistic.

I was astonished. After four years of searching, questioning, and wondering, I hadn't really expected to get any
diagnosis from him, much less so quickly. I had only a vague
sense of what autism was, but I didn't see how it could be
any worse than mental retardation, or not knowing what
was wrong with her. Dr. Parmalee felt quite certain of the
diagnosis, given Adri's history, her lack of language development, and her behaviors. However, since no one else over
the years had suggested autism, he recommended that we

get a second opinion. He gave us the name of another doctor at NPI, a specialist in autism, Dr. Ornitz.

A few days after I made the appointment, we received in the mail a very long, very extensive questionnaire from Dr. Ornitz. I was flabbergasted as I filled it out. Besides all the questions detailing her lack of responsiveness and lack of language development, there were many others that dealt with behaviors I'd always assumed were unique to Adri.

Did she walk on her toes? Yes. Did she lead you by the hand to things she wanted? Yes. Did she open her hand, letting go of objects, without seeming to notice? Yes. Did she spin and run in circles? Yes. Of course, there were some characteristics that didn't apply to Adri, such as could she remember and recite long strings of information? Only in my dreams.

Certainly normal children exhibit some of these behaviors, too, but in passing and as part of a larger repertoire. Now it seemed that these behaviors were defining, not just for Adri but for a whole population of people. These were behaviors typical enough to be included on a questionnaire. It was strangely reassuring—Adri wasn't the only child in the world who acted like this. We weren't the only parents trying to deal with this particular situation.

Unlike Dr. Parmalee, Dr. Ornitz was a bit brusque and distant during our appointment. He observed Adri for a few minutes, glanced through the questionnaire, and then confirmed the diagnosis: Adri was indeed autistic.

Even though I knew autism was serious, from the moment we had a name for Adri's condition, I began to feel some sense of relief. I'd read a little bit about autism in my college psychology textbooks. I knew autistic kids were considered to be mysterious, aloof, unable to connect with others. And I also seemed to remember that they were considered quite intelligent. If Adri was autistic, I reasoned, then she couldn't be retarded. That was enough for me. For the time being, I didn't want to know more. With this diagnosis surely we'd be able to find the people and the services she needed. Now Adri could begin to make real progress.

Rodrigo, on the other hand, wanted more information right away. He quickly found some books on the subject and began reading. After a few weeks I reluctantly picked them up too. For the most part the information was discouraging. Nevertheless there were no studies linking autism to brain damage. That seemed hopeful. On the other hand it appeared that statistically the chances for recovery from autism were about nil. But if the doctors didn't know why or how people became autistic, how could they know that the condition was permanent? And even if it wasn't reversible, how could they possibly judge how far any individual autistic person might be able to advance? The door seemed wide open.

In our research we learned that there was no known physiological marker or test for autism. It is what's called a "spectrum" disorder, one that is both characterized and diagnosed by the presence of a certain number of typical behaviorisms—primarily speech and language difficulties, lack of sociability, and lack of eye contact. Reading on, I was surprised and dismayed to learn that most experts actually did consider the vast majority of autistic persons to be retarded as well. Was the psychiatrist at NPI right after all? Was this a case of double jeopardy? It still didn't feel right.

Some of the books suggested that "functionally retarded" might be a better way to describe autistic people. I found that easier to accept. Adri had mastered very few daily living skills and even fewer academic skills. And clearly she was not skilled in IQ test taking. But did that really mean she was intellectually impaired? What about her apparent inability to learn, as opposed to just being a slow learner? What about those odd moments of total competence that emerged spontaneously from time to time? Didn't those characteristics distinguish her from someone who was retarded? I didn't want to see her labeled as permanently limited. She was only four years old—she had plenty of time to prove them all wrong.

Over and over we kept reading about how little we might expect from Adri and how likely it was that she would need lifelong care. The books described her behaviors accurately, so I did not doubt the diagnosis. But because she was so personable, charming, and affectionate, I couldn't really believe or accept the prognosis. Underneath all that sophisticated language and all those carefully designed studies, it was apparent that none of the experts understood what caused autism. Everything they reported was strictly observational.

Well, I was observing Adri, too, and although I certainly saw what they saw on the outside, what about the person on the inside? What about her bright, sparkling eyes? Hadn't anyone looked into them? There was a whole world in there. However, not wanting to appear unrealistic or naive, I kept my hopes close to my heart.

Rodrigo, too, was keeping his thoughts to himself. Although he supported my optimism, he later told me that he'd found the reading disheartening and depressing. It had never occurred to him that there were people in the world who might never learn to speak or to communicate in any manner. Now he was reading that not only was that possible but it was highly probable in the case of his own daughter.

Almost immediately we began seeking help for Adri. We simply assumed that there would be countless programs designed to serve autistic children, and now that we had the "access code," we could begin to avail ourselves of them. I had really expected Dr. Parmalee or Dr. Ornitz to hand us a list of resources.

Instead what we discovered was that not only was there no list, there seemed to be no programs. Dr. Parmalee knew of nothing, and Dr. Ornitz, when pressed, came up with only one possibility, a program, also at NPI. We investigated and learned that because it was part of an ongoing research project, only children under four were accepted. Adri was too old. Our one lead was dead.

Even with our shiny new diagnosis, we were floundering. Despite the fact that some experts advocated integrating children with developmental problems into the public schools, I didn't bother to call them. I felt certain they wouldn't have the resources or training to work with a child like Adri. I couldn't see why integration was such an important factor. Adri had been more or less integrated these last two years in her classroom of emotionally and behaviorally disturbed children. Many of those children were far more "normal" than she, yet their behavior had never rubbed off on her. In a regular classroom wouldn't she simply be left alone, ostracized, or worse yet, mocked, by the other children? I set out to find a program geared to autistic children.

In the resource section of one of the newer books on autism, I was excited to discover that there was a national advocacy group. I called the headquarters of the Autism Society of America, and they sent me several pamphlets, their newsletter, and a notice of their upcoming annual conference to be held in July. It was a three-day conference, and top autism experts and representatives from successful programs from all over the country were going to speak. Rodrigo and I made plans to attend.

At the conference, surrounded at last by some of the most knowledgeable autism experts in the world, we felt as though we'd found an oasis in the desert. What we didn't learn until several years—and several conferences—later is that because there are so few advances in the field, the meetings change very little from year to year. Perhaps that explained why many of the other parents at the conference seemed so discouraged, even cynical. But unlike those conference veterans we still had hope. I thought that surely here in Mecca someone knew how to "debug" what looked to me like a neural system gone awry.

Among the various presentations, we were particularly impressed with one from the Language and Cognitive Development Center (LCDC) located in Boston. The directors of that program showed videos of children who, like Adri, jumped, spun, flapped their hands, and were for the most part nonverbal. But while these children were clearly autistic, they were still participating in the classroom activities. Most of those activities seemed to involve completing some sequential action.

For example, a child might pick up a cup, bring it to the faucet, turn the faucet on, put the cup under the tap for water, turn the faucet off, return to his seat, and finally take a drink. It sounds simple to the average person, but for an autistic person that could be a very difficult sequence to master. I knew Adri wouldn't be able to perform such a complex set of tasks without assistance. Surely this would be true of many of these children as well. Yet the tapes showed how much the children improved over time. I was impressed.

The LCDC program was trying, in effect, to help autistic people reprogram their brains. With the help of a teacher the children repeated an action until it was extremely familiar. Then the teacher interrupted that action. The hope was that the autistic person could continue the routine on his or her own momentum based on the newly established pattern. Unlike other programs LCDC didn't limit their programming to just teaching basic skills, such as eating, buttoning, and sorting. Instead their method was aimed at addressing what they assumed to be the "underlying language and cognitive deficits" of autism. I liked that. It sounded very scientific. Though I wanted Adri to master basic skills and be able to function in the world, I also thought she was capable of learning more than that. After the conference presentation we met with the director and set up an evaluation appointment for Adri.

A couple of weeks later Rodrigo, Adri, and I flew to

Boston. On the drive over to LCDC we were somewhat disconcerted to discover that the school was not located in the best of neighborhoods. We pulled up in front of a rather gloomy-looking redbrick building, its windows protected by bars. Fortunately it wasn't as bad inside. But still I shuddered at the thought of Adri spending all her time in such a dismal place. I was determined, however, to keep an open mind. We were here for the program, not the building.

The evaluation was unlike anything Adri had ever participated in before. She was not asked to roll a ball or stack blocks. Instead they had all kinds of gadgets and custom-built wooden equipment. Although we weren't sure just what they were assessing, it was fascinating to watch Adri do things like walk across a board with different-shaped holes cut into it. The first time, in order to not fall through, she actually looked down, paying close attention to the holes. She made it across without a stumble. After that she didn't bother to look down again—she just walked calmly and purposefully across, gazing out into space.

Next they placed her in front of a tether ball, and a staff member pushed it toward her. Rather than putting her hands up to hit it back or protect herself, Adri just let the ball hit her. In another activity, with only minimal assistance, Adri was able to take items from a basket and throw them, one at a time, down a small children's slide.

In a cup test a staff member placed a plastic cup in front of Adri and asked her to pick it up and stack it on the pile. The staff person observed how Adri picked up the cup and then noted if she was able to orient it in the right way in order to stack it. I assumed this would be an easy task for Adri, but it wasn't. Sometimes she could position it correctly, but at other times, while she seemed to be trying, she just couldn't do it.

At one point a staff member asked me to leave the room so that she could assess how Adri responded to separations. I watched from a TV screen in the adjoining room as Adri looked toward the door but made no effort to follow. She showed no fear or discomfort at my absence. After a few minutes they motioned me back in.

When it was over, the director told me that he agreed with the diagnosis and thought Adri was a good candidate for the LCDC program. I breathed a sigh of relief. Here were people who understood enough about autism to develop this very unique and imaginative series of assessment tests. Surely if they understood autism that well, they must have created a good program to deal with it. Back in our hotel room that night, Rodrigo and I made the decision to move our household and his business to Boston so that we could enroll Adri in the program.

Chapter 5

Boston

I was eight months pregnant when we arrived in Boston. Adri started at her new school, and I began looking for a house and an obstetrician. In her classes she worked on activities similar to those in the assessment. However, she also began to learn a rudimentary sign communication system that LCDC had developed based on a simplified version of standard sign language. It was taught through a combination of videos, modeling behavior, and actual physical manipulation of her hands. The number of signs any particular child might learn varied greatly, but all the children seemed to know at least a few basic signs such as "Hello," "cracker," "bathroom," "eat," and "finished."

After a month of steady searching we moved into a house in the suburb of Brookline, just fifteen minutes from the school. Though Rodrigo and I often talked to Adri about the baby and rested her hand on my stomach, we really didn't know if she had any inkling of what was going on. She would lie in bed between us and pat my stomach, but since she patted lots of things, we really couldn't tell if it meant anything. Still, I liked it.

At about six A.M. on the morning of November 7th, I woke up in labor. Around eleven A.M. we headed to the hospital, and our son, Sebastian, was born about two hours later. He was a big, healthy boy with black hair. When the nurse laid him on my chest, he began to nurse immediately, a good sign indeed. Though difficulty with nursing is not uncommon, and it is certainly not a precursor of autism, I did find out, long after Adri's birth, that doctors consider difficulty with sucking to be a "soft" neurological sign that may indicate potential problems. Though no one has proved that autism is genetic, there is evidence suggesting a genetic link, so I felt very relieved that Seby, as we nicknamed him, was nursing properly.

When Adri first came to visit us in the hospital, she virtually ignored her new brother. We held her hand and helped her touch him, but when we let go, she wandered off. Then history began to repeat itself. The day before we were scheduled to go home the doctor became concerned about Seby's bilirubin count. As far as I knew, jaundice was not statistically associated with autism, but I was concerned. I didn't want Seby to be isolated in a nursery incubator. On discharge day, when his count was neither down nor up, we pleaded with the doctors to let us take him home. They finally agreed. Giving them no time to reconsider, we quickly bundled him up and left the hospital.

At home Seby recovered quickly, and we soon began to recognize that life with him was going to be quite different from life with Adri. First of all he nursed voraciously. And although he certainly cried, his was a normal infant's cry—loud, angry, demanding, and crescendoing over time. Adri's piercing screams had come out of nowhere and continued unabated, despite all our efforts. Seby cried for attention; he cried for food; he cried to be changed; he cried during "fussy" periods. But when he got what he needed, his crying subsided.

Another good sign was that even in those first months, Seby looked us straight in the eye. He would smile at me and try to engage my attention. He knew who I was, and he wanted me to be there with him. When I left him, he wailed with displeasure. When I returned, through his gestures and expressions he showed his great pleasure. Rodrigo and I knew that we were important to him. In many ways Seby taught me about being a mother, and Rodrigo about being a father. Though Rodrigo had always doted on Adri, there was a difference in his interactions with Seby. Seby's face just lit up when he saw his dad, and Rodrigo responded in kind. This was a duet performance, not a solo.

For her part Adri ignored Seby most of the time except for the occasional surreptitious attempt to pinch him. I tried to spend plenty of time alone with her, too, so she wouldn't feel left out. Though we experienced no major mishaps between the two of them, there was also little indication of any developing attachment. They were more like two different satellites orbiting the same planet.

In December Adri turned five. She was still beautiful, graceful, and petite. She was also still in diapers, still not speaking, and still, in that mysterious way, "very far away" from us. She went to school every day, and we religiously followed the LCDC model at home. Whenever possible in conversations with her we would both sign and say our words. We had all expected that by now she would be signing, at least a little bit. But so far she hadn't independently signed at all. We yearned for Adri to repeat a sign, even just once, to let us know she understood what we were trying to do with her.

One day in late January about five months after she had

begun at LCDC, Adri was playing at home with me. As she often did when she wanted something, she took my hand and led me to the front door, showing that she wanted to go out for a walk. I bundled her up, got my own coat, and we both walked back to the door. Through each step of this sequence I had been saying the words, signing them myself and then physically helping her make the sign. Before opening the door I did what had by now become automatic for me: I stopped, turned to her, and said, "What do you want me to do?" I paused expectantly. Then, just as I was about to model the "open" sign myself, I looked down and saw Adri's little hands suddenly come together and apart to make the "open" sign. "Adri, you did it," I shouted, hugging her. "You said 'open.' I can understand you!"

Laughing, almost crying, I quickly opened the door. It was Adri's first independent sign communication, and I wanted her to experience the effectiveness of it immediately. Yet I didn't want to walk too long, because I was eager to get back to the door to see if she'd sign again.

So after a short, brisk walk we returned to the door and I repeated as usual, "What do you want me to do?" I held my breath for only a moment before her hands once again came together and apart to form the "open" sign. She had signed twice. This was no onetime miracle. This was bona fide communication. I dashed to the phone and called Rodrigo. He couldn't wait to come home and see her sign. That night we had a joyful "communication" celebration in our home.

Over the next months Adri went on to learn about six more signs. She could consistently sign "give," "more," "cracker," "close," "eat," "finished," and of course "open." After that she simply couldn't or didn't learn any more signs. Though I certainly wished for and worked for additional signs, it really wasn't so surprising that she couldn't master more. Though her gross motor skills had always been excellent—she could run and jump as well as any child—

her fine motor skills were pretty inadequate. She wasn't able to hold or manage utensils very well. She could not grip a pencil or crayon properly to form letters or draw. She couldn't button a shirt or pull a zipper up or down. Grasping something between two fingers was difficult for her and often required more control than she could muster. With food such as popcorn or potato chips she always made a mess by reaching in and grabbing a handful or two and then trying to scoop it all into her mouth.

Given this degree of fine motor impairment, it was actually pretty amazing that she'd mastered any signs at all. So, while more signs would have been nice, we were thrilled and excited by what she'd been able to accomplish. It told us that at some level she could both understand and initiate communication. This was a major development in our understanding of Adri and, we thought, in her ability to be part of this world.

Despite Adri's successes at LCDC, Rodrigo and I still continued to search for more information and for new approaches to autism. That January we heard about a program in Japan where autistic children were integrated with regular kids. We were told that in their classrooms, observers could not tell the autistic children from the normal ones. We found that hard to believe but intriguing enough to want to check out. Rodrigo and I made arrangements to visit the Higashi School that following month.

It was like visiting another world. For one thing it was spotless. The children, we were told, kept it that way. In one classroom we were treated to a musical performance. I could pick out the autistic children only because, when you looked closely, you could see an adult crouching behind each one, ready to intervene if necessary. In general the curriculum seemed more academically advanced than the average American school. They seemed to have much higher expectations for both their "normal" and their autistic students.

In a separate classroom I met about nine or ten American autistic students ranging in age from about four to seventeen. They were being taught by Japanese teachers in English. Because of the language barrier Dr. Kitahara, the founder of the school, did not feel the American children could be integrated into Japanese-speaking classrooms. Nevertheless the American autistic children were also well behaved and, like their Japanese peers, they were being taught academic subjects. It was very impressive and encouraging.

The staff pointed out one four-year-old autistic American girl who had almost died before coming to Japan. She had refused to eat and had only been kept alive by intravenous feeding through a tube inserted into her stomach. There was certainly no evidence of any such tube now. We were also told that because many of the students had been self-abusive head bangers, they had arrived at the school in helmets. How desperate all the parents of these children must have been. Adri was neither self-abusive nor suicidal, but if she were, would we have had the courage to send her away? I just couldn't imagine life without her in our home.

Dr. Kitahara believed that autistic children were far more capable than they could or would demonstrate. Her goal was to help them develop, through the school structure and routine, a "daily life rhythm." And though they might not be able to show it, she also believed they learned by example. So at Higashi the students worked almost exclusively in groups, as opposed to the one-on-one interactions typical in American settings.

The daily routine included several periods of calisthenics and sportslike exercise activities. The staff also had strict behavioral requirements. It was expected that all the children would learn basic social skills, such as sitting quietly, waiting, walking in line, and table manners. And everyone was taught some academics, according to ability. Some received only kindergarten-level instruction, while others participated in sophisticated high school lessons.

Toward the end of the visit we learned that the Higashi School planned to open a U.S. branch in, of all places, Boston. They hoped to begin classes the following fall. Although I still had some serious questions about their methods, because no one could or would explain to my satisfaction how they got the results they did, clearly the program was effective. On that basis alone I knew we had a responsibility to Adri to investigate further.

By spring, with Seby smiling, sitting up, and vocalizing right on schedule, and Adri settled at LCDC, I wanted to get back into social services work. With a start-up grant from Rodrigo's company we established two foundations: the K.I.D.S. (Kids In Disadvantaged Situations) Foundation, whose purpose was to provide housing, advocacy, and educational support to single welfare mothers struggling to become self-sufficient. And the Adriana Foundation, which we hoped might serve as a national resource center for autistic people and their parents, with a particular emphasis on early diagnosis and intervention.

Late that summer Rodrigo and I discovered, to our mutual delight, that I was pregnant again. We'd talked about having another baby even before Seby was born. We wanted a third child, close in age to Seby. We also thought it important that Seby not be expected to carry by himself the potential burden and responsibility for Adri's care in the future.

In the fall of 1987, as Adri began her second year at LCDC, the Boston Higashi School opened its doors. Rodrigo had wanted to send Adri to Higashi right away, but I wasn't ready to enroll her yet. She was still progressing at LCDC, and I wanted more time to learn about the Higashi methods. This wasn't easy. The Boston Higashi staff were primarily Japanese, and while they were learning English, their ability to communicate in it was limited. Nor were they accustomed to having to explain their methods. We discovered that unlike American parents, Japanese parents do not question their children's educators. Nevertheless whenever I visited, I could see that the children under their care were indisputably making progress. Even more convincing, the parents, traditionally the harshest of critics, were almost unanimous in their support and enthusiasm for the program.

By the spring of 1988 I was beginning to feel discouraged with LCDC. The second year of the program seemed to be simply a repeat of the first. She was stagnating. At six and a half she was not yet toilet trained, still nonverbal, and still spending her days doing what seemed to be in some ways "nothing" kinds of activities: sorting colors, repeating the task routines, and watching and practicing the signs. Certainly the activities had value in terms of the philosophy of the program. But I was coming to agree with Rodrigo that they didn't seem to have much value in terms of helping Adri learn and progress in her real life.

Before we could take action, though, nature intervened. On the night of April 10, 1988, our family was gathered in the TV room watching *Dumbo* before bed. Just as the stork swooped down, I felt a contraction. Our third baby was arriving right on schedule. Neither Seby, at seventeen months, nor Adri, at six and a half, showed much interest in the developing events. Sabrina was born early on the morning of April 11th. She weighed in at a healthy eight pounds fifteen ounces and, like Seby, nursed from the beginning without difficulty.

Just as we had worried, before Seby was born, that he might be autistic, we faced the same fears with Brie. Do we dare risk it? we asked ourselves. Could we handle another autistic child? For myself at least, I knew the answer had to be yes, because as difficult as Adri could be, I loved her completely. And despite all the tears and struggles I recognized that I was opening up and expanding because of her, growing and changing in positive ways.

In my own upbringing I had learned to value intelligence above almost all else. So how does a person like me learn to love and mother a person like Adri, who appears to be sorely lacking in that very capacity? Somewhere along the line I rearranged my value system. I didn't do it consciously. It wasn't an intellectual decision. It just happened. I valued Adri more than anything on earth. Yet by all appearances she was not intelligent, therefore I could no longer hold intelligence as a primary value. Loving kindness, tolerance—simple "humanness," if there is such a thing—became vastly more important. I began learning some important lessons, one of which was that if I did not want Adri, or myself, to be harshly judged, then I'd better stop judging others so harshly. Who was I to pass judgment on anyone?

Although I'd always considered myself a compassionate person, one who believed that those with more advantages had a clear responsibility to care for and protect those with less, before Adri came into my life, my compassion had more of a patronizing quality. My unspoken assumption was that I was doing all those less-advantaged people a favor. I didn't yet understand that we all have the right to occupy our own space on the earth simply because we exist. I didn't realize that it was possible to really love someone even though they lacked all the qualities you considered worthwhile. I had no idea what unconditional love was. I didn't even know how much I didn't know.

Before Adri I deeply believed that I was not only in charge of my own life but that I could control the lives of others as well. Adri pulled the rug out from under me. She taught me that the world was not my oyster. This was a painful lesson, and one I've really struggled with. But it came to me because I desperately needed it. Under Adri's tutelage I've learned to recognize myself as simply a person becoming.

We took Brie home from the hospital a couple of days after she was born, this time even escaping the jaundice scare. Brie slipped into our family and into our lives with ease and joy. In fact her first day home she performed an amazing feat. I put her in her crib on her stomach, and when I returned a few minutes later, she was lying on her back. I literally jumped. I yelled to Rodrigo to come and see. Had he turned her over? I asked. He said no, he'd been downstairs. There was no other possibility. At three days old she had turned over on her own. I had to conclude that, like her sister and brother, Sabrina, too, was an extraordinary being.

In May, after Adri tested lower on the standardized tests at LCDC than she'd tested at NPI some two years earlier, I decided that it was time to schedule an interview for her with Dr. Kitahara, Higashi's founder, who was visiting Boston at the time. As we entered the hotel suite where the interview was to take place, Dr. Kitahara came forward to greet us, smiling warmly. She bent down, took Adri's hands into her own, looked directly into her eyes, and murmured something in Japanese. Adri pulled away and went to a corner of the room. Rodrigo and I glanced at each other. Surely that couldn't be the kind of behavior Dr. Kitahara was looking for?

Then Dr. Kitahara went over and spoke with her Japanese colleagues. After less than a minute one of the men came over to tell us that she had accepted Adri into the school. That was it. Adri had met Dr. Kitahara's sole criterion, the "look into the eyes" test. She could see the depth and intelligence in Adri's eyes, and that was enough for her. In that moment she earned my lasting respect. She had looked for Adri in the one place that no other professional had ever sought to find her.

We enjoyed a relaxed August at the lake house in New Hampshire that we had bought the past spring. The children spent hours at the beach. Adri loved being in the water, being tossed in the air, swimming to the raft. She would sit, running her hands or a stick through the sand for long periods of time, occasionally jumping up to scamper along the water's edge, or to trample over Seby and Brie's sandcastles, giggling and shrieking with joy and excitement. Though annoyed at seeing their creations ruined, Seby and Brie were used to this kind of behavior. They seemed to accept it as part of life with Adri.

When we returned to Boston in September, Adri began attending Higashi School. It was housed in a recently abandoned public school building that Higashi had rented from the state of Massachusetts. I liked to think of Adri in those corridors. They reminded me of my own childhood school—a regular school built for regular kids. When I brought Adri there the first day, I saw several of the children walking down the halls in an orderly fashion, their hands resting lightly on the shoulders of the child in front of them. I shook my head in disbelief. Did they really think they could get Adri to do that? Maybe the others, I thought, but not Adri. I was sure that they had finally met their match.

After school had been in session for a month, I was invited to come and observe. I hadn't known what to expect, but I certainly didn't expect that the first thing I'd see would be my daughter walking in a line, her hands resting lightly on the shoulders of the child in front of her as they all made their way into the gymnasium. It seemed a miracle, the first of several we experienced in her first six months at Higashi.

The most momentous of these accomplishments was that Adri, at almost seven, was finally potty trained. The school didn't use any special tricks, just common sense. They took her diapers off and wouldn't put them back on, no matter how many accidents she had. They took Adri to the bathroom on a regular schedule, and they helped her clean up when she missed the toilet.

At home, Rodrigo assumed the responsibility for nighttime potty training. As the school had instructed, Adri went to bed without diapers, and Rodrigo woke her up and brought her to the bathroom every night an hour after she had fallen asleep, and again in the morning an hour before her usual wake-up time. Within about a month Adri became aware of when she needed to use the bathroom and began to wait, trusting that we'd take her. Sometimes at school she even went by herself.

Adri also learned to sit still and eat lunch with minimal assistance. Although she couldn't seem to learn any of the daily calisthenics movements the students practiced together, she nevertheless stayed in her place in line while the others performed the movements. The secret of the school's approach, I learned, is perseverance. Higashi teachers are more persistent and stubborn than even the most impaired and/or stubborn autistic child.

As part of the Higashi curriculum the children practiced all year learning specific motor skills such as walking on a balance beam, dribbling a basketball, riding a bicycle, using roller skates, and so on. Then, at the end of the year the students showed off their newly acquired skills in a dramatic three-hour performance complete with elaborate costumes, music, and sets. A hall was rented, and parents, relatives, friends, and invited officials—some even from Japan—attended. Initially I had my doubts about the value of this extravaganza. It wasn't until I saw Adri in her first year-end celebration that I began to appreciate just how much effort it represented and how much it meant to her and to us.

Sitting in that audience, holding my breath, crossing my fingers, I found it breathtaking watching our oldest daughter performing on that stage. Adri was so proud of herself. There was a radiant glow in her eyes when we all rushed up to hug and congratulate her afterward. For the first time in her life she had received public praise and recognition for her achievements.

What other school or program would dare attempt such a major production? Most wouldn't consider working as hard as it takes to ensure success, nor would they be willing to risk yet another failure in the lives of autistic children, who have already experienced more than their share of it. No wonder the parents so passionately supported the school.

It seemed as though Higashi, unlike other schools, had the knowledge and the experience to create appropriate programs for the children over a long period of time, not just for the first or second year. And since they had achieved such astounding success with Adri in her first months there, it seemed possible that she, like some of the other students, might eventually be able to engage in academic work and perhaps even play a musical instrument. At Higashi Adri traced letters or numbers rather than simply sorting colors and pegs. It was an important distinction. Here her day came close to a normal school day.

With Adri settled into her routine, two-year-old Seby enrolled in a morning program, and with only Brie at home, no longer nursing, I started part-time in the master's program for social work at Boston College. I soon discovered that graduate programs in social work were not advocacy oriented as I had anticipated, but clinical. So instead of learning how to be an effective voice for the disadvantaged, I received training in psychotherapy. This wasn't a path I would have chosen for myself, but I found that I was enjoying my studies immensely.

Though she continued to improve her second year at Higashi, Adri's accomplishments were far less dramatic. Unlike some of the other children she didn't master any of the exercises, nor did she improve academically. Still, we were shocked and disappointed when she was placed in a class for children who were not progressing very well—the nonachievers, so to speak. It was like getting a jolt of reality. Even here, in the best of schools, Adri was one of the very worst students. If Higashi couldn't teach her, maybe she just couldn't learn. Rodrigo had never been overly hopeful. I slowly began to resign myself to the possibility that this preschool level—a picture of an igloo drawn on the blackboard and the word *cold* spelled out beside it—might be Adri's maximum level of intellectual achievement.

Of course I knew I'd never quit looking for answers, but I stopped expecting to find them. Perhaps all the experts were right after all. Perhaps the light that shone in Adri's eyes wasn't light at all but only my own wishful projection, a mirage in the desert. Perhaps, as the experts suggested, there could be no breakthrough because there was nothing to break through. It felt like a deadweight in my heart.

Rodrigo and I spent long hours talking about Adri's future, about how we could ensure her safety and well-being once we were gone. Over the years the moderate-mental-retardation diagnosis had even begun to appeal to us. At least then we might expect her to reach the so-called age of reason, a mental age of about seven. At that level she could possibly learn enough rudimentary reasoning skills to get along in the world. But now, five years beyond her diagnosis, with the best help the medical and academic communities could offer, she was functioning, optimistically, at a two-year-old level. The likelihood that Adri would ever reach the "age of reason" seemed very remote.

Chapter 6

ACCESS

The last thing we expected was a miracle.

For some months we'd been hearing about a new breakthrough therapy for autistic children, but we didn't pay much attention. It was something about autistic children communicating through typing, and demonstrating sophisticated literacy skills. I assumed that if anything like that was happening, it could only be with "high functioning" autistic people, those who had already demonstrated some language skills. These children were a breed apart from Adri.

However, in January 1991 I was amazed to hear, via the Higashi grapevine, that one of our own had tried this new technique. A child I knew had typed the word *earth* in response to a question about what planet he lived on. A little younger than my daughter, he was nonverbal, self-abusive, and as "low functioning" as Adri. I was puzzled. The father of this boy knew the rules. He knew better than to use words like *miracle* or *breakthrough* about anything to do with autism—words that raise false hopes.

I thought there must be some critical piece of the story that I just wasn't hearing about. But when I checked around, it held. Using a method called Facilitated Communication, or FC, this father had seen his child type the word *earth*. I couldn't ignore that. The man to contact, I was told, was Dr. Douglas Biklen, a professor at Syracuse University who specialized in integrating special-needs children and adults into schools and communities.

I contacted Dr. Biklen, and he sent me a paper he'd just written on FC. It described how the method originated in Australia with a woman named Rosemary Crossley. It involved a trained person, a facilitator, lightly supporting the hand or arm of a "handicapped" person in a manner that enabled him or her to type. Ms. Crossley had first used the method with people who had cerebral palsy. Then one day, on a whim, she tried it with an autistic person and, much to her amazement, it worked. She soon began facilitating successfully with other autistic persons. Sometime later Ms. Crossley contacted Dr. Biklen. Though skeptical, he agreed to visit her program during one of his trips to Australia. As the initial several days extended into several weeks of observation at her center, Dr. Biklen became convinced of the authenticity of FC, and returned to the United States determined to introduce it to autistic people here.

Intrigued, though still skeptical, I spoke with Dr. Biklen again. He told me that FC was being used with many autistic children in Syracuse and that he had trained a group of facilitators, some of whom were available to do workshops. I approached the Higashi School about hosting such a workshop. When they agreed, I called Syracuse again and was put in touch with Annegret Schubert and Marilyn Chadwick, two experienced facilitators. We set up the workshop for February 22 and 23, 1991. They would see as many children as time would allow in those two days. Higashi would select the children who would participate. Adriana was one of the fourteen children chosen.

I brought her to school the morning of the twenty-second excited, but expecting very little. Marilyn was Adri's facilitator. She greeted Adri pleasantly, steered her to a chair, and then sat down beside her, expertly boxing her in. I sat behind the two of them. Marilyn began the session by showing Adri pictures of other autistic children and adults pointing to letters, their hands, wrists, or elbows lightly supported by the facilitator. This was Facilitated Communication, she explained, and Adri could do it too.

Adri didn't even look at the pictures. Ignoring her indifference, Marilyn took Adri's hand and showed her how she intended to support it. The whole thing was beginning to look pretty farfetched to me. To type, Adri would have to know not only how to think and process information but also how to read and spell—and she wasn't even paying attention. I glanced at Marilyn, half expecting to see embarrassment or some acknowledgment of failure. But she seemed perfectly at ease, continuing to converse with the air around Adri.

Marilyn then took Adri's hand and rested it in the palm of her own. She isolated Adri's index finger while gently suppressing her other fingers. She showed Adri a piece of paper on which were drawn groups of toys and food and animals, then she asked Adri to point to the animals. I waited, not even hopeful enough to anticipate disappointment. After a moment, to my complete astonishment, Adri moved her hand forward, letting her index finger come to rest on the animal grouping. I moved in closer. Was this a fluke?

Marilyn then asked Adri to show her the food. Before I could even summon my doubts, Adri easily and correctly responded. I couldn't believe what I was seeing. Adri was demonstrating awareness and intent. Was this my child?

After that I listened incredulously as Marilyn told Adri that she knew this work was probably very easy and boring for her, but that she intended to introduce more difficult material very soon. Although I've always talked to Adri in a respectful way, I never spoke to her as if she were a perfectly normal nine-year-old child. I felt like Alice in Wonderland—as if I'd slipped into a dream world where the extraordinary becomes ordinary.

Marilyn then read a description to Adri: "This animal has whiskers and short ears." She showed Adri a page with about sixteen line drawings of different animals and asked Adri to indicate the one she had described. Without hesitation Adri's finger went to the drawing of the cat. Before I even had time to register my shock, Marilyn brought out a Canon Communicator, a portable typing device about the size of a calculator, and asked Adri if she would like to write the word for that animal. I began to cry soundlessly. Through my tears I watched in disbelief as Adri typed the letters C . . . A . . . T. I didn't even know she knew what a cat was, much less how to spell it.

Marilyn carried on as if this were an everyday event. She brought out another page, containing sixteen words that corresponded to the animal line drawings. She pointed to one of the words and asked Adri to read it, then point to the corresponding animal. Adri's eyes swept over the page and after a moment she correctly pointed to the pig and then typed on the Canon the letters PIG. Not only could she spell, she could read. I was in a state of shock—numb, I was almost out of touch with what was going on right before my eyes. Marilyn asked a series of questions, and Adri answered all of them, typing that she liked books, books were found in libraries, and that she enjoyed bologna sandwiches.

Marilyn finished up the session by asking Adri, "Is there anything that you want to tell Mom?" From my trancelike state I watched as the letters emerged one by one:

"IEEJUSTWANTEDTOTELLMOMSHEISTERRI . . ." At this point I fully expected that "TERRI" would finish with the letters BLE. But I figured I'd take whatever I had coming to me. Instead Adri absolved me forever with the letters FIC.

"I JUST WANTED TO TELL MOM SHE IS TERRIFIC."

I was crying and laughing, on the edge of hysteria. Not only could she think, spell, and read—she forgave me, she cared about me. I only remembered later that, through my sobbing and hugging, I apologized to her, repeating over and over, "I'm so sorry. I'm so sorry. I didn't know. I love you. I love you, Adri."

Other people started milling about, and the next child arrived for his session. A teacher came to take Adri back to her classroom. I wanted to grab Adri up into my arms and take her home. She shouldn't just return to the classroom as if nothing had happened. But I was still so numb that she was gone before I could react. I rushed into the school office and called Rodrigo's secretary, asking her to tell Rodrigo that I was on my way over. I had to tell him this news face-to-face.

The Canon prints the typed message in a narrow strip of paper. Marilyn had pasted Adri's communications onto a sheet of typing paper, and it lay on the car seat beside me. As I headed for Rodrigo's office, I replayed the scene over and over in my mind, glancing at the tapes every few minutes to prove to myself that I wasn't dreaming.

When I told Rodrigo and showed him Adri's words, he just started to cry. And I cried, too, a thousand tears of joy and relief. As we emerged from our daze, we began to call around Boston and then New York, finally locating a Canon Communicator we could get within two days. I had already made an appointment with Marilyn to come to our home the following day to type again with Adri and to train us to facilitate. The next twenty-four hours seemed interminable. I desperately wanted to make contact with Adri again, to talk to her. I needed to reassure myself that what we had experienced the day before was real.

The next day Rodrigo and I watched, fascinated, as Marilyn once again facilitated Adri. Even though the questions Adri answered, about geography and the solar system, were easy, I was still astonished. Where or how could she have learned this information?

In one rather humorous exchange Marilyn asked Adri a question about "baking with Mom." Adri typed that she did *not* like to bake cakes with Mom. The most extraordinary surprise of all was her math skills. I would never have dreamed of asking Adri math questions, but Marilyn's work with other autistic children had taught her that they are often adept at math. So, calmly, without skipping a beat, Marilyn gave Adri problems in addition, then subtraction, then multiplication, and finally division. Adri correctly answered every one. Rodrigo and I were absolutely stunned. Marilyn was not. In her experience this level of competence wasn't all that unusual.

Adri fidgeted throughout the session and tried to throw her Canon on the floor or push the table over several times. Marilyn simply remained calm and alert, averting disasters before they happened or quickly reorganizing when they did occur. About halfway through the session Marilyn asked us if we wanted to try. Though Rodrigo was eager to learn, there was only enough time for one of us, so he let me go first. I just couldn't wait. Marilyn started by facilitating my facilitation. With her help I was able to facilitate Adri as she typed one- or two-word responses to questions. It was extraordinary. It was heaven.

Then Marilyn let go, and now I was facilitating Adri on my own. All along I'd felt convinced that Adri was doing the typing, yet, almost in spite of myself, doubts kept creeping in. Was it really Adri, or could Marilyn be influencing things? It just seemed too good to be true.

I was holding my breath as I supported Adri's hand, poised above the keyboard. Then suddenly I felt it. Pressure, as she directed her finger to the letter she wanted and then to the next and the next. It was the most incredible sensation of my life. Her hand was pushing mine. I could feel it. She was asserting her own will. She was communicating. She was in there, my daughter, Adriana Noelle Rocha.

In the hours and days after Marilyn left, things in our house might have looked the same to a casual observer. But things were not the same—and they would never be the same again. Adri still ran around the house without any particular direction, dropping things wherever she might be, listening to "snow" on the TV, blaring the radio, and drawing on any surface with any writing utensil she could find. But now I knew that these were purely and simply autistic behaviors. They didn't necessarily reflect anything that was going on inside Adri. Our child was far, far more than the embodiment of her physical actions—more than a figment of her father's or my imagination, more than our wishful projection. She was her own unique person.

Almost immediately we began to relate to Adri differently. I stopped talking to her in just one- or two-word sentences, and I also stopped talking to myself in her presence. Now I used complete sentences and looked directly at her as I spoke. I felt light-headed and lighthearted. I knew she understood me.

Seby and Brie noticed the new atmosphere in our house. They began to treat Adri differently too. And although Adri didn't respond any differently on the outside, she seemed to radiate joy, love, and even gratitude. She was becoming known in the world.

Adri's new Canon Communicator arrived the next day. From then on I began to facilitate with her daily. At the outset I didn't try to facilitate complete sentences with her. For me, as for most beginning facilitators, a training period was necessary. Holding Adri's hand, I began as instructed with "shared knowledge." I asked her questions like "What planet do we live on?" This gave us a chance to get comfortable with FC. As Adri moved her index finger toward the keys, my task was to pull back. This slight resistance helped to slow and stabilize her forward movement toward the keys.

It was extraordinary getting to know Adri, even little things like what she wanted for breakfast, what she wanted to do that day, what she wanted to wear. After school we'd sit together an hour or more working on a study program I'd put together for her and talking. It was during this period, as more and more typed evidence accumulated, that I became truly and irrevocably convinced that this phenomenon was indeed true. This typed voice was the voice of my missing daughter.

Adri's typing could be fluid and fast-paced, but more often it was slow and arduous. We often sat for long minutes, our hands entwined above the keyboard, waiting for her to initiate the movements to the key. With frequent breaks it sometimes took an hour just to get one sentence. Adri would often interrupt a session by crashing her Canon to the floor, or by trying to bite or scratch me, or by impulsively grabbing the tape emerging from the Canon and pulling it out. Each time she seemed to be rebelling against typing, I'd ask her if she wanted to stop or take a break. Almost always, even though her body seemed to be communicating the opposite message, she said she wanted to continue.

As hard as it sometimes was, I decided that my task was to listen to Adri, not to her body. Anything else seemed disrespectful. If I stopped because she lost control of her body, what message would I be sending her? That I really didn't believe in her words? That I really wasn't interested enough to stick by her? That I was willing to stand by her only when it was comfortable for me to do so? She deserved better than that. She deserved my respect and my total commitment. So even though there were times when I'd insist on a break, I never just dropped the subject. We always returned to it so that she could complete her thoughts.

At times Adri and I typed sitting at a table, especially when we were doing schoolwork. More often, though, we sat side by side on the sofa, or on the floor in a corner. Sometimes when we typed, she would clearly be looking at the keyboard. But most of the time she appeared not to be looking at all. One day, when we were doing math with the Canon and I was tired of asking her to look at the keys, I asked how she could type without looking. She replied,

"I SEE THE NUMBERS IN MY HEAD"

During our first month or two of typing, Adri and I worked together on some simple standard academic workbooks that I'd found in a school supply store. I also created several personal subject categories with questions under each one. I had no trouble coming up with topics, because I didn't know any of the things about Adri that you'd expect to know about your own child. I asked her questions about food, sports, TV, toys, clothes, family, school, and memories. Some of the questions were about her thoughts and feelings, others were simply to gather information. Almost daily Adri would tell me that she wanted to learn more. Over and over she'd type:

"I NEED NEW WORK"

And she did. She was still doing kindergarten work in school because, strangely enough, although the staff at Higashi had been willing to host the workshop, they weren't willing to recognize how remarkable the results had been. Despite the fact that all but one of the workshop participants had successfully typed using FC, the school was now acting as if there hadn't even been a workshop. They never even told some of the parents that their children had typed. They wouldn't talk about FC. They wouldn't allow it in the classroom. They wouldn't acknowledge Adri's academic progress and promote her to a higher level.

In spite of my disappointment I continued to trust their integrity. I knew that, like me, they had to be reeling from the shock. They could hardly have expected to see children they thought they knew so well do something so completely extraordinary—especially using a technique that wasn't even their own. Incorporating FC into their overall program would create a lot of upheaval, too, especially since it would require changes in their "Daily Life Therapy" philosophy and program. To them this was almost sacrosanct. Still, I thought, in time they'd come around. How could they eventually not do what was best for the children?

Meanwhile Adri and I felt frustrated. One day I read Adri her own Individual Education Plan (IEP). Required by the state for every special-needs child, IEPs outline achievement goals in a variety of categories. Adri's plan contained lots of functional-skills goals and hardly any academic work. When I asked her what she thought about this, she quickly typed:

"SERIOUSLY NOT WORKING   I NOT STUPID"

I tried to compensate for the lack of challenge she was getting in school by giving her harder, more interesting academic work at home. We studied geography, math, and science using second-, third-, and fourth-grade workbooks. Adri breezed through them, and in fact she seemed prepared to answer the questions even before she'd had time to read the material. I kept encouraging her to take longer until it finally dawned on me that she didn't need more time because she reads very quickly. On average it took her about seven seconds to read a two- to three-paragraph page. And then she was generally able to answer all the comprehension questions correctly.

I let Adri choose what she wanted to talk about or study each day. Usually she chose to start out a session with academic work and finish it up with a brief personal discussion. I sensed a reluctance in her to open up too fast, and I didn't want to push her. I felt that this all had to be pretty scary for her. Let her ease into this interpersonal world at her own pace. Besides, she'd been intellectually starved these last nine years, so the schoolwork was interesting and important to her.

Sometimes Rodrigo came home in time to catch the end of a session. I knew he wanted to try facilitating. But I didn't want to put undue pressure on Adri. I also felt—incorrectly as I later learned—that the fewer facilitators the better. So I insisted that Rodrigo let me become proficient with her before he began trying it.

Not wanting to lose a single word Adri said, for the first time in my life I began to keep a daily journal. While my days were spent with all my children, engaging in all the daily activities of living, in my journal I focused on Adri. My journal was my therapy. I recorded my questions and taped Adri's typed responses on the page. The first month contains lots of "getting to know you" moments—little things meant so much. Like the first time Brie wanted to wear her hair like Adri's. That was the day Adri really became a big sister. Or the day we went to McDonald's and Adri ordered for herself—not Chicken McNuggets, thank you, but a hamburger! And what a surprise when Adri asked for dresses, patterned if possible, instead of the pants that her mom preferred. As to her hair, she likes it long, and in a ponytail. Adri's favorite color, I learned, is red, although, she says: "I LIKE PURPLE TOO."

For me each revelation was a gift—the gift of my own child after nine long years. It was also the gift of having my own life back. I no longer needed to be responsible for making choices that Adri could now make for herself. Suddenly we were free. It's hard for anyone who hasn't been in this position to appreciate what such freedom means. Letter by letter, word by word, she was reclaiming her space in this world.

Some of our exchanges that first month were painful, some were perplexing. One afternoon Adri chose the "memories" category. I didn't expect that she'd be able to recall much about her first three years of life—not many people can. Still, I thought we might as well start at the beginning. That afternoon we had the following conversation:

KRISTI: Adri, do you remember anything about the first school you attended?

ADRI: YES

Before I could ask another question, she continued typing.

ADRI: JENNIFER

KRISTI: Who was Jennifer, a teacher?

ADRI: YES

KRISTI: Where were we living at that time?

ADRI: NU YORK

KRISTI: What school did you attend in New York?

ADRI: MONTESSORI

I was stunned. Adri was less than two years old when we lived in New York. How did she remember that time? How did she remember "Montessori"? And her teacher's name? I couldn't remember it myself. Hiding my discomfort, I continued on as if this were just a typical discussion.

KRISTI: Did you like the school?

ADRI: YES

KRISTI: Was it easy or hard?

ADRI: EASY

KRISTI: Did your teachers know you thought it was easy?

ADRI: NO

KRISTI: Did they think you thought it was hard?

ADRI: YES

KRISTI: Were you trying to talk then?

ADRI: YES

KRISTI: What happened when you tried to talk?

ADRI: NOTHING CAME OUT

How would it feel to try to talk for all those years and have "nothing" come out? My heart went out to her.

The subject of talking came up again in early March. That day as we typed, Adri was making lots of sounds. Finally I asked her about it.

KRISTI: Adri, are you trying to talk?

ADRI: YES

KRISTI: Would you like to work on making sounds to learn to talk?

ADRI: YES

I demonstrated very slowly the "d" sound, one that we had often heard her make on her own. And then I asked her to try to repeat it. To my total delight she did. At the same time, I thought she was also trying to say something.

KRISTI: Adri, what are you trying to say with that "d" sound?

ADRI: I DON'T TALK

I assured her that she was making progress. If she'd been able to speak those words to me rather than type them, I might have heard the pain in her voice, and then I might have known how she was feeling. But instead I continued on, excited by her "d" sound, not noticing anything amiss until she abruptly jerked out of her chair, upsetting the table. She began screaming in a high-pitched voice and jumping up and down. I couldn't imagine what was wrong, I only knew she was desperately upset. I quickly put my arms around her and pulled her into my lap.

KRISTI: Adri, tell me what's wrong. Why are you screaming?

ADRI: I SCREAM BECAUSE I WANTED TO TALK

I felt like crying. How could I be so insensitive? I hugged her and apologized for not "hearing" her. I told her that I would never give up trying to help her speak if that's what she wanted so badly. When we had both calmed down, I asked her if there was anything else she wanted to say.

ADRI: SOON I TALK WITH MY TONGUE

Before Adri began communicating, bedtime was one of the hardest times of the day. I would sit with Adri in her room, talking to her or reading as she flitted about, fiddling with the tuner on the radio, flipping the pages of a book, or running a stick over the carpet. It was at these times, when we were alone without distractions, that I felt most keenly my yearning to connect with her. In her presence I missed her most.

But after she began typing, I'd bring the Canon in so that we could talk. Even when she was tired and typed only "NOT NOW," or "GOOD NIGHT," it was enough. Reassured of our continuing connection, I was flooded with a sense of peace. On many nights I would feel so overcome with gratitude and love that I'd begin to sob and not be able to stop. It felt as if a long journey was over. I was finally home.

As monumental as all those early communications were, this was only the beginning of our developing relationship. Facilitating with Adri over the next days, weeks, and months, I began to discover my eldest daughter—an extraordinary human being, part child, part nymph, part angel, part seer. And as Adri came to trust me, she began to teach me and to open my heart. What I have learned from her has utterly, irrevocably, and joyfully altered the course of my life. In the following chapters I turn to my journal to allow Adri's story to unfold for you as it did for me during those transformative months from March to September 1991.

Part Two

EMERGENCE

Chapter 7

"I HISTORY"

MARCH 1991

Saturday 3/16/91

Adri is amazing. Lately I've been thinking a lot about how I can best teach her. But I've realized that anything I can teach Adri is really just peripheral to what I'm learning from her. Adri may need me to find her books and materials, but she learns on her own much faster and more comprehensively than I can possibly teach her. She's much smarter than I am. I just have to follow her lead rather than trying to set my own agenda.

Sunday 3/17/91

I'm obsessed with the idea that Facilitated Communication has to be made available to autistic people right away. Being able to communicate should not be a luxury. The Adriana Foundation needs to sponsor FC training sessions as soon as possible.

Adri has been wet almost every morning lately. I really wonder how much bodily control she has. Last night before she went to bed, I asked her about it.

KRISTI: Adri, could you stay dry and use the toilet during the night if you needed to?

ADRI: YES

KRISTI: Good. So, you feel you have control. Will you be dry tomorrow morning when I come in?

ADRI: YES

This morning, lo and behold, she was dry. So why did she have all those wet nights? It's hard to reconcile these discrepancies. I know she's a capable person, but at the same time I have to remember that physical control is difficult for her. Maybe making progress in one area means regressing in another? After all, Adri's moving and changing so fast—how much can one person do at a time?

Monday 3/18/91

This morning before school Adri chose her clothes for the first time. I supported her hand and she pointed to what she wanted to wear. It was fantastic. Tonight I watched her play in her room. Her favorite toy is a Sit 'n' Spin—you sit on it and spin around by shifting your body weight. She spun at top speed, nonstop, for at least three minutes. Her eyes were closed and she was smiling blissfully. It was amazing.

KRISTI: Adri, does that make you feel dizzy?

ADRI: YES

KRISTI: Do you like the feeling?
ADRI: YES
KRISTI: Is the spinning calming for you?
ADRI: YES I EZY

I guess that means it relaxes her.

The other day Adri told me she wanted to read "other men's stories." I think she meant biographies. I'd already bought a biography of Helen Keller for her, and we're reading it together. She seems to enjoy it, but she also likes the much simpler Sesame Street books just as much. Again, the juxtaposition is puzzling.

Tonight as usual Adri wanted to listen to her radio before going to bed. I taped the volume knob to keep her from blasting us out and then went to my room. A little later she pulled the tape off and I heard loud rock music blaring from her room. She loves the beat of rock or Latin music. I went in to check on her, expecting a wild dance scene, but she was sound asleep. How can she tune out that level of noise? Can it possibly relax her?

Tuesday 3/19/91

I've been thinking about my sense of coming home. Have I been lost? I know that in losing Adri to autism I lost me. So then maybe in finding her I've found me. Still it will take some effort—or maybe noneffort—for all the fears of those years to dissipate.

I told my sister, Jan, that Adri had typed "SOON I TALK WITH MY TONGUE." It made me think about that possibility. Adri can make sounds. Maybe there isn't any damage to the language centers of her brain, just some kind of blockage. How can I help her get around, get through, or get over that?

And yet I have a lingering sense that I need to slow Adri's emergence into the world so that she doesn't lose the aspects of her "autism" that she might need. If the process goes too fast, she might retreat back into the autism out of fear. If FC had been available before, I wonder if Adri would or could have emerged earlier, or is there something special about right now? And if so, are we talking about this point in her development, or mine, or this point in history?

We read Helen Keller together tonight. I asked Adri:

KRISTI: Do you like her story?
ADRI: YES
KRISTI: Does this brave girl remind you of anyone?
ADRI: YES ME

Thursday 3/21/91

"Normal" people have developed a reductionist way of looking at autistic people. We observe them, and describe and categorize them. And then, taking a huge, illogical leap, we define the whole human being on the basis of our narrow observations. In a sense we limit autistic people through our own limited perceptions. And they have no recourse, they're totally at our mercy. No human being can function without an emotional and mental life, not even if they're in a coma. But because of our arrogant need to define and control, we've created and sustained such a myth about autistic people.

Autism cannot be purely physiological. There's no such thing. There have to be emotions and where there are emotions, there have to be emotional repercussions. You can see it in the mother-child relationship—as intensely as I've loved Adri, there was an emotional distance between us that could not be bridged until we had FC. I didn't create the chasm, nor did Adri—the autism did that. But FC enabled me to see through appearances.

That must be our lesson: If we care anything about truth, we cannot limit the universe solely to what we think we perceive with our five senses. The world is not as it appears. From moment to moment Adri is a living demonstration of this truth, and this has begun to shape all my thinking. The far-out, the impossible, even the foolish, can be more real and more true than all the logical, measurable, reality-based beliefs our culture holds in such reverence.

Friday 3/22/91

This morning Adri and I worked in our sunroom turned schoolroom on her third-, fourth-, and fifth-grade workbooks. As usual she answered all the questions correctly. When we finished, Adri said she wanted to talk.

ADRI: YOU UNDERESTIMATE ME

I thought she must be talking about the schoolwork. I could see it was too easy.

KRISTI: You're probably right. Do you mean this work? What would you like to work on?

ADRI: I WORK ON ENGLISH SPELLING

KRISTI: Do you know what we're planning to do today?

ADRI: WE GO TO NINJA TURTLE MOVIE I EAT POPCORN

That was our plan. Like her mom, Adri loves popcorn.

KRISTI: Anything else you wish to say?

ADRI: YOU NOT KNOW TOO MUCH NOT TO ME

KRISTI: I don't know too much about you? Is that what you mean?

ADRI: YES

Adri had been calm up till that last comment, but then she tried to bite me. I know it's hard for her to be so misunderstood all the time. But still the biting made me angry, and I told her so.

ADRI: NO BITE SORRY

Sunday 3/24/91

I was with Adri in her room before bed, and we were reading about Helen Keller again.

KRISTI: Do you know what it means to be blind?

ADRI: YES THEY CANNOT SEE

I was thinking about my next question when Adri began to type spontaneously.

ADRI: YOU WORRY

I try not to worry all the time, but I know there's so much change in store for Adri, and I want to do the right thing. I guess it shows. I told her she was probably right. Then I told her I was going to write a note in her curriculum notebook for school.

KRISTI: Do you want to tell Mr. T. anything? If you do, start with Dear T., so he knows you're addressing him.

ADRI: DEAR T I NEED WORK TEN TIMES TEN HARDER I TOO EDUCATED I NEED NEW WORK

Pretty sophisticated communication! I certainly got the message, although I wouldn't have expressed it quite that way. Adri is very clever.

Monday 3/25/91

We were in the sunroom working on Adri's workbooks. She said she'd like to do "MULTIPLICATION," so we did some math. But toward the end of the lesson she became aggravated and tried to bite me. I asked her if she'd like to take a break. She said "YES," so we headed to the kitchen for a snack.

As I carried her out of the sunroom, we passed by the light switch and I asked her to turn it out. I've done this before and she'd never responded. But today she suddenly reached out and flipped it. I was so excited. This is the first time she'd ever just done what I've asked her to do. Is it motivation and not control that she's lacking—at least some of the time?

In the kitchen she continued to surprise me by typing that she wanted a root beer, then walking over to the fridge, opening it, and taking one. Wow! I got her a glass and helped her open the can. Then she poured the drink into the cup. We were making history. While she was drinking, though, she became very excited, probably from all the praise I was lavishing on her, and spilled her root beer. I gave her some paper towels, and she cleaned it up herself. Another landmark moment!

The ramifications of even these small changes seem enormous. How different would things be if the parents of autistic children knew from the beginning that despite appearances their children were smart and capable of understanding, and treated them accordingly? And what if these parents were to tell their autistic children that they knew they were bright but were trapped inside a body that couldn't always be controlled?

And rather than assuming from the autistic behavior that these children didn't really like or care about other people, what if their parents recognized that the problem might not be insensitivity but actually supersensitivity? How many years of misunderstanding, loneliness, heartache, and confusion might be avoided or at least alleviated for both these children and their families? It's a challenging task for parents even with FC; sometimes it's really hard to look beyond the behaviors. Yet to free our children, we have to be able to rise above the limitations of our own perceptions. I hope I can do that.

Tuesday 3/26/91

Once again, before bed Adri chose to read about Helen Keller. After we finished, I asked her what she was thinking about.

> **KRISTI:** Adri, what is Helen Keller trying to do?
>
> **ADRI:** SPEAK

Though that's the most relevant thing for Adri, I thought that maybe she hadn't understood all the concepts. I decided to check.

> **KRISTI:** Adri, are you blind?
>
> **ADRI:** NO
>
> **KRISTI:** Deaf?
>
> **ADRI:** NO
>
> **KRISTI:** Why can't you speak, do you know?
>
> **ADRI:** I AM AUTISTIC

That stopped me in my tracks. I don't know what I expected, but not that. I really do underestimate her.

> **KRISTI:** Do you know about autism?

As soon as the question was out of my mouth, I realized how stupid it sounded. So I quickly said of course she knows about autism, she lives with it. I apologized to her and then somehow got started on a little lecture about autism and other disabilities. After a few minutes I asked Adri if she had anything she wanted to say.

> **ADRI:** GO

That was either short for good night, or she was trying to tell me she didn't appreciate my lecture.

Wednesday 3/27/91

After school today Adri said she wanted to do double-digit multiplication. I wrote a problem for her: 15 x 8.

KRISTI: Adri, do you know the answer?
ADRI: NO
KRISTI: Do you know how to figure it out?
ADRI: NO

I showed her how to do the math steps. Then I wrote another problem: 13 x 3.

KRISTI: Adri, what's three times three?
ADRI: 9
KRISTI: Three times one?
ADRI: 3
KRISTI: What's the answer to the problem?
ADRI: 39

We did several more problems of increasing difficulty. She answered them really fast.

KRISTI: Eleven times twelve?
ADRI: 122

It wasn't till later that I realized she got that one wrong. Even so I'm not sure whether she got it wrong or if she accidentally hit a 2 rather than a 3. Anyway it's nice to see her get a few wrong.

KRISTI: Do you understand multiplication now?
ADRI: YES
KRISTI: Do you want to stop now or do more work?
ADRI: SOLAR

We worked in her solar workbook for a while and then stopped for the day. On the way out of the room I once again asked her to flip out the light. She did.

Thursday 3/28/91

We were driving up to our house in New Hampshire, and Adri and I were talking in the backseat:

KRISTI: Did you like the Ninja Turtles?

ADRI: YES

KRISTI: Who is your favorite?

ADRI: DONATELLO

It was early evening. I began to comment, at length, on the beautiful sunset.

KRISTI: Adri, what do you think about the sunset, isn't it beautiful?

ADRI: ROTTEN

I looked at her, surprised. That sounded like something her brother, Seby, would have said. Adri started giggling. It was a joke. I'd underestimated her once again. Did I think autistic people had no sense of humor? I gave her a big hug.

It's hard to be expressive using FC, there's such a stilted quality to it. You have to write out your thought, wait for an answer, and then type your next idea. Sometimes I just get so intense. I need to lighten up.

KRISTI: Anything you want to say to Daddy?

ADRI: HI DADDY

KRISTI: Do you want to talk more?

ADRI: YES SOON I TALK WITH MY TONGUE

I agreed that that was our goal. She looked thoughtful.

ADRI: YOU TOO SENDING ME TO SCHOOL

I wasn't sure what she meant, but I thought I'd give it a stab.

KRISTI: Are you asking if we're thinking about finding another school for you?

ADRI: YES

KRISTI: Do you want another school?

ADRI: NO

That surprised me because she'd been talking so much about getting more advanced schoolwork. Since Higashi still refused to acknowledge Adri's academic ability, we'd been discussing other school options, particularly switching her to one of the Brookline public schools. Adri had been talking about wanting friends who weren't autistic. That couldn't happen at Higashi. So I'd just assumed, underestimating her feelings yet again, that she was ready to move on.

KRISTI: Do you want to stay at Higashi School?

ADRI: YES

KRISTI: But isn't the work too easy?

ADRI: YES

KRISTI: Then don't you think it would be better to go to a regular school?

ADRI: NO

KRISTI: Why not?

ADRI: I NOT NORMAL

It was another one of those comments of hers that stop you dead in your tracks. Everything is so hard for her, but I just don't get it a lot of the time. Of course she'd have all the normal fears about leaving an old, secure place where she's been understood and accepted and switching to a new place where she'll be different from the other students and perhaps not accepted by all of them.

The prospect scares me too. And that's probably what I should have told her. Instead I tried to bolster her self-esteem. I told her she wasn't abnormal. She was a normal person with autism. A disability doesn't make a person abnormal. I told her that she was wonderful and fun and smart, and anyone would like being around her and being her friend. Then I asked:

KRISTI: Are you scared?

ADRI: YES OTHER SCHOOL

KRISTI: I know it's a big change to move to a new school, especially a regular one. It takes a lot of courage and strength. But you've already demonstrated that you have a lot of courage and strength.

I told her that we'd never just stick her in a new school

without her permission. Ultimately it would be her decision. Then I told her about my recent visit to Syracuse, where I'd seen autistic students, each with his or her own facilitator, well integrated into regular classrooms, socially and academically. I told her we were walking a unique path at this time. It might be difficult, but it would give us all the opportunity to learn and to grow.

That sounded pretty patronizing—I realize that now. I spoke as if our experiences were the same, as if I could understand what she was feeling. The truth is that her experience is far more difficult, demanding, and painful than mine or Rodrigo's. She has to live in a body that continually betrays her. She inhabits a world in which she is totally dependent on others even to express a simple need. How could I ever know what that feels like? How could I even suggest that I did?

Then, out of the blue, Adri typed:

ADRI: I HISTORY

I wasn't at all sure what she meant, and she wouldn't clarify it for me. My first thought was that she was predicting her own death, but I don't really think that was it. Was she referring to this huge change in her life? Does she mean that the way in which she's lived these last nine years is now history? I don't know. It was getting dark, and we had to stop typing.

Friday 3/29/91

We were in the kitchen of the lake house. There were lots of distractions, so Adri wasn't very focused.

KRISTI: Do you want to talk?

ADRI: YES   MOM XIT

She usually says this when she'd finished with something. I was confused.

KRISTI: You just said you wanted to talk. Why are you telling me to "xit"?

She tried several times to respond, but I couldn't really make it out. Then she started to scream.

KRISTI: Adri, what is it? Why are you screaming?

ADRI: I WANT TO TALK

It's so frustrating for her. Sometimes, even when she wants to type, she can't. Typing requires enormous concentration. It's very difficult when there are distractions, regardless of whether they're internally or externally generated. She's making such an enormous effort to be part of the world.

*C*hapter 8

"I WANT IDENTITY"

APRIL 1991

Monday 4/1/91

The kids started back to school today after spring break. Adri seemed happy to be at Higashi.

Tonight while I was reading to her, she kept leaving the room. Finally I got aggravated.

KRISTI: Adri, if you don't want to stay with me, I'll stop reading.

Adri stomped back in. I asked her if she had anything she wanted to say.

ADRI: GOOD NIGHT

Rather cryptic, I'd say. I gave her a kiss and a hug and went off to my own room.

★ ★ ★

I've been thinking about how much Adri wants to talk. She can think, she can move her muscles. Talking shouldn't be impossible. So why can't she? About half of all autistic people do talk. But why do some begin to talk and not others? Statistics show that if an autistic child hasn't begun speaking by about age five, it's unlikely that they ever will. But why is that true? Somewhere, someone must understand this phenomenon. Speech pathologists know a lot about helping people improve their speech and language, but we need to find someone who knows how to teach people to talk! Anybody out there?

Tuesday 4/2/91

After school today Adri and I went to the sunroom to talk as usual. But before I could even ask a question, she started to type.

ADRI: XIT

KRISTI: We just started to talk and you want to go? Are you still mad at me?

ADRI: YES

I assumed this might be about last night.

KRISTI: When I'm reading to you and you wander all over the place, it makes me feel that you don't care if I'm reading or not. That makes me feel very unappreciated. If you do that in school, you might offend other people too. Is this why you're angry with me, from last night?

ADRI: YOU NOT TENDER

KRISTI: I'm sorry. I don't mean to be not tender, but I think I also have to be tough sometimes. What do you think? Do I need to be both tender and tough?

ADRI: YES

Then she added:

ADRI: YOU TOO WORRIED

KRISTI: I know I worry too much. Don't you worry too?

ADRI: NO

That's amazing. I don't know how that's possible, but it sure is great.

Wednesday 4/3/91

Yesterday I promised Adri that I'd come home early from work so that we could type in the afternoon. But I was finishing a paper for school and didn't get in until just before supper. Rather than running to greet me, Adri totally ignored me. I went to her and hugged her anyway. Then I got the Canon and asked if she'd like to talk.

ADRI: XIT

She pushed me away. And when I tried to hug her again, she scratched me.

KRISTI: Are you mad at me for being late?

ADRI: YES

I explained about my paper and apologized. But she continued to be angry with me and showed it by pouring her soda all over the floor. After we finished eating, I asked her if she wanted to work, and she typed a definite "NO." I asked if she'd like me to read to her, and she said "YES."

Up in her room I talked to her about expressing her anger through words rather than scratching. She seemed very upset. More upset than I would have anticipated. I asked her several times if she was angry about anything else besides my being late. Finally she answered me.

ADRI: I YET NOT TALKING

I said it must be horribly frustrating and painful for her

to want to talk so desperately, and to be trying so hard, and yet be unable to get the words out. As I spoke, she was making lots of sounds.

KRISTI: Are you mad about anything else?

ADRI: YES EVERYBODY

I said I could understand that too. I told her that anger can be a shield for pain. And sometimes if the pain is too great, we just want to lash out at everybody. While I was talking, Seby came into the room and sat down beside us.

KRISTI: Anything you want to say to Seby?

ADRI: I LOVE YOU

This is the first time she's said "I LOVE YOU" to anyone! I was so excited. She hasn't even said it to me yet. Seby beamed. Adri hasn't really been interested in talking with the other children much, and I'm sure Seby had no idea whether Adri loved him or not, although we often told him that she did. I could see he felt very special.

After Seby left, Adri's typing became jumbled. Her answers to my questions didn't make sense, and I could see she was just letter pushing. I told her I was concerned about that because how would she get along in school if she didn't type clearly. She replied:

ADRI: I EDUCATED

KRISTI: Yes, I know you are. Why are you bringing that up now? Are you having a problem at school?

ADRI: YES

KRISTI: With someone or something?

ADRI: YES MR T

Her teacher! This makes me so angry. Why won't they acknowledge her intelligence? Why won't they listen to her? It's such a betrayal. Adri climbed into our bed, and I went over to her.

KRISTI: Are you tired, honey?

ADRI: YES AND GOOD NIGHT

★ ★ ★

Today I got calls from several excited parents responding to my "Letter to Parents" in the autism newsletter about Adri's first FC session. Luckily the Adriana Foundation has already scheduled our first FC workshop for the end of the month. I'm also giving everybody Doug Biklen's number in Syracuse. I hope he's okay with that. I feel such a sense of urgency. Now that we have FC, autistic children and adults shouldn't go one day longer without being able to communicate. The workshops are essential.

Thursday 4/4/91

Tomorrow I'm going to visit one of our local elementary schools. I described what I knew of it to Adri and asked her what she thought.

ADRI: YES I NEED NEW WORK SCHOOL

KRISTI: So, you're comfortable with me checking it out. I don't want to jump ahead of you. Are you still feeling scared about it?

ADRI: YOU TOO WORRIED

Friday 4/5/91

I told Adri all about my school visit and my discussion with the director of the special-needs program there. I asked her if she thought it sounded interesting.

ADRI: YOU WANT TO SEND ME TO NEW SCHOOL?

KRISTI: Do you want to go?

ADRI: YES I WANT NEW WORK SO I NEED TO CHANGE

Saturday 4/6/91

Adri worked well this morning. I showed her a new work-book on money and laid several coins out on our sunroom table. At first she didn't seem to understand the value of the coins, but she learned very quickly.

At one point she picked up her book and threw it across the room. When we're working with new material, I have a tendency to repeat a lot, and I think she gets bored. I talked to her about the need to express herself through typing, not by throwing things. No sooner had we started to work again than she hit me on the nose and tried to bite me. It was exasperating, but before I had a chance to say anything, she typed, "SORRY."

Sunday 4/7/91

Before bed I went up to talk with Adri in her room. I asked if there was anything on her mind.

ADRI: HI I NEED NEW WORK YES I EDU-CATED

I agreed with her. Then we picked up a book we've been reading together. It's by Temple Grandin, an autistic adult who describes the temper tantrums she used to have when she was a young girl. I asked Adri whether she felt she had a bad temper too. She said, "NO." But when I reminded her about throwing things and biting and hitting and scratching on purpose, she agreed that at times she has a bad temper. By this point Adri seemed to be getting tired, and she indicated that she wanted me to go.

KRISTI: Don't you want to say good night first?
ADRI: GOOD NIGHT
KRISTI: I love you.
ADRI: TENDER

Tender isn't a word I use very often. It gives me such a warm sense coming from Adri.

Monday 4/8/91

Dinner tonight was chaos. Seby and Brie were being very noisy and jumping out of their chairs and pushing at each other. Adri was eating her food with her hands. And each time we'd give her a fork, she'd use it for one bite and then go back to using her hands. I lectured the younger kids about their manners and then turned to Adri and said, "You too! Autism is no excuse for eating like a pig!"

When I said that, Adri just rolled her eyes, like any normal kid. It makes me realize how much I unconsciously edit my interactions with Adri, never quite daring to say the A-word. I need to stop doing this. Otherwise I'm responding to the autism, not to Adri.

Tuesday 4/9/91

Today, after we did schoolwork, I asked Adri if she had anything on her mind.

ADRI: YES YOU TOUGH WITH ME
KRISTI: Is that good?
ADRI: YES

We reviewed our earlier coin lesson, and Adri correctly identified all the values. Then I gave her a written problem, asking her to figure out which was the more expensive of two items and what the difference in cost would be. She figured it out accurately in her head ($4.98 - 1.29 = $3.69). Better than I could do.

Friday 4/12/91

I came home from work tonight feeling very rushed and guilty. Adri'd had the day off from school, and it would have been a perfect opportunity for us to work. But with the FC workshop coming up, and papers for school, and an autism news conference in Washington, D.C., where I was scheduled to speak about FC, I didn't have a minute today—or all week for that matter.

Tonight in her room, after fifteen minutes of trying to apologize and coax Adri into typing, I just stopped trying. Then she typed "I'M SORRY." I don't feel good about this. I've been so immersed in autism work that I've neglected Adri. Am I turning into one of those parents who lives her life through her child's disability? I need to keep my priorities straight.

Saturday 4/13/91

This morning I went to the sunroom with Adri, and we really talked for the first time this week. It was a great session. At first she seemed angry and had a difficult time typing accurately.

KRISTI: What's wrong?

ADRI: YOU TALKING DECISION

KRISTI: I talking decision? Do you mean that I'm making the decisions about your talking, about when we use the Canon?

ADRI: YES

KRISTI: I know we haven't talked much this week. I'm sorry. Would you like to be the one to decide when we should talk?

ADRI: TALK I WANT YES

KRISTI: I understand that you want to talk whenever you wish. I think it would help if you were facilitating with more people. Would you like everyone to be able to facilitate with you?

ADRI: YES

KRISTI: Then you have to be very careful in choosing the letters so everyone can understand you.

ADRI: TOO EDUCATED YOU HIGH EXPECTATIONS

KRISTI: You think my expectations are too high for you?

ADRI: NO

KRISTI: Do you think you can do what I expect?

ADRI: YES

I'm not sure what she was trying to get at here. Is she talking about school, or maybe about life?

ADRI: EDUCATE ME

KRISTI: I'm trying to! I'm also trying to understand what you might mean by what you're saying here.

ADRI: YOU TOO WORRIED

KRISTI: About what?

ADRI: SCHOOL

I told her I was worried because she seemed so frustrated by her lack of progress in school. I want her to get what she needs, wants, and deserves from school.

ADRI: YOU SOMETIMES TOO MOST MIDDLE ROAD

SOMETIMES DECIDE MY LIFE

KRISTI: I do sometimes decide your life—a lot of the time in fact. But you have to remember, you're only nine years old.

Adri shrugged. Maybe she's saying the decisions I make are too middle-of-the-road for her. I'm not sure.

KRISTI: You would like to decide your own life more?

ADRI: YES

KRISTI: Okay. From now on we'll talk about everything together, and you'll have a voice in everything

that has to do with your life. As much as possible, we'll
let you make the decisions that affect your life. Is there
something in particular that you're frustrated about just
now?

ADRI: I WANT EDUCATION

This, after she's just told me I'm too worried about
school. Is she really talking about school? I don't know.
We've discussed switching to home schooling. Is that what
she wants?

KRISTI: Where do you want to be educated?

ADRI: SCHOOL

KRISTI: It must be very upsetting to have everything
change in your life, everything opened up, your intelligence revealed, and still not have this acknowledged and
supported at school. But I don't know what to do about
it. I can't force them to facilitate. And because it's so late
in the school year, it doesn't make sense to switch to a
new school right now. Maybe the best we can do is just
to work more at home.

ADRI: HOME MORE WORK

The battery ran out on the Canon, so we stopped. At
bedtime I read to her as she walked around the room pulling the string of her talking Bugs Bunny toy. I don't know
if she was copying what Bugs Bunny was saying, or if it was
just spontaneous, but I heard her say aloud: "Nigh-nigh."

KRISTI: Adri, you talked with your tongue again. I
understood you. That's great!

Is she trying to talk every time she verbalizes? If so,
what enormous perseverance she has. I sat on her bed. She
took a copy of *101 Dalmatians* from a pile of books on the
floor, brought it to me, and then curled up beside me while
I read it to her. She's never done that before.

Friday 4/26/91

At breakfast Adri was calm and indicated she wanted to talk.

ADRI: YOU DEDICATED NOT

KRISTI: Do you mean that you think I'm not dedicated?

ADRI: YES I NEED NEW WORK

I explained to her that I did consider myself dedicated, but some things took time and she needed to understand that. I was doing the best I could.

KRISTI: Do you mean you want to quit learning?

ADRI: NO

KRISTI: Do you mean you want to move to a harder class, quit the class that you are in?

ADRI: YES

After school Adri and I had our usual study session in the sunroom. She wanted to work in her "Sound and Light" workbook. At the end of the book there were several examples of Japanese haiku poetry. Adri seemed interested.

KRISTI: Do you understand what a haiku is?

ADRI: YES

KRISTI: Would you like to write one?

ADRI: YES

Then she wrote slowly and carefully.

ADRI: TENDER ENDINGS ARE
DECIDED BY THE DAWN
NOT IN THE NIGH

I was absolutely stunned. What a beautiful haiku. Adri's first creative work. Getting the words out took a lot of focus and concentration, but she stayed with it. I told her that her poem was amazing and beautiful and that I would remember it forever. I was so proud of her, and she seemed proud of herself too. Is a haiku like that typical for a nine-year-old? I doubt it.

Sunday 4/28/91

Tonight while we were reading together, Adri was making lots of sounds. I heard her say, "Mama," quite distinctly. It was music to my ears. We'd had a busy day, and Adri seemed tired.

KRISTI: Are you ready for bed?
ADRI: NO
KRISTI: Well, do you want me to leave now?
ADRI: YES GOOD NIGHT MOM
KRISTI: I love you Adri. Anything else you want to say?
ADRI: YES I LOVE YOU

This was a first! Never in this lifetime had I expected to hear that from Adri. I felt blessed. I hugged her tightly and told her how much I loved her, too, and how wonderful it was to hear those words from her. I floated from the room.

Tuesday 4/30/91

Last night was our FC workshop. Marilyn Chadwick, Adri's facilitator from Syracuse, was the presenter. Despite some minor mishaps with the video, everything went great. This morning, with no prompting and very little hesitation, Adri typed a lot.

ADRI: I WANT IDENTITY I NEED EDUCATION NEED NEW SCHOOL
I NOT EDUCATED I NOT STUPID

She was late for school, so we didn't have time to continue, but I told her that it was an important subject and we would talk about it later. She wants to be her own person and be recognized as such. Is that so much to wish for?

After school she continued to be expressive. Instead of working on her third- and fourth-grade workbooks, we used the encyclopedia. She answered several of my questions correctly after reading entries in the encyclopedia. I thought the work was going well, but during a pause Adri changed the subject.

ADRI: OTHER DAY I NOT MAD

I thought she might have been talking about the other day when she said I wasn't dedicated enough, but I couldn't get her to clarify. Then she started typing again.

ADRI: I MEDICINE EDUCATED

KRISTI: You want to be educated in medicine—to be a doctor?

ADRI: YES

KRISTI: What do you want to study?

ADRI: NEUROLOGY   YES   I   MANAGE NEUROLOGY   NOT DIE   LEGHY CLINIC

I was surprised and more than a little bit impressed. How did she know about neurology and the Lahey Clinic?

KRISTI: Do you mean you want to be involved with the Lahey Clinic somehow?

ADRI: YES   I DIE HAPPY HELPING OTHERS PEOPLE HAPPY WHEN I HAPPY

KRISTI: What do you mean "people happy when I happy"? Why?

ADRI: BECAUSE I FIND A CURE FOR CANCER CANCER ACTS AS AN AGENT FOR THE BRAIN AND SENDS A MESSAGE TO THE CELLS

I was shocked. Whatever was she talking about? Where did this come from? It sounded so complex, so sophisticated. Trying to appear calm, I continued.

KRISTI: Do you know where you want to study?

ADRI: YES   MIT   I EDUCATED

I praised her ambition and her choice of schools. How did she know about the Massachusetts Institute of Technology? It's so strange, I have no idea what she knows. Our baby-sitter said there had been a documentary on TV about cancer the other day, maybe Adri had been watching it. Still, her language seems pretty uniquely her own.

Chapter 9

"I Smart Not Stupid"

MAY 1991

Saturday 5/4/91

I met with the special education director for the town of Brookline the other day. She could not have been nicer or more supportive and helpful. She looked at Adri's academic work and expressed amazement but not doubt—at least not to me. She told me to go ahead and look for a full-time facilitator for Adri. My hope is to hire someone soon so that he or she can be trained and get to know Adri over the summer. Then the transition to having that person as the classroom facilitator in the fall will not be so difficult.

Adri said she agreed with the plan, but then made a strange comment.

ADRI: DOES NOISE MAKE YOU EDUCATED?
KRISTI: No, I don't think so, what do you think?
ADRI: NO I EDUCATED WITH NOISE AT
SCHOOL

I'm not sure what she meant, but perhaps she was referring to the high noise level with so many autistic children
at Higashi School. Or maybe she was being sarcastic, suggesting that so far "noise" was the only education she had
received.

Sunday 5/5/91

Today before we began with Adri's workbooks, I asked her
why she always turned the TV to the "snow" channels.
   ADRI: I XCITED
I asked her to try to keep the sound level down when
she does that because it hurts everyone else's ears.
   That settled, we moved on to the science. I asked Adri
if she knew who discovered the concept of gravity.
   ADRI: YES NEWTON
   KRISTI: Right. And how did you know about cancer,
Adri?
   ADRI: I SEE IT ON TV
   KRISTI: How did you know about MIT?
   ADRI: YES WITH YOU
   I don't remember discussing MIT with her, but I guess
I could have mentioned it. Then I wanted to review some
material with Adri, but she didn't want to do it and she
threw her machine on the floor and tried to bite me. I got
very angry with her and told her that I wouldn't put up
with that kind of behavior. She could do better. I asked her
if she had anything to say.
   ADRI: YOU TOO TOUGH   YOU XIT
   KRISTI: You can't just throw things and bite when
you're angry. Remember, I'm supposed to be both ten-

der and tough. That's what you told me. Anything else you want to say?

ADRI: YES   YOU MAKE ME MAD

I was actually pretty thrilled that she was able to tell me that directly, without backing down.

KRISTI: It's fine that you're mad, but isn't there another way that you could express that without throwing your machine or trying to bite me? The machine is very precious. It's your voice.

ADRI: TELL

KRISTI: Yes, telling would be much better.

She still seemed angry.

KRISTI: Is there something else you have to say?

ADRI: I SMART AND I RICH

She sounded like a spoiled brat. How amazing. It makes me realize how much I still see her single-dimensionally. She is a sensitive child who wants to help others, make friends, and be a neurologist. She is also a little nine-year-old girl who, like most kids, can be stubborn and petulant at times.

Monday 5/6/91

Tonight at the dinner table the children talked about their day at school. When I asked Adri about gym class, she said:

ADRI: NOT YET EDUCATED   WE RODE BIKE

It's nice to have her participating in family conversations.

Tuesday 5/7/91

Once again we had the Canon at the dinner table and I asked Adri about her day. She gave what might by now be considered a standard reply.

ADRI: NOT YET EDUCATED

She vacillates between "I too educated" and "not yet educated." I'm still not sure what she means. Suddenly she started making high-pitched screams and then threw her body against the table.

> **KRISTI:** Adri, what's going on? Are you mad about something?

ADRI: YES ME

Does she blame herself for her autism? Does she really suffer when she, or maybe just her body, acts out? I talked to her about the need to express her feelings to help vent the frustration. I told her that no one was to blame for the autism, least of all herself.

Wednesday 5/8/91

This morning Adri and I talked before school.

ADRI: YES YOU WEREN'T TENDER TO SEBY LAST NIGHT

What a surprise and what an intuitive comment. Last night I'd been putting Adri to bed when Seby, who I'd already put to bed about four times, came in again. I told him, in an angry voice, to get right back to his room. I hadn't given it a second thought and I didn't think Adri had either. I was wrong. She is always paying attention whether she appears to be or not. I told her she was right. I was angry with Seby, but I needn't have sounded so harsh.

> **KRISTI:** How do you think Seby felt when I talked to him with that harsh voice?

ADRI: YES HURT   I TOO SENSITIVE

I told her that she was not too sensitive and I was proud of her, that that kind of caring was wonderful and special. This, from a child who, according to the tenets of the current understanding of autism, lacks sensitivity and feelings toward others!

Thursday 5/9/91

We were having a lovely afternoon together. Adri had played outside and then we started working on her vocabulary words. She was typing them all correctly when suddenly she began to scream. She lunged for her machine and threw it on the floor. She was so upset that I started shaking. I put my arms around her, trying to calm both of us.

KRISTI: Adri, what is it? What's wrong?

ADRI: I WANT TO TALK

Of course she does! She wants to participate in the world, not be on the outskirts. I can't imagine what it's like. What if all our thoughts stayed trapped inside our heads or if we had to choose just one word or thought to express from among the hundreds in our brains? And although Adri can communicate now, she still needs a facilitator and a keyboard to do it—even then she can't always get her fingers to press the right keys. Sometimes I forget what she's struggling with every minute of every day. I can be so matter-of-fact, so goal driven, even when I think I'm acting in her behalf. I forget how hard this must be for her.

Friday 5/10/91

Today I've been thinking about an old article I reread about an autistic "savant" who could read a page in the encyclopedia and recite the answer to any question from that page. I wonder if Adri can do that. I'm almost afraid to find out. Still I need to know as much about who she is as I can, no matter what I discover.

Saturday 5/11/91

I'm writing this tonight for catharsis. After school today Adri agreed to read and answer questions from a children's encyclopedia. I placed it on the table between us, holding her hand so that she could indicate when she'd finished a page. She read each page in an average of only five seconds, then answered all the comprehension questions correctly.

It frightened me. I don't want her dismissed as some kind of a freak savant, just as I've never wanted her dismissed as a freak idiot. She's her own person, and I'm only just now getting to know her. I don't want to lose her again, not to anything. I want to learn about her, but I want to learn beside her. I don't know if I can understand her if she learns so differently than I do, in a way that's so outside my own ability to comprehend, so beyond me.

I don't quite fully understand my own fears, but I certainly don't want to infect her with them. I want to show her total confidence, to feed her courage, to believe in her a hundred percent. Today I was thinking about the night after our first FC session. I was sobbing uncontrollably in her room, feeling relief, happiness, and terror all merging—terror at the thought that it might somehow not be true, that she might disappear from me again at any moment. Her world is still so alien to me. And yet if I expect her to enter into mine, I must also be willing to enter into hers.

For tomorrow I've asked Rodrigo to read sections of the regular encyclopedia and prepare some multiple-choice questions. Adri can read the sections, and then I'll simply facilitate her without knowing any of the answers myself.

This whole thing is so huge and overwhelming. I know I'm afraid and I don't want my fear to impair my judgment. I keep thinking back to those first weeks after we started facilitating. The fear that this wasn't real was so strong—even though I could feel her pressing the keys. Even though she talked to me about things I didn't know. Even though she'd refuse to type when she didn't want to no matter what I wanted. Even though she said some amazing things, in amazing ways, that went far beyond my own thinking. Even though I had all this evidence, it was still hard to believe because appearances and reality were so much at odds.

Just writing this helps me to relax and breathe easier. I know I have to simply allow things to unfold, to stay out of the way. I need to remember that this is a process. Most of all I have to keep reminding myself that the fact that I don't or can't understand the nature or workings of the process doesn't invalidate it in any way. I am, after all, neither omniscient nor omnipotent. My fears are my problems, not Adri's.

Sunday 5/12/91

Today Rodrigo, Adri, and I worked together in the sunroom using the questions he'd prepared from the encyclopedia. They were about Siberia and Sierra Leone. I sat with Adri and turned pages for her as she read the material on Siberia. She answered one of the two questions I asked her correctly.

Then right away, before we'd even had a chance to do the reading, Rodrigo asked her the questions about Sierra Leone. Adri got two out of three correct. Although she'd flipped the page over once and gotten a glimpse of the Sierra Leone section before I turned it back, it's hard to imagine that she could have read it that quickly. The results were both confusing and inconclusive. We'll just have to try it again.

I assured Adri that I wasn't trying to test her.

ADRI: YOU TOO SENSITIVE   NOT NECESSARY

Sometimes she can be so reasonable. Then she added a comment.

ADRI: YET NOT EDUCATED

KRISTI: That's what we're doing right now. When do you think you'll be educated?

ADRI: WHEN I HAVE MORE HOURS OF EDUCATION

How true.

Monday 5/13/91

Marie, Adri's old teacher from LCDC, came over this morning. I had hoped that Adri would type with Marie and show off her abilities. Instead, when I asked Adri if she had anything to say, she typed her usual "NOT YET EDUCATED" and then couldn't or wouldn't write anything else. Adri was flitting around the room acting no different from the way she had as Marie's student. It was exasperating to me, but I realize now how much more exasperating it must have been for Adri. Why should she perform to satisfy my ego? Will I ever learn?

Tuesday 5/14/91

Adri and I had a very good session today using more questions Rodrigo had prepared from the encyclopedia. We did four pages of reading, and she got fifteen of the eighteen questions right. Tonight while I was putting her to bed, she was playing with her Speak and Spell toy. I watched fascinated as she pressed the lever over and over.

KRISTI: Adri, why do you keep pushing the lever without even giving it a chance to speak?

ADRI: HAPPY

KRISTI: I'm glad it makes you happy, but is it good for you to do that over and over?

ADRI: YES GOOD NIGHT

Wednesday 5/15/91

I found an article written in 1983 about a "talking type-writer." It was about FC, although they didn't call it that. Since then several more individual examples of the success-ful use of FC, again unnamed, have been recorded. And they've been using the method for five years in Australia. Cumulatively there is quite a history of Facilitated Commu-nication, yet people are talking about it now as if it's some-thing new. What a disservice to autistic people. It must never happen again.

Saturday 5/18/91

I haven't talked to Adri since Wednesday. I'm beginning to realize that on the days that I talk to her, I feel good and peaceful, but on the days that I don't, I feel agitated and up-set. I need to connect with her every day.

I worry so much about Adri, thinking I have to protect her from unpleasant experiences. Worrying that she's angry with me or upset about something. I speculate all the time. But she just seems to let go of things—I really need to learn that from her.

Today Seby felt sick. I asked Adri if she knew about that.

Adri: YES STOMACH

Once again she was more aware than I gave her credit for. This child has eyes in the back of her head.

Sunday 5/19/91

Today we went to a play entitled *Tandy's Bishop,* based on a true story about an autistic nineteen-year-old who uses facilitated handwriting to write absolutely beautiful and

amazing poetry. "Tandy" also plays chess, hence the title of
the play. The play documents her and her mother's struggle
to get her intelligence and competence recognized by her
school, to no avail. Needless to say, I was very struck by the
story.

According to the play—and apparently Tandy consulted
closely with the production—she attributes her autism to
the trauma of her C-section birth, which she remembers,
and to her mother's seven-week absence when she was just
an infant. The director told me that Tandy says her autism
was "chosen." For most of the play Adri was pretty atten-
tive, only going out for a couple of breaks. At the end I
asked her what she thought of the play.

ADRI: I WAS MOVED BY IT
KRISTI: Adri, did the play remind you of anyone?
ADRI: ME
KRISTI: Can you remember a long time back? Like
when you were born?
ADRI: YES

Tuesday 5/21/91

Adri and I had never discussed any of the circumstances of
her birth, so I didn't really expect her to be able to answer
my questions. But still, because of the play, I wanted to ask.

KRISTI: Adri, do you know where you were born?
ADRI: GREENWICH CONNECTICUT
KRISTI: Adri, do you know what time of day you
were born? Morning, noon, or night?
ADRI: NIGHT
KRISTI: Do you remember how you felt at the time
of your birth?
ADRI: SCARED

I've heard that some people can remember their births,
but I've never met anybody that could. I really wonder if

this is for real, or if Adri somehow learned about her birth? I don't know. She didn't want to type more, but I hope she'll come back to this later.

Wednesday 5/22/91

Before school this morning I asked Adri if there was anything she wished to say, thinking she might want to comment on our discussion of yesterday. She did have a comment, but not what I expected.

ADRI: YES DOG GONE

Tuesday afternoon someone left the gate of our yard open and our dog had run off. We hadn't been able to find him. I didn't know Adri was even aware of his disappearance. Does she care about the dog? I've never seen her spending much time with him, but I should know by now that with Adri appearances are deceiving.

Our work today after school was very frustrating. Although Adri said she wanted to type, she was fighting me and pushing the machine away. Maybe she was as bored with the encyclopedia work as I was. Nevertheless I spoke firmly to her, explaining that if she really wanted an education, she had to try hard to focus her attention and do the work. I also reminded her that I was trying to find appropriate and interesting materials for her to learn from.

KRISTI: Adri, are you sure you don't want to take a break?

ADRI: NO

KRISTI: What do you want to study?

ADRI: SCIENCE

I went to our bookshelf and found a science book that we hadn't worked on yet. I opened it and read her a question from that page.

KRISTI: Adri, what drugs destroy bacteria?
ADRI: ANTIBIOTICS

How did she know that? I picked the question out of the blue. Then she typed that she wanted a break. We went to the kitchen. I'd just taped a new poster up on the wall with about thirty drawings of children with different expressions on their faces and a word to describe that expression written underneath.

KRISTI: Adri, which one of those pictures describes how you feel?

I expected her to pick happy or something like that. Instead she went straight to the picture labeled "Terrified" and then, without pausing, pointed to "Ashamed." I took her in my arms and hugged her tight.

What is she terrified of? Being part of the world? That I might stop talking to her or stop trying to help her? And what is she ashamed of? Her behavior? I reassured her that I would always be there for her no matter what.

Thursday 5/23/91

I asked Adri at breakfast if there was anything she wanted to say.

ADRI: YOU WONDERFUL   NEED YOU

Perhaps she was trying to apologize for the hard time she'd given me the day before.

KRISTI: Anything else you want to say?
ADRI: NOT YET EDUCATED

Back to business as usual. I told her that today, as requested, I would try to buy some new science books for her.

KRISTI: Adri, I'm not sure which level to get. What do you think? Third-, fourth-, fifth-, sixth-, seventh-, eighth-, ninth-, tenth-, eleventh-, or twelfth-grade books?

ADRI: YES COLLEGE

KRISTI: You want college level?

ADRI: YES

I went to the Boston College bookstore and bought three college-level textbooks: Precalculus Math, Contemporary College Physics, and Human Anatomy and Physiology.

My brother, Jamie, who has just completed his M.B.A. in Minneapolis, is visiting us. He wanted to see Adri type, so he joined us for our after-school session in the sunroom. I started with one of our third- or fourth-grade workbooks. Adri did several pages from it with no difficulty.

Jamie was absolutely stunned. It reminded me of the first time I watched Adri type. All he could do was apologize, telling her how sorry he was for having misunderstood her all these years. I asked Adri if she knew who Jamie was.

ADRI: YES BROTHER

Then I brought out the new college texts. She chose the Human Anatomy and Physiology textbook, the hardest of the three because of all the terminology. I held the book open, waiting for her to indicate when she'd finished a page. She seemed very distracted, and when we got to the chapter questions, she got most of them wrong.

KRISTI: Adri, you didn't get too many correct. What's up?

ADRI: YES   TOO HARD

That's a first. The first time she's said that the work is too hard. In a way I'm disappointed. After all, it would have been fun to show her off to Jamie. But in another way I'm relieved.

KRISTI: Yeah, I think so too. Anything else you want to say?

ADRI: YES TENDER   YOU TOUGH   I SMART NOT STUPID

Did she think I might think she was stupid because she

couldn't do this work? I assured her that that wasn't the case. We opened some of the less technical science books and she answered a few questions. As we were finishing up, I asked Adri if she wanted to tell her shell-shocked uncle Jamie what she planned to study.

ADRI: NEUROLOGY

Chapter 10

"Today I Ready to Go to School"

JUNE 1991

Monday 6/10/91

Last night I tried again to talk with Adri, but she just hasn't wanted to type these last couple of days. I'm not sure why. Perhaps she's angry that I was away—Rodrigo and I had gone to Syracuse University to meet with Doug Biklen and some of the children facilitating in schools there. Or maybe it just takes a little time for us to adjust to each other again. However, she's been typing with our baby-sitter, so I don't feel so bad. I hate to think of Adri's going through even a day without the opportunity to talk.

Tuesday 6/11/91

Finally Adri typed with me this morning. We were watching a cartoon on TV.

KRISTI: Adri, what do you think?

ADRI: I CREATING ON TELEVISION STORIES PEOPLE YOUNG THAT HAVE AUTISM

KRISTI: You want to create programming for or about young people with autism? What would you tell people through your television stories?

ADRI: I TELL THEM NEED EDUCATION

KRISTI: Adri, do you know what special day this is?

ADRI: MOMS BIRTHDAY 35

Thursday 6/13/91

Tonight I had my first phone conversation ever with Adri. Rodrigo had taken me to a health spa in California for a week for my birthday. Our sitter had Adri's Canon, and while I talked, telling her how much I loved and missed her, I could hear Adri pressing the keys. After I finished talking, Claudia read me Adri's message.

ADRI: LOVE MOM AND DAD HI

Claudia put Adri on again, and I told her how much it meant to me to hear those words from her. Claudia asked Adri if she had anything else she wished to add.

ADRI: CLAUDIA TENDER

Claudia, too, is part of our lives forever. Adri was all right, in Claudia's tender care.

Today I met another couple from Boston, Joan and Miron Borysenko. She's a writer and he's a scientist. They conduct mind-body workshops together around the country. The four of us went hiking together, and I had such a good time talking to Joan. She's very smart. I got the feeling she could talk about anything and everything. Since she was interested in spiritual subjects, I mentioned a book I'd heard about, *Many Masters, Many Lives*, by a psychiatrist whose patient, under hypnosis, began to speak of her past lives.

Joan knew the book very well, and in fact she knew a lot about what happened to the psychiatrist in the aftermath of the book. The conversation was really interesting. There's something unique and extraordinary about Joan. I hope I get the chance to know her better.

Friday 6/14/91

Tonight we attended a presentation on self-hypnosis. First the presenter gave an overview of the benefits of self-hypnosis, and then she tried it with our group. I'd gone to a hypnotist once before to help me lose weight, it hadn't worked. I was too tense. This time, though, I really wanted to let go, so I made an effort to relax and set aside my fears.

As the group leader talked, I felt myself slide into a state of deep relaxation. It seemed that only minutes later she was instructing us to come back. When I was fully conscious again, much to my disbelief, I realized that twenty minutes had passed. She described some of the key feelings and sensations of being hypnotized, and I realized I'd done it. I was amazed and proud of myself.

I hope I can do this on my own. I feel I must open up if I'm to know Adri, if I'm to understand her.

Sunday 6/16/91

This morning I went on a silent meditation hike, and it was totally different from anything I've ever experienced in my life. It makes me nervous even to write about it, but I want to get it down before I forget things or question them away.

Early on, as we walked silently up the mountain, I slid into some kind of reverie in which I was feeling keenly attuned to nature. I sensed the earth beneath my feet—I felt it was supporting, even carrying me. Then I began to feel the air wrapping around my body, sustaining me too. I felt such a profound sense of gratitude.

At the top of the mountain we stopped to rest for ten minutes or so. Each of us found a quiet place to sit in solitude. I was perched on a giant rock, feeling peaceful and very open. Suddenly I saw this little blackish spermlike wisp to the left of my line of vision. I blinked and shook my head. When it didn't go away, I brushed my fingers through my hair and rubbed my eyes suspecting that it might be a bug of some sort. But still it remained there at the edge of my line of vision. I began to feel frightened, a little panicky. Was I seeing things? Was I crazy?

But then I took a deep breath and just watched as it moved slowly across my visual path and out of view. Then several more wisps appeared. Because I could literally see them, I assumed they were physical. But then I realized that they weren't, at least not in the sense I had always understood physical. They couldn't be touched, yet they were real.

As I continued to watch, I began to see circles, like drops. It seemed as if I was seeing the air itself composed of water droplets and little rivulets. The air, I suddenly understood, is not static but living, and it truly does sustain us. Regardless of which direction I turned my head, the droplets and rivulets were there.

I no longer felt any alarm. In fact I felt more like I was floating in that state of reverie again. Suddenly, in that same enigmatic way, I just understood what I was seeing. This was simply a part of all that is, but it exists outside of our normal range of perceptions. Just as Adri challenges my perceptions of the seen versus what's real.

On the walk down, still dazed, my thoughts drifted to my children. An image of a triangle formed with Adri at the top of it, and I understood that she was the teacher, the wise one. Seby was at the left lower point, and Brie completed the triangle at the right. I had a strong sense that I need to do more than just love and care for my children. I must begin to talk to them about the incredible gift of love we receive from God and how we must give it to others.

Tuesday 6/18/91

It's good to be home. Everybody's fine. I feel rejuvenated and healthy. And while I don't really know what happened to me on the mountain, I know that it was a blessing and related to Adri's unfolding.

Wednesday 6/19/91

This morning Adri and I had our first real conversation since my return.

KRISTI: Adri, anything special on your mind this morning?

ADRI: DIE EDUCATED

That made me nervous. Why was she talking about death?

KRISTI: Yes, I'm sure by the time you die, you'll be educated. That'll be a long time from now, I would think. How many years do you think?

ADRI: ZILLION YES

That's reassuring. Spontaneously she continued typing.

ADRI: I WISH THAT I UNDERSTOOD AUTISM WANT TO FIND WAY TO CURE PEOPLE WITH AUTISM EINSTEIN EDUCATED TENDER

There was a kind of wishful quality in her words. Adri's fascinated by Einstein and brings his name up frequently. There wasn't time to ask her what she meant because we were running late for school. But I told her that she was in a unique position to really understand autism both personally and intellectually and that if she worked hard to educate herself, she would certainly be able to contribute a great deal to the field. And I really believe that. Adri has a lot to offer the world. I'm going to look for some books on Einstein for her.

Today I finally wrote a formal letter to Higashi withdrawing Adri from the school. I told them that she would not be attending their summer program, nor would she be returning in the fall. I feel very relieved that the decision is finally made.

Thursday 6/20/91

I've been looking for a facilitator for Adri, and today one of the candidates came for an interview. Adri was a bit edgy, pushing the machine away and spitting up. I think she feels the pressure of all these major shifts in her life. Nevertheless she did manage to ask some good questions.

ADRI: SHE WANTS TO BE MY TEACHER?

Karen said she did.

ADRI: YET NOT EDUCATED

Karen told Adri a little bit about herself and her education. She seemed uncertain of how to act around Adri.

ADRI: DO YOU LOVE EDUCATION?

Karen answered yes.

ADRI: DO YOU SELECT YET YOUR OWN EDUCATION?

I think that Adri was trying to find out what subjects Karen herself was interested in, but Karen thought she'd already answered that by saying she studied special education. Finally I changed the subject and asked Adri what personal qualities she felt she needed in a facilitator.

ADRI: TOUGH NOT TOO TOUGH TENDER BUT TOUGH

Karen assured her that she was capable of being tender but tough. Adri typed "GOODBY." She had worked hard in that interview and I was really proud of her.

Friday 6/21/91

Today Adri had a sore throat, so I took her to see our pediatrician. When we'd moved to Boston, we'd chosen him to be our doctor because of his experience diagnosing and working with autistic children. I'd told him about FC some months earlier, and he'd been wanting to see a demonstration. So, even though Adri wasn't feeling well, she agreed that this seemed like a good opportunity to type for him. When we arrived at his office, I asked Adri if she wanted to say anything, but although she tried, she managed to type only one word and a lot of random letters. Although the doctor was polite, I think our visit only served to strengthen his initial skepticism. I learned a lesson the hard way: Adri is not a display model.

Tuesday 6/25/91

It feels like a long time since I've written. I just haven't had the heart. Over the weekend and for these last two days Adri hasn't been willing to type much with me. Maybe it's because I was gone for a week or, more likely, our visit with the pediatrician. I think she might have felt used by that, or perhaps ashamed or disappointed that she hadn't been able to live up to my expectations. I've apologized. I've assured her many times that I was the one at fault, not her. I shouldn't have put her in that position.

One good thing, yesterday we hired Wei to be Adri's facilitator. She starts July 1st, and I think she'll be terrific. She seems mature, calm, bright, and capable. Adri likes her very much.

Wednesday 6/26/91

Annegret, the facilitator from Syracuse who is here doing the Adriana Foundation workshops, has been staying at our house this week. Last night Adri sneaked out of her room and went down to the sunroom. Annegret was working there. She brought Adri to the computer, thinking she might want to talk. But Adri told her:

ADRI: I CAME DOWNSTAIRS TO DRAW NOT TO TYPE

I love that. I've been speaking to Annegret about the possibility of her taking a year's leave of absence from her job as a speech therapist and coming to work for the foundation. If we had someone full-time, we could set up workshops all around the country and teach FC to a lot of people.

She's considering it. With all the traveling, plus the energy it requires to introduce FC to people physically and emotionally, this would not be an easy job. But it would certainly be worthwhile and rewarding. I know Annegret feels as strongly as I do about spreading the news about FC. But I'll just have to wait and see whether she can arrange it.

Today Adri attended the end-of-the-year party at Higashi. When her teacher came over, I asked if she had anything to tell him.

ADRI: DEAR T I MISS YOU

I handed him the message, but as usual, although he was friendly to Adri, he didn't really say anything. It's a good thing we're moving on.

Tonight I asked Adri how she felt visiting the school now that she was no longer a student there.

ADRI: YES   I FELT EMPTY

KRISTI: You felt empty? What do you mean by that?

ADRI: NOTHING

KRISTI: Empty feels like nothing?

ADRI: YES

I'm not sure if she meant she felt sad/empty or if she means she's no longer upset by the prospect of leaving.

KRISTI: Adri, how do you feel, in general, about your time at Higashi? Do you feel you benefited from the experience?

ADRI: YES

KRISTI: What do you feel you've learned?

ADRI: I LEARNED I INTELLIGENT   NOT STUPID

KRISTI: That's a very important thing to have learned, and if Higashi taught you that, they served you well.

I'm glad that even though Higashi didn't come through for Adri in the end, she can still appreciate their contribution to her development. I'm going to include this conversation on Adri's thank-you letter to her teacher.

Thursday 6/27/91

Today was very traumatic, sad, and poignant. But at the same time it was also amazing and wonderful. I had taken Adri to the foundation office to do an FC consultation with Annegret in order to teach Wei how to facilitate. Adri was very agitated from the start. Possibly she had assumed the session would be at her school, like last time. She might have expected to see her beloved Mr. T. In any case, from the beginning she appeared angry. She was throwing her body, trying to scratch, kicking, and biting in a way that she hadn't done for a long time. Annegret, Wei, and I gathered close around her and held her and encouraged her to talk about why she was so upset. I tried to stay calm and communicate that quiet to her. Finally, after a lot of holding, talking, and stroking, Adri was able to type.

I don't have the specific transcript from that session, just my notes and the videotape. With Annegret facilitating, Adri typed that she was very sensitive to the upcoming change but not afraid of it. She said that she loved T. and wanted to be with him. The depth of her emotion really moved me. Her eyes welled up several times, and I began to cry too. Mr. T. was a friend, and he'd been a source of strength for Adri all those years. The whole session was extraordinary. Though I'm sure Adri has experienced loss, she'd never been able to cry about it. The experience, I think, was cathartic for her. By the end of the session she was calm.

Friday 6/28/91

Today I took Adri to see Felice for her third cranial-sacral-massage session. This therapy is supposed to correct fluid imbalances in the brain that might create sensory, motor, and intellectual difficulties. Since Adri has these kinds of problems, when another parent of an autistic child told me that it had helped her child, it seemed a logical thing to try.

Felice worked on Adri, making very gentle, very subtle physical adjustments around her neck and head. Although I hadn't noticed any effects from the first sessions, we continued to come because Adri seemed to like it. Felice said she was able to get in much deeper this time. I'm not sure what that means. At the end of the session I asked Adri if it had hurt.

ADRI: NO

Felice asked if it had made her sad.

ADRI: YES

KRISTI: Why does it make you sad? Does it make you think of anyone?

ADRI: YES

KRISTI: Can you say who?

ADRI: YES T

KRISTI: Can you tell Felice who T. is?

ADRI: MY TEACHER

KRISTI: Adri, do you have anything else you want to say?

ADRI: I HAVE TODAY EDUCATION

Tonight before bed the kids and I were in the TV room watching a video. Everybody was being a bit noisy, especially Brie. Adri suddenly got up, walked over to Brie, and very deliberately pulled her hair. Brie started to cry. I told Adri that pulling hair like that was simply not allowed.

KRISTI: Why did you pull Brie's hair?

ADRI: I DON'T ENJOY HER TALKING

KRISTI: Is it too loud?

ADRI: YES

KRISTI: Even so, we can ask her to speak more softly. We don't just pull somebody's hair. Is there anything you would like to say to Brie now?

ADRI: SORRY BEE

Before bed I went into Adri's room to say good night and see if she wanted to talk any more.

KRISTI: Adri, do you have anything else to add about T. or anything else you want to talk about?

ADRI: YES YOU NEED TO TELL T THAT ADRI WISHES HE WOULD SEE HER SPELL

KRISTI: Anything else?

ADRI: YES NO ONE UNDERSTANDS TENDERNESS LIKE T

Again I see how much I've underestimated the depth of her attachment.

KRISTI: Adri, would you like me to call T. and invite

him over so that you can spell with him and show him the video of your session with Annegret, Wei, and myself?

ADRI: YES

KRISTI: Should we buy a thank-you present for T.?

ADRI: YES

KRISTI: What should we buy?

ADRI: EDUCATIONAL MATERIALS TOYS

I told Adri that we could go shopping together for these things.

KRISTI: What do you think about going to school with children who do not have autism?

ADRI: YES TODAY I READY TO GO TO SCHOOL

Saturday 6/29/91

Tonight I was planning to read *Charlotte's Web*, but Adri wanted to talk to Daddy.

ADRI: WISH HE WOULD READ STORY ABOUT HIMSELF

KRISTI: Do you mean you'd like Daddy to talk about his own life?

ADRI: YES

KRISTI: I'll tell him.

Sunday 6/30/91

Today we had a brief scare. Adri had been playing outside for a few minutes, but when we went to check on her, we couldn't find her anywhere. We panicked. I raced out to the swimming pool, my mind filled with terrifying visions of a child floating facedown. She wasn't there of course, but because the water was murky and I couldn't see the floor of the pool, I began to imagine that somehow she had sunk to the bottom. Horrible thoughts.

Heading back to the house, I heard Annie (our babysitter) shouting from down the street that she'd found Adri. I ran over and hugged her. She had found her about a block away walking *toward* home. We went inside, and I got Adri's Canon.

KRISTI: Adri, where were you?

ADRI: I TAKE A WALK

Of course she only wants what the rest of us take for granted—a little bit of freedom and independence.

Chapter 11

"I HAVE DIED...
OTHER LIVES"

JULY 1–18, 1991

Monday 7/1/91

Mr. T. came to dinner this evening. At first it didn't seem as if things would go well. He seemed pretty distant and defensive, and Adri wasn't typing very clearly. Things lightened up, though, when T. began throwing her in the air and tickling her.

After dinner, T., Adri, and I watched the video of the session when she typed about her sadness at leaving him. The tape is so revealing—Adri's facial expressions correspond directly to her words. There's no mistaking that she's speaking from the heart. T. could feel it too. He was surprised by the intensity of her emotion and her capacity to show it. We were all mesmerized, and as usual I was crying. T. asked for a copy of the tape. Maybe he'll share it with the rest of the Higashi staff.

I talked to Adri about the evening:

KRISTI: Adri, are you pleased with how the visit went?

ADRI: NO   I YET NOT TALK WITH T

I said I thought she'd done very well. Typing had been difficult because she and T. were both nervous. But he'd seen her type quite clearly on the video, and he'd seen how much she cared about him. As far as I was concerned, the evening had been a success.

ADRI: YES

KRISTI: Anything else you want to say?

ADRI: I LOVE T

Tuesday 7/2/91

This was Adri's first day of home schooling. We were in the sunroom waiting for Wei, her new facilitator. Adri was so excited that I asked her if she'd like to get started.

ADRI: YOU NOT TEACHER

I guess she wants to keep our roles straight. We haven't been doing much academic work together lately, but I'm feeling easier about that because at least she's typing with me again. Wei arrived a few minutes late, and formal lessons began, although for this first session I did most of the facilitating.

In social studies Adri wasn't interested in answering the content questions, but she was willing to express her opinions about the information. She seemed to find the math much too easy, but she was excited about the science. Tomorrow we'll plant some bean seeds together. Still I think her favorite time was recess.

Tonight we had a barbecue birthday dinner for Annie. It was a beautiful evening. After cake and presents each of the children said something nice to Annie. Adri typed:

ADRI: I DEARLY LOVE ANNIE

Annie was thrilled and is keeping the tape. I'm always moved by the attachment everyone who comes into our orbit feels to Adri.

Annegret phoned and told me she'd been able to make arrangements to take a leave from her job and would like to come and work for the Adriana Foundation doing FC workshops around the country. This is great news.

Thursday 7/4/91

Joan and Miron Borysenko came for dinner tonight. It was a wonderful evening. They met all the children, and although Adri didn't really want to talk, she stayed downstairs with us for a little while. At one point in the evening I remember Joan's speaking to us about the "universal lesson of Adri." She saw Adri and/or autism as the "dramatization of the paralyzed heart in each of us."

Saturday 7/6/91

I suddenly find myself treading on strange waters. I must really take care to make sure I know exactly what Adri means when she tells me things—especially what she talked about today. The morning started out pretty much as usual. I spent the early part of my day preparing a lesson plan for Adri and Wei for next week while I'm away at the autism conference in Indianapolis.

KRISTI: What do you think about the work for the week?

ADRI: EASY YOU MAKE TEACHER I EDU-
CATED

I wasn't sure what she meant by that.

KRISTI: Would you like me to give you some tests so
that we can figure out just what kind of work would be
the most interesting and challenging for you?

ADRI: NOT NEED TEST I NEED EDUCATED
TEACHER

KRISTI: Well, Wei is educated. She's had many years
of college, and she also knows a lot about autism.

Adri bit me. Wrong answer, I guess. But it hurts to be
bitten, and I told her I was angry with her.

ADRI: I SORRY

Again, I repeated that Wei was intelligent and educated
and was qualified to act as her teacher. I was still puzzling
over what she meant by "EDUCATED" in this context, when
she began to type again.

ADRI: DEAD I BEEN DEAD

I was stunned. Where did that come from? I tried not
to show my discomfort.

KRISTI: Adri, I'm not sure what you mean. Is there
some relationship between being educated and having died?

ADRI: I HAVE DIED

It wasn't a mistake. That's what she meant to say. Grasping for a reasonable explanation, it occurred to me that
perhaps she was referring to having lived a kind of "living
death" these last years, being autistic and isolated.

KRISTI: Adri, do you mean you feel dead in this life?
Or is this about something else?

ADRI: OTHER LIVES I HAVE LIVED LONG
ERES

KRISTI: Do you mean eras?

ADRI: NO

KRISTI: Years?

ADRI: YES

I tried to remain calm and steady. I told Adri that I'd read and heard about such things. That there were people who said they could remember their past lives. And I added that if this was what was on her mind, I was glad she could share it with me. Inside, though, I was shaking.

ADRI: YET YOU ACCEPT THAT I SEE DEATH UNDER SIDE   UNDERNEATH

KRISTI: I'm not sure what you mean by underside, underneath. Can you clarify it for me?

ADRI: I MEAN IN HISTORY

KRISTI: Do you mean you have lived before in history?

ADRI: YES

KRISTI: You've lived before? You think you have? Who were you?

I was blurting out questions, trying to gain some time for myself. I wanted to believe her, but I couldn't, not that fast.

ADRI: YES   SAILOR

KRISTI: Do you like sailing?

ADRI: YES

KRISTI: Do you remember how you died?

ADRI: YES I DIED IN A FIRE ON RENEA TEMACIJ

I tried several times to get her to be clear about that last word. While she was telling me these things, I had a sense of déjà vu, but I couldn't quite place it.

KRISTI: Do you remember where you lived?

ADRI: TURKEY

KRISTI: How old were you when you died?

ADRI: 85

Adri had begun to struggle in my arms. I asked her several times whether she would like to stop or take a break, but each time she forcefully typed "NO!" I held her to help her stay calm. When she had quieted, we continued.

KRISTI: Some people believe that we chose our present lives for a particular reason. What do you think?

She started to struggle again, but was working hard to maintain enough control to type.

ADRI: I AUTISTIC BECAUSE I ANGRY AT YEEEE

We tried several times, to no avail, to help her clarify who or what she was angry with.

KRISTI: Adri, do you think you became autistic before or after you were born?

ADRI: AFTER

I'm not sure why I even asked that question. Is it possible for a fetus to be autistic? In *Tandy's Bishop* that girl said her autism was partly caused by her mother's absence. I caught my breath. Could it have been something I did that caused Adri's autism?

KRISTI: I remember your birth very well. The delivery was very fast. Was that traumatic for you? And then with the jaundice, you had to be alone under those lights in the incubator for several days. Did that upset you? Are you angry with me or with Daddy?

ADRI: I CHOOSE TO BE AUTISTIC BECAUSE I AM ANGRY AT MYSELF

I was flabbergasted. I can't even recall what I said then. Adri chose autism—out of anger at herself? Why? How? What did this child understand about herself? What was going on? This all felt very surreal to me. I didn't feel capable of talking much more about it, but I felt I should continue if that's what she wanted.

KRISTI: Adri, do you want to say more now?

ADRI: NO

I was incredibly relieved.

KRISTI: Would you like to talk with me again later about it?

ADRI: YES

I promised her that I would not show the tape or share

the information with anyone else except Daddy unless she okayed it first. Adri went to play with the other kids. I needed to be alone for a while. I went into my room and closed the door. I was almost in shock. The world around me suddenly seemed to be in motion. Where was the ground?

As I lay down on the bed, thoughts started running through my mind. If Adri's right and we live again and again, the implications are absolutely staggering. To me it was such an amazing idea. But Adri knows things that I probably never will. She experiences life differently. She could know about this too.

I wondered how Rodrigo would react to this. What if he dismissed what she said, just brushed it off? I felt as if I might be getting a glimpse of something very important. But it was fragile—Adri was fragile. If her ideas were not supported, if they were dismissed, what effect might that have on her newly emerging sense of self?

I asked Rodrigo to come up and showed him the tapes. Though it's possible he felt differently on the inside, outwardly he just looked at me and commented that it was pretty interesting. Such a different reaction from mine. I just let it go.

I wasn't able to get much accomplished the rest of the day—I really needed a break from my thoughts—so Rodrigo and I went to an early movie. When we got back home, everyone was gathered around the table, finishing dinner.

As I walked into the kitchen, Adri looked at me, picked up her plate, and flung it across the room. She hasn't done that in a long time. I must have really upset her. Maybe she thought I was taking our conversation lightly. The whole thing was so strange because no one else at the table knew there was anything unusual happening, except Rodrigo, who already seemed to have forgotten.

I brought the Canon over.

Kristi: Adri, why did you throw your plate?
Adri: YOU NOT HERE

I guess it was pretty selfish of me to go to a movie after she'd just shared something so important. Again, I had underestimated the intensity of her emotional life. After apologizing I held her and assured her that I am always there for her.

Adri: I CALM

Just before I went to bed. I suddenly realized what my déjà vu feeling had been about—the psychic at my friend Kathy's shower in California. He described Adri living a life at sea and had talked about her being in a fire. I hadn't connected the two things at that time, and I don't think he did either. But now it seemed pretty clear. How strange—that whole thing happened six years ago. What's going on here?

Monday 7/8/91

This morning Adri and I talked in the sunroom. I could hardly wait to get back to Friday's conversation. But I didn't want to pressure her, so I'd also prepared some questions from her textbooks. I asked her, in the usual way, if she wanted to work or talk.

Adri: CHOOSE TO NOT MONRR
Kristi: Adri, I'm not sure what you mean. Can you say that another way?
Adri: NEED NOTHING
Kristi: Adri, do you mean you choose to "need nothing"?
Adri: YES
Kristi: Why? Sometimes people feel that way if they've been hurt. Is that why?
Adri: YES
Kristi: Who hurt you?
Adri: MYSELF

KRISTI: You hurt yourself? When did you do that?

ADRI: I HURT MYSELF WHEN I WAS IN THE WOMB

She hurt herself in the womb? I'd wanted this discussion, but it had barely begun and I was already feeling anxious. Even the word *womb* seemed strange coming from a child. I tried to set aside my fears and uneasiness. I wanted to stay with Adri, just to stay with her wherever she was going.

KRISTI: Do you know how you hurt yourself?

ADRI: YES BY NOT EATING

KRISTI: How did the not eating hurt you? This is really hard to understand.

ADRI: IT ATTACKED MY ENDOCRINE SYSTEM

I had to stop for a minute. What was she talking about? Where was it coming from? She was way over my head.

KRISTI: I don't know anything about the endocrine system. What is it?

ADRI: IS THE SYSTEM TIED TO NEEDING NUTRIENTS

KRISTI: What happens to the endocrine system if it doesn't get nutrients?

ADRI: TAKES AWAY BODIES ENERGY

KRISTI: If the endocrine system doesn't get proper nutrients, it takes away the body's energy? Is that what you're saying? Adri, how would you know something like that?

ADRI: I AM EDUCATED

KRISTI: Yes, I can see that you are. But how did you learn so much?

ADRI: IN OTHER LIVES

I was already at the saturation point. I needed breathing space.

KRISTI: Adri, do you want to stop for today?

ADRI: YES

KRISTI: Will you talk about this again another day?

ADRI: YES

Is Adri being straight with me? It's not a joke, I know that. But it's just so unbelievable—unclear too. What does choosing autism "after" mean? After birth? After conception? She chose to hurt herself by not eating in the womb? Is it possible?

I believe she's communicating something important, but it's so difficult for her to put what she wants to say into language, and it's so difficult for me to grasp these concepts. Still, my task is not necessarily to understand everything she says but just to stay with her wherever she's going.

For the last two weeks Adri has been spitting up a lot. Just a little bit at a time, but almost every day. I'm not really worried, but I wonder if she's nervous about all these things she's been telling me. I asked her about it.

KRISTI: Adri, are you spitting up on purpose or accidentally?

ADRI: ON PURPOSE

KRISTI: Why would you want to do such a thing?

ADRI: I THROW UP BECAUSE IT MAKES A NATURAL DRAWING PAINT

I would never have thought of that.

KRISTI: If I give you some pencils or markers and some paper in here will you stop spitting up?

ADRI: YES

KRISTI: Will you also promise to confine your colorings to the paper and not decorate the walls and books?

ADRI: YES

KRISTI: Shall I get some now?

ADRI: YES

I brought some material into her room.

KRISTI: Now, what's our deal?

ADRI: NO THROW UP

Great! Even if she does decorate the walls, I think I'd

rather have her doing that than spitting up all day. I can't
believe how much my relationship with Adri has changed,
and is changing, both on the day-to-day level and because
of these ideas she's sharing with me. I told Rodrigo that I
thought even throwing her plate was a good thing. It means
she's expressing herself, fighting back, growing.

Tuesday 7/9/91

I went through all my pregnancy and childbirth books, and
none of them even mentioned the endocrine system except
Dr. Thomas Verney, who writes quite extensively about it
in his book, *The Secret Life of the Unborn Child*. He suggests
that a mother's state of anxiety or nervousness during pregnancy can somehow be communicated to the fetus, possibly
creating a physical basis for increased anxiety in the child.

Verney also discussed a study about the effects of malnutrition on the endocrine system. Could this be related to
Adri's reference to "not eating"? I'll have to study all this
much more. Adri uses sophisticated terminology and intro-
duces complex concepts, but it's hard to piece what she says
together. And I'm never even certain if a word has the same
meaning to her as it does to me. There's so much to
consider.

It's probably good that I'm going to the Indianapolis
ASA conference for a few days. If nothing else, I'm really
looking forward to hearing Doug Biklen speak. For the
time being, though, I think I need to keep much of what
Adri is telling me to myself, at least until I understand it
better. I'm excited, but frightened and concerned too.

Adri is only nine. What ought one to expect from a
nine-year-old? I don't know many, but I don't think this is
typical. She's too advanced, and too regressed, all at the
same time. But in spite of everything I really trust my
daughter. I just trust her. My instincts tell me that whatever

this is, it's for real. I feel that a path is unfolding before us. There's no reason to rush, we just need to keep going.

Saturday 7/13/91

The conference was great. The kids picked me up at the airport today. I've really missed them all. Adri was very responsive, actually scrambling to hug me as I got into the van. They said she hadn't spit up all week. I complimented her on this.

ADRI: I TENDER   I DON'T PAINT

Later, talking in her room, I asked about her week. She'd not been happy with her home schooling.

ADRI: I EDUCATED   NEED NEW EDUCATION I SMART

I explained again, as I have several times, that I think we need to cover material she may already know just so that we can have a better picture of where she stands academically.

All of a sudden Brie walked in and started talking. Adri immediately became agitated and scratched her. I scolded Adri, telling her I understood her need for my attention, but it was still not okay to scratch Brie.

ADRI: I SORRY   ENEMY

KRISTI: Do you mean Brie is an enemy?

ADRI: YES BRIE   NOT ME BAD

I explained that neither of them was bad. But Brie needed to respect Adri's need for privacy, and Adri needed to learn to talk to Brie, rather than to lash out at her. I also explained that Brie was not her enemy. Brie just wanted to be with us, to share in what we were doing.

ADRI: BECAUSE BIG ANGER   LOVE BRIE

Does Adri feel frightened by her own "big anger" toward Brie? Does she really see Brie as an enemy of hers, or herself as an enemy of Brie's?

ADRI: I ANGRY BECAUSE YET YOU TENDER

KRISTI: You are angry because I am tender with Brie?

ADRI: NO WEI TOO TENDER WITH BRIE

Oh . . . that was it. Something must have gone on this week between Wei and Brie that made Adri jealous.

ADRI: NOT ONE IDENTIFIES WITH I

KRISTI: You don't feel that anyone understands and supports you?

ADRI: NO ONE CARES EDUCATION FOR ME

She was feeling left out. I tried to explain to her that all of us cared very much about her even though it might not always seem like it. This was all new, and we were still trying to figure out the best course. As I spoke, Adri became more and more distraught and emotional. She was fighting me and throwing her machine as I struggled to hold her in my arms. I kept trying to reassure her, repeating over and over again that I loved her.

Then suddenly, in the intensity of the moment, Adri cried out, "MAMAMA." Tears began to stream from her eyes and she clung to me. I held her tight, and I began to sob too. She cried and cried until her whole body just collapsed. It was an extraordinary emotional breakthrough. This is simply not the same child I had before. The old Adri didn't cry. She didn't allow herself to feel so deeply or to express those feelings. I have no words to describe what it feels like to see this beautiful person fighting to emerge.

Before bed I talked to Adri a little longer. I told her about the autistic adults that I had met at the conference who said that they had come to terms with their autism. They told me that in a sense they even identified with it. They didn't want to be changed, only to be accepted for who they were.

I asked Adri if she thought that there were any positive aspects to being autistic. Adri smiled and typed her own unique response:

ADRI: YES I CAN ESCAPE WHEN THE MECHA-NISM FAILS

Sunday 7/14/91

I bought a book the other day about people remembering their births. It said that little children, younger than four years old or so, can often remember their births. So I decided to ask Seby and Brie if they could remember theirs.

Sitting with Seby on his bed after I'd read him a story, I asked if he remembered being in Mommy's tummy and being born. He immediately replied, "Yes. I saw Mommy's blood. I saw Mommy's backbone. I saw Mommy's tummybone."

What a surprise! Do we just need to ask our children? His description was so specific and his choice of words so unusual.

Brie didn't seem to understand the question. However, when I asked her if she remembered whether she came out of Mommy's tummy feetfirst or headfirst, she decisively and correctly answered, "Head." We seem to lose so much as we age—memories, thoughts, abilities, knowledge. Does it have to be that way? Is this biologically determined, or a result of our cultural socialization process, one that Adri, by virtue of her autism, escaped?

Monday 7/15/91

When Wei came this morning, I asked her if anything had happened between her and Brie that might have upset Adri. She looked startled and explained that in fact one morning she had spent time talking with Brie before greeting Adri. She said Adri had seemed upset and angry at the time, but they'd talked about it, and Wei had thought it was resolved. We agreed that from now on she would focus her attention on Adri before greeting the other kids.

Adri came into the room, and I asked if anything was on her mind.

ADRI: WEI IS QUIET

KRISTI: Does that concern you?

ADRI: YES

Wei said she was happy to see Adri again and that nothing was wrong, she just felt quiet.

We all went to the sunroom schoolroom and sat down at the table. I opened her geography book, but Adri started turning her head and trying to jump up from the table, refusing to read.

KRISTI: Adri, what's wrong? I thought you wanted to learn.

ADRI: I NEED NEW WORK   TOO EASY

KRISTI: Okay then, let's just open your geography book anywhere. I'll ask you questions and you see if you know the answers.

I opened the book randomly to the glossary section. The words were unfamiliar, but Adri knew all the definitions except the one for *papyrus*. Maybe she was right. Why was I so intent on being so methodical in my approach to her studies? I needed to "chill out," as Brie would say.

While Adri took a short break, I went to the bookshelves in search of some science or math materials. I found a college-level SAT biology preparation textbook and thumbed through it. Each chapter consisted of about six densely packed pages of information and terminology followed by about twenty-five multiple-choice test questions. For example: "An organic compound in which H and O are present in the same ratio as in water is (a) fat; (b) protein; (c) amino acid; (d) nucleic acid; (e) carbohydrate." It was pretty complex, but it was the only book with the right format, so I brought it over.

It took Adri about ten minutes to read the five pages of chapter 1. Then I read the test questions while Wei facilitated Adri. This was college biology material. Adri got about 90 percent of the answers correct. Wei and I were both stunned. No wonder she found the other work boring.

Tuesday 7/16/91

I talked again with Adri this evening before bed.

KRISTI: How was your day, Adri?

ADRI: GOOD

Then she volunteered what was on her mind.

ADRI: YOU LIVE TO LOVE

Sometimes she sounds so expansive. Did she mean me, or all of us in general? I decided just to tell her how much I loved her. Then I asked her if she would like to talk about what we'd been talking about before—other lives, her birth, autism.

ADRI: YES

KRISTI: I know I asked you about your birth before, but I want to ask you again if you remember.

ADRI: YES

KRISTI: What was it like?

ADRI: IT WAS VERY SCARY

KRISTI: Who was there?

ADRI: MOM DAD DOCTOR

KRISTI: Anyone else?

ADRI: NO

KRISTI: Were you autistic before you were born?

ADRI: NO

KRISTI: Did you become autistic after you were born?

ADRI: YES I . . .

She wasn't able to complete her thought. She was moving around and spitting up a little.

KRISTI: Is this very hard for you to talk about?

ADRI: YES

I told her that in the book I'd been reading about birth memories, it says that most people remember the experience as very frightening. That's supposedly why so few of us are able to recall it.

KRISTI: Do you want to stop for tonight?

ADRI: YES

She was spitting up almost steadily.

KRISTI: Does all of this make you nervous?

ADRI: YES

Me too.

Wednesday 7/17/91

Today was another emotional roller coaster. In our morning session I'd had to speak to Adri several times to get her to focus. She didn't want to do math, so we ended up doing another chapter from the Biology SAT book. Adri read through most of the chapter, but then suddenly became very agitated and angry.

KRISTI: Adri, what's going on? Do you want to talk about why you're so upset?

ADRI: NO   I ANGRY BECAUSE YOU TOO NICE

KRISTI: Let me try to understand this. You are angry because I'm too nice. You don't think you deserve it. Is that what you mean?

ADRI: NO

KRISTI: Adri, do you mean that I'm too nice, or not too nice?

ADRI: NOT

Oh, I told her that I didn't mean to be inflexible or too demanding. But I wanted to help her learn to focus her attention and to persist with her studies so that she could become, in her own words, "educated."

Big tears started to roll down her cheeks. I wasn't expecting that. I took her in my arms and held her while she cried. Sometimes she seems so tough, and sometimes so incredibly vulnerable. We just sat together for a while, and when she was calmer, I asked if there was anything she wanted to say.

ADRI: I NEED LOTS OF LOVE

Sometimes she just takes my breath away. She's so honest, so open and trusting. I held her close and told her again how deeply I loved her.

Tonight before bed I read Adri a book about Thomas Edison. She seemed to enjoy it. Then I said good night and went to bed myself. When I was just about asleep, Adri came in and actually crawled into bed with Rodrigo and me and stayed there, snuggling, for at least fifteen minutes before she grew restless. Then I brought her back to her bed and tucked her in again. It felt so nice. Of course the other kids like to snuggle all the time. They'd sleep with us all night if we let them. But Adri has never been willing to cuddle for more than a minute or two. Something is really changing in her.

Thursday 7/18/91

Today Wei and I worked together with Adri in her new math book. It was a regular fourth- or fifth-grade textbook. At first when she saw it, she seemed excited. However, as we worked on common denominators, she soon became bored and, I think, disappointed. Either she already knew how to do common denominators or she understood them very quickly.

Once again we switched to the Biology SAT book. At first Adri didn't want to read, but once she realized that Wei and I weren't going to give up, she settled in and read the chapter even more quickly than the day before. She answered almost all the test questions correctly, until the last grouping, where she got four out of seven wrong. I think it was because she hadn't finished the reading or studied the chart on the last page. Or maybe she just wasn't interested in that part because it was about plants, not people.

Before bed I watched Adri with her radio. She often adjusts the tuner every few seconds or so. Now I realize that this isn't as random and unintentional as I'd thought. When she finds music she likes—music with a strong beat—she stays with it for a much longer time.

Personally I've been feeling depressed lately. I've been thinking a lot about Coreece. It's hard to understand why someone like Coreece would get cancer, and I feel so helpless. I encouraged Coreece to be honest with me and tell me how she's really feeling. But it's so hard to hear the truth because I want to believe that everything's fine. At least tonight I was able to cry about it. It feels to me like Adri's opening up is a catalyst for my own. I look at her and think, If she can risk it, so can I.

Chapter 12

"I VERY YET WISE"

JULY 19–31, 1991

Friday 7/19/91

I left for my office before eight this morning so that I could get a couple of things done before ten, when Adri, Wei, and I planned to meet. But work took more time than I expected, so I rushed in guilty and late. Wei had managed to do some math with Adri and she had tried to start on science, but Adri refused.

    ADRI: I WANT MOM

    We got right to it. Adri completed a science chapter and then knocked over her glass of soda.

    KRISTI: Adri, it looked like you did that on purpose. Why?

ADRI: BECAUSE I WANTED TO TAKE A BREAK

That made sense, but I explained as we cleaned up the spill together that there are better ways to communicate. The Canon was right in front of her. She could have just typed that she wanted a break. A while later she wet her pants.

KRISTI: Adri, was that accidental or on purpose?

ADRI: ON PURPOSE

KRISTI: Did you do that to get a break too?

ADRI: YES

I was exasperated with her and I told her so. As we cleaned up together again, I explained that it may have been necessary to communicate in such a physical way before she had access to FC, but now there was no excuse for that kind of behavior. How would she feel, I asked, if other kids at school saw her do that?

ADRI: SAD

KRISTI: And embarrassed too.

This afternoon we went for another cranial-sacral appointment with Felice. This session was quite extraordinary. As Felice worked on Adri's skull, she began to describe a session she had participated in the week before. One of the therapists working on the client with her, a man named Ben, had chanted in what sounded like an Indian dialect. I asked if Ben was from India, and Felice said something like, "Not in this lifetime."

So far I hadn't told anyone except Rodrigo about Adri's past-lives communication. But with this kind of opener I decided to tell Felice, asking her to keep it confidential for the time being. Unfazed, Felice asked Adri if she'd like to hear about some of her own past lives. Adri typed "YES." So, here we were, in a respected therapist's office, chatting about past lives. I realized that my world had turned upside down.

Felice briefly described several of her past lives, including one in India that she said she'd shared with Ben. Felice asked Adri if she had been Indian in any of her past lives.

ADRI: YES

FELICE: Did you know me?

ADRI: YES

Then Adri surprised me by giving Felice a big hug. I was feeling a bit funny, like the odd man out. I'd been keeping these new and strange ideas on hold, feeling uncertain about them and fearful of how others might react. And here's Felice embracing them as a normal part of her reality. Either a lot more people than I thought believe in past lives, or else Adri and I landed, by some serendipitous chance, in just the right place. It was a good lesson for me.

Saturday 7/21/91

Before I forget any of this, I need to write it down. Last night I prepared some questions based on information about the developing fetus in Verney's book and some of Adri's earlier revelations. But I wasn't going to ask them unless Adri started talking about this first. The session began as usual.

KRISTI: Adri, do you have anything you want to say?

ADRI: YES   I TOO TENDER

KRISTI: Why? What makes you too tender?

ADRI: MY WILLINGNESS TO TRUST YOU

I launched into a discussion about the difficulty of trusting others. Trusting someone, I told her, makes us vulnerable, but at the same time it's only by trusting people that we learn to open up. I told her that I thought she was opening up these days, taking the kinds of courageous risks that bring tremendous rewards.

During this discussion Adri typed "YES" several times. I was feeling relaxed and comfortable with the subject, happy to be in the role of teacher for a change. And then I asked Adri if there was anything else she wanted to say.

ADRI: JESUS XIT FOR ME   HE DIED EDUCATED

I couldn't respond—I was too stunned. My illusion of safety had just been shattered. Why was she talking about Jesus? It wasn't a subject I talked about, that's for sure. What could she know about Jesus? I picked up the conversation as best I could.

KRISTI: Jesus was an educated person?

ADRI: HE TELL ME THAT YOU EDUCATED

KRISTI: Jesus told you that I'm educated? When did he tell you that?

ADRI: YES IN A DREAM I CHOOSE YOU FOR ME

KRISTI: When was this dream, in this lifetime or in another lifetime?

ADRI: YES THIS LIFETIME

KRISTI: When? When you were four, this year, in utero?

ADRI: WHEN I WAS A BABY

KRISTI: You had a dream as a baby, and in that dream Jesus told you that I was educated?

ADRI: YES

KRISTI: Adri, why is it so significant? What is so important about education?

ADRI: YOU EDUCATED SO BABY EDUCATED TOO

KRISTI: But I still don't understand. What is so important about being educated? Why is it so important to you?

ADRI: BECAUSE IT IS THE WAY TO HAPPINESS

KRISTI: Happiness?

ADRI: YES

I felt so mixed up and frustrated. Just what does she mean by "educated"? And "happiness"? And who is "Jesus" to her? How are these ideas linked? I asked her if we could go over some of the things she'd said.

ADRI: YES

KRISTI: Adri, you said before that you decided not to eat in utero and that that affected your endocrine system. Now you're talking about a dream you had as a baby when you learned I was educated. Is there a relationship between education and the fact that you are autistic?

ADRI: YES BECAUSE I DO NOTHING ABOUT SOYBEANS

How can I possibly take this seriously? I do of course, but just what is she talking about? Where did the reference to soybeans come from? Then I remembered that when she was an infant, I switched her to soy formula because she couldn't tolerate cow's milk. Did the soy itself cause some effect, or was the need for soy formula just one of the repercussions of her not eating?

I tried unsuccessfully to get her to clarify this for me. We were both frustrated, and I was feeling a little light-headed and having trouble organizing my thoughts. It seemed like a good time to bring out the questions I'd prepared on the endocrine system. I told her that if they were crazy questions, she should just tell me to stop.

KRISTI: Adri, what does the endocrine system produce, do you know?

ADRI: YES NEUROHORMONES

KRISTI: What part of the brain controls the endocrine system?

ADRI: HYPOTHALAMUS

KRISTI: What part of the brain can be viewed as the emotional regulator, do you know?

ADRI: HYPOTHALAMUS

KRISTI: Does the hypothalamus also regulate food intake?

ADRI: YES

KRISTI: Okay, Adri. I don't know if I've got this right, but my understanding from what I've read so far is that extreme maternal stress in the second trimester of pregnancy can trigger a mother's endocrine system to overproduce neurohormones. These can then affect the developing fetus by creating possible physical or biological changes that could result in emotional vulnerability later on. Could such a change be extreme enough to create a physiological basis for a disorder as serious as autism? Is this possible?

ADRI: YES

KRISTI: Is this what happened to you? Extreme stress in me during the pregnancy triggered an overproduction of neurohormones that created the basis for your autism?

ADRI: NO

I'd tried to be as objective as possible. I didn't want my fear of what her answers might be to influence my questions. But when she said no, I felt so relieved. And yet, if it hadn't been my stress, what did cause it? I was groping for possibilities.

KRISTI: Did you somehow trigger my emotional system so that I would overproduce neurohormones?

ADRI: NO

I wasn't sure whether I was making sense or not. But I persisted because thoughts kept entering my mind.

KRISTI: Did you trigger your own emotional system somehow?

ADRI: NO

KRISTI: Adri, this is very difficult for me to understand. What I read about the relationship between "starving" and the hypothalamus said that malnutrition can create a biological basis for the inability to regulate food intake and growth in a developing fetus. Is this true?

ADRI: YES

KRISTI: Is this what happened to you? Did inadequate nourishment in the womb create in you an inability to regulate food intake? Did this affect your growth later? Is that why you're small for your age?

ADRI: NO

Another dead end. I was struggling to stay with Adri, to make enough sense of what she was saying to keep the dialogue going. I had no idea whether any of it was scientifically sound.

KRISTI: Adri, if a fetus is undernourished, can that somehow also create the basis for the emotional vulnerability? Is some kind of cross-influence possible?

ADRI: YES

KRISTI: Yes? Is that what happened to you? You somehow starved yourself in utero and that increased your emotional susceptibility to such an extent that you developed the cluster of behaviors that we now call autism?

ADRI: YES

Unbelievable. Still, on some level, it doesn't seem so crazy. Though many people would like to believe that autism is a purely physiological disorder, nothing is purely physiological. Human beings are not machines. Autism is related to sensitivity. Perhaps autism is even a kind of survival mechanism designed to protect hypersensitive people from this world. I don't know—but something about all this feels very real.

KRISTI: Adri, can you explain anything further?

ADRI: I WAS KILLING MYSELF IN UTERO

It really hurt to hear her say that, but I kept going.

KRISTI: By somehow "not eating"?

ADRI: YES

KRISTI: Why were you killing yourself in utero?

ADRI: BECAUSE PLACE WAS WRONG

The air just went out of me. Still, I didn't want to stop her. We were going for truth.

KRISTI: You were killing yourself in utero by not eating because you believed you were in the wrong place?

ADRI: YES

KRISTI: But you didn't die. Yet the deprivation created a physiological change that resulted in autism?

ADRI: YES

KRISTI: Are you glad you're here now, Adri?

ADRI: YES

I was so relieved. I couldn't tolerate the thought of her still being that unhappy.

KRISTI: Is there a reason you're here, Adri? Something to learn?

ADRI: YES

Adri got up and walked around for a few minutes. I followed her to the table. There was another question I was dying to ask.

KRISTI: You said that I was educated, do you mean in another lifetime?

ADRI: YES

KRISTI: Did you know me?

ADRI: YET U

She pulled away from me and couldn't finish. Enough. We were both talked out. I was exhausted, absolutely drained—and she was too.

Later in the afternoon I reread the tapes of our conversation and tried to piece it all together. Did Adri stop eating in the womb because she was angry with herself? Did starving herself deprive her of the energy needed for normal development? Why was Adri angry at herself? Because she didn't die? Or because she was in the wrong place?

Hypothesis: Adri found herself in utero in what she perceived was the wrong place. She became angry and decided not to eat. The effect this had on her endocrine system created the physiological basis for her autism.

But that's only the beginning, there's so much more. Did the trauma of her birth or the jaundice treatment in some way trigger a predisposition to autism in Adri's vulnerable system? After she was born, did the soybean formula somehow affect her adversely? Or is she intimating that what appeared to be her inability to breast-feed may have been a deliberate withdrawal from life on her part? Did she choose this particular method to create her autism? Did she ever waver from her chosen course in utero or as a young infant?

Then there's the question of where Adri's understanding of Jesus comes from. Did she decide to start eating after he came and told her I was educated? I also wonder why all this is coming out now. Is it because Adri's finally able to communicate, or does the very fact that she is able to communicate now mean something else entirely? These are big questions. And I don't know if she'll ever be able to answer them. But I'm going to keep asking as long as she's willing.

I want to understand Adri, to enter her world. I know that somehow what she says will make sense if I can just unravel it. All this is real. It has to be, because it all makes me feel alive in a way that I've never felt before—surrounded by possibilities, by hope.

This afternoon my younger brother, Jamie, came over. I haven't told him about the things that Adri has been saying. I just don't feel I know him well enough. He's on an M.B.A. money/power/success path. But I must say, it doesn't seem to suit him very well.

Jamie's been really great with Adri. Today when she saw him, she ran to him with her arms outstretched. He lifted her up and to his absolute amazement, she said softly, with her *voice*, "Uncle," into his ear.

KRISTI: Adri, did you say something to Jamie?
ADRI: UNCLE
KRISTI: Wonderful, Adri. It certainly seems that soon you will be talking with your tongue.
ADRI: YES

Monday 7/22/91

Very early this morning, about a quarter to five, Adri came into our bedroom and crawled into bed with us. After about ten minutes she got up and started running around the room. Rodrigo took her back to her own room, but by then we were both wide awake.

I know Rodrigo feels neglected, and he thinks I'm neglecting our other kids too. I worry about Seby and Brie, but if they're upset about the time I spend with Adri, I don't see it in their behavior. I set aside time with each of them every day, too, trying to make sure they don't feel left out. They seem to understand that Adri needs extra time right now.

Adri and I only talk about an hour a day. Is that too much for a child who's been neglected for nine years? Now that she finally has a voice, how could I possibly tell her I don't have time for her? Maybe there will come a time when things will ease up later on, but by then she'll have said those things that she desperately wants to say, and we won't need that hour. But for now she needs me. And I've got to be there for her.

In spite of her middle-of-the-night activity, Adri was back in our room by six-thirty. She and I decided to go out for a walk around the reservoir near our home, leaving Rodrigo to sleep.

It was a mind-clearing walk. I realized again that Adri is a catalyst for me, an agent of change. Nevertheless all this is affecting our family dynamics. Both Adri and I are changing, but Rodrigo's desperately trying to maintain the status quo.

Tuesday 7/23/91

We've just come back from another of Adri's cranial-sacral-massage sessions. Today three therapists worked on her simultaneously: Felice at her head, Maria on her chest and back, and Ben at her stomach. As they gently rested their hands on her, Adri began to tense up more and more until her body was completely rigid. Then suddenly the tension broke and she relaxed completely. This happened several times over the course of the twenty-five-minute session. Mounting tension and then complete surrender.

From time to time Ben would suddenly start verbalizing in the Indian dialect. Adri appeared to listen intently. When the session was over, I asked her if she understood what he was saying.

ADRI: YES TENDER WORDS
KRISTI: Do you know this language?
ADRI: NO
She was quiet and calm, remaining close to Ben.
ADRI: I OTHER CAME
Felice asked if Adri meant her "higher self."
ADRI: NO
KRISTI: Adri, do you know Ben somehow?
ADRI: YES
She turned directly to Ben and put her arms around him, giving him a big hug.
KRISTI: Adri, how are you feeling now?
ADRI: EXSTATIC
Wow! Whatever this work is, it's very powerful.
KRISTI: Do you want to come again?
ADRI: YES

★ ★ ★

I did some work in my office and didn't get home till eight o'clock. Adri was still awake but very tired after her busy day. I think she was waiting up because she wanted to talk about this afternoon. I asked her if she had anything she wished to say.

ADRI: YES XET TOO TENDER

KRISTI: Who or what is too tender?

ADRI: I DEAD BY RISEK   PAKISTAN EDUCATED IN INDIA

Who or what is Risek, and what happened in Pakistan? Is she talking about a past life? Did Risek kill her? Did she die beside him? I couldn't get a clear response from her, so I went on.

KRISTI: Did you know Ben in another lifetime?

ADRI: YES

KRISTI: Did you and he share a lifetime in Pakistan?

ADRI: YES

KRISTI: What was his relationship to you?

ADRI: MY MENTOR

KRISTI: He was your mentor. Was he male or female in that lifetime?

ADRI: MALE

KRISTI: Do you know what year that was?

ADRI: 55 AD

KRISTI: Do you know the name of the city you lived in?

Adri had great difficulty spelling what she was trying to say. She tried twice, and both times the letters were the same letters she had typed in Felice's office in the afternoon. But I still couldn't make them out.

ADRI: DEWEMDSDEIEYIES DEEETEEYEEO

KRISTI: Did you understand what Ben was saying to you?

ADRI: YES   I SENSITIVE ABOUT TELLING

KRISTI: You're sensitive about saying what the tender words were?

ADRI: YES

KRISTI: Can you tell them just to Mommy here?

ADRI: YES

KRISTI: What did he say?

ADRI: TENDER WORDS   MEMORY TOO REAL

KRISTI: When he said those words, the memory seemed very real to you, too real?

ADRI: YES

KRISTI: Adri, you seem very tired. Do you want to stop now and continue talking about this tomorrow?

ADRI: NO

We were sitting on the floor of her room, and her eyes were literally closing even as she typed.

KRISTI: Do you want to type more now?

ADRI: YES

But even as she was typing the last word, her eyes began to close, and she drifted off to sleep. I carried her to her bed and she slept soundly the entire night. I'm feeling excited and intrigued, but also frightened and confused. Adri and I are on a journey without a map. At least I don't have a map. I am operating purely on faith now—faith in Adri.

Wednesday 7/24/91

This morning Adri wanted to continue where we'd left off yesterday. I offered her the Canon.

ADRI: INDIA

I told Adri we could talk right after breakfast. When she'd finished, we went into the sunroom and I asked Adri what she wanted to do or talk about.

ADRI: I CHOOSE MATH

I was disappointed, but I tried not to show it. I got her

math book, and we started working. But she seemed very agitated, jumping up several times and running out of the room. I brought her back into the room, sat down beside her and told her firmly that I was going to sit by her and help her get control of herself so that she could work.

ADRI: NEED HELP TRY

KRISTI: Do you mean you need help today, you're trying?

ADRI: YES YOU YET TOO TENDER

KRISTI: You think I'm too tender. I should be more firm with you?

ADRI: NO YOU YET TOO SENSITIVE

KRISTI: I am too sensitive?

ADRI: YES

KRISTI: And you, too, are too sensitive?

ADRI: YES

KRISTI: We're alike in that way?

ADRI: YES YET NOT EDUCATED

KRISTI: Maybe not, but we're working on it.

ADRI: I TELEPHONE TO DECZE

KRISTI: Who or what do you want to telephone to? I don't understand.

ADRI: YES DESEY

KRISTI: Is Desey a person?

ADRI: YES

KRISTI: How do you know Desey?

ADRI: FROM TALKING

I felt like a detective searching for clues.

KRISTI: When did you talk to Desey?

ADRI: YESTERDAY

KRISTI: Is Ben Desey?

ADRI: YES

KRISTI: Do you want me to call him for you?

ADRI: YES TENDER DESEY

KRISTI: Was Desey your mentor?

ADRI: MENTOR

Kristi: Did you like the experience yesterday?

Adri: YES

Kristi: Do you think it helped you?

Adri: YES

Kristi: Could you physically feel the energy that they talked about?

Adri: YES

Kristi: How did it help you?

Adri: IT HELPED ME TO XET TENDER WORDS

Kristi: I'm not sure what you mean.

Adri: YES TENDER I EMPTY TENSION TENSE

Kristi: Did you feel warm when they touched you?

Adri: YES ENERGY

Kristi: How did you feel when Ben spoke with you in the ancient tongue?

Adri: I FEEL INTELLIGENT

Kristi: He spoke to you like the intelligent person you are rather than the way you are perceived and spoken to in this lifetime?

Adri: YES NOT EDUCATED

Kristi: Did you have a particular area of interest at that time?

Adri: YES SCIENCE

Kristi: Did you have a job?

Adri: NO

Kristi: Were you a teacher of some sort?

Adri: NO

Kristi: Were you a philosopher?

Adri: YES ADRI STUDIED SEOY

I couldn't make it out.

Kristi: Did you have an area of particular interest and expertise?

Adri: YES NEUROLOGY

Kristi: Did Desey have a job?

ADRI: TEACHER

KRISTI: Would you like to have the three of them work on you again soon?

ADRI: YES

These conversations leave me excited but uneasy. Sometimes Adri is so clear, and other times so garbled. It makes me uncomfortable when she's not clear because what she's talking about is so outside the mainstream, and I need the reassurance of all the clarity I can get.

Today Adri was frustrated with her math. She seems familiar with some of the principles of geometry, or at least pregeometry questions. So instead of spending time going over all the lesson material, we went directly to the questions at the end of the chapter. She answered them all correctly.

ADRI: POLYGRAM INFINITE RAYS AREA PENTAGON OCTAGON HEXAGON RADIUS DIAMETER

Then, suddenly, she paused and spontaneously began typing again—not about math.

ADRI: MENTOR IS RECEIVING IT

I found that rather unnerving, particularly because she seemed to snap to attention.

KRISTI: Can you clarify what you mean? What's "it," what mentor?

Adri then typed her response quickly and accurately, without pausing once.

ADRI: I MEAN THAT EVERY DAY I WORRY INTENSELY ABOUT MY YOUR NETWORK OF GUIDES

KRISTI: Adri, what do you mean by network of guides? How would you describe them?

ADRI: SPIRITS

KRISTI: I have a network of spirit guides?

ADRI: YES

This was so amazing. A million questions went through my mind, but I couldn't think of a single one to ask.

KRISTI: Do you know them?

ADRI: YES

KRISTI: Why are you worried about them and me?

ADRI: BECAUSE YOU DON'T GO TO THEM

Once again I was on automatic pilot. I floundered around, trying to come up with a question.

KRISTI: Are they good, my spirit guides?

ADRI: YES

KRISTI: How do I go to them? How should I? What do I do?

ADRI: YOU TELL THEM TO TEACH YOU

KRISTI: I just tell them that?

ADRI: YES YOU TELL THEM YOU NEED THEIR HELP

KRISTI: How will they communicate with me?

ADRI: THROUGH YOUR THOUGHTS

KRISTI: Will I know when it is them speaking and not just my own thoughts?

ADRI: YES

KRISTI: How?

ADRI: BECAUSE SPIRITS TONE IS IDENTIFI-ABLE

KRISTI: Will I recognize it if I experience it?

ADRI: YES (big grin)

KRISTI: Are you a guide of sorts for me?

ADRI: YES

KRISTI: Are there people around here who could help me with this? Do you know anyone who is involved with spirit guides?

ADRI: YES

KRISTI: How do I find them?

ADRI: YOU CAN IDENTIFY THEM BY TEST-ING THEM

I tried to get her to explain what such a test would be, but I couldn't make sense of what she was typing. Something about a "sonygram." I decided to change tactics.

KRISTI: Do you know the people I should talk to?

ADRI: YES

KRISTI: Do you know their names?

ADRI: NO

I thought about everyone I knew and gave her five names, trying to describe the people as I named them. Adri confirmed that I might call my friend Gail, who had often told me about her own spiritual pursuits. Ben could also be of help, and of course Joan, whom I hadn't spoken with since she'd been over to dinner.

KRISTI: Anything else?

ADRI: I NEED BATH

This whole thing is so strange and confusing. I don't know how to perceive Adri, this brilliant girl/woman/man/ being in her out-of-control nine-year-old body. And I don't know how to perceive myself in relation to her. Am I mother, student, friend—all three? Our roles keep shifting all the time.

When we were leaving the sunroom, Adri paused at the globe that stood in the corner. I asked if she could point to where she had lived in the "Desey" lifetime. I facilitated her while she turned the globe and, without paying much attention, pointed to Bangladesh, formerly Pakistan, on the border of India, and then wandered off. I wondered if she'd purposefully selected Bangladesh, or if it was some kind of fluke. Trying to sound nonchalant, I asked her a few more questions.

KRISTI: Was it around Nepal?

ADRI: NO

KRISTI: By the sea?

ADRI: YES

KRISTI: Does the city still exist?

ADRI: NO

KRISTI: What is the nearest existing city?
ADRI: CALCUTTA

Quite obviously, she'd been paying attention.

Thursday 7/25/91

I need and want to write about what I am, what I am becoming . . . the blossoming, expanding me . . . the awareness of life beyond and around the body and personality . . .
the expression and certainty of the experience . . . the im-
mersion and dispersion. It is powerful. Truly powerful.

This afternoon I had lunch with Gail. I hadn't seen her
for more than a year. I brought my journal along, and after
we had finished eating, I began to tell Adri's story, quoting
her as I went along.

As I talked, Gail began to cry. I started crying too. Since
we'd lost contact, her life had changed a lot. Her business
had dropped off considerably, she was in a difficult marriage,
and had been too busy and worried most of the time to attend to her spiritual growth. She'd even stopped doing the
volunteer hospice work with the dying that had been so vi-
tal to her. The effects were immediately apparent. Although
she looked fine physically, the light in her eyes, which had
always defined Gail for me, was gone.

Ironically I had come to Gail for help. Now it was clear
that our meeting was as much for Gail as it was for me. Gail
needed to hear Adri's story. She needed a spiritual boost, a
reaffirmation of her own beliefs. As we talked more, I felt a
resurgence of the old Gail. And she noticed the change
in me.

Tonight while I was typing with Adri, Rodrigo came in to
watch us. We didn't talk much, but somehow I ended up
asking Adri if she knew Daddy from other lifetimes.

ADRI: YES

And that was that. Rodrigo didn't ask her anything else.

Adri is such a gift to me and to everyone around her. Today I thought about how all of this was changing my life so radically. I wondered how I could make sure that I would never use any of what she's teaching me for selfish purposes. But then I realized that if I'm in contact with my guides, the things I need to know or to do will be made clear to me. It had also occurred to me that it's very possible that Adri is revealing all of this information because her story must be shared with others. Even as I'm typing, Adri comes in to lend perspective—she needs me to plug in her radio for her. The autism and the wisdom coexist. It isn't supposed to be easy, I guess.

Friday 7/26/91

This morning Adri was up bright and early, wanting to talk.

KRISTI: Do you want me to tell you about my visit with Gail?

ADRI: YES

But then I started asking her questions instead. I was curious why Adri had suggested talking to Gail.

KRISTI: Do you know Gail from a past life?

ADRI: YES

KRISTI: Who was she?

ADRI: SHE WAS YOUR DAUGHTER

KRISTI: Were you present in that lifetime?

ADRI: YES I WAS YOUR WIFE

KRISTI: I was the father, the husband?

ADRI: YES

KRISTI: Where did we live?

ADRI: YOU YET LIVED IN MINNESOTA

KRISTI: Adri, do you remember all of your lifetimes?

ADRI: YES
KRISTI: Adri, can you remember them because you
are autistic or because you are evolved?
ADRI: BECAUSE I AM EVOLVED
KRISTI: Is my network of guides the same as yours?
ADRI: YES
KRISTI: Do you hear them all the time?
ADRI: NO
KRISTI: You call them?
ADRI: YES
KRISTI: Can all autistic people do what you do?
ADRI: NO
KRISTI: So, this isn't an aspect of your autism or of
FC? But even autistic people who are not spiritual are
still intelligent, aren't they? They can still learn to
do FC?
ADRI: YES

This afternoon I read an article suggesting that many gurus
are charlatans and that people should be wary about getting
trapped in cults. It made me think about the fine line between reality and fantasy and how difficult it is to figure out
what's real. Rodrigo's doubts unsettle me. But then I think
about Adri. In her highly sheltered life she's certainly had
no spiritual or religious training, so how could she have
learned these ideas? She couldn't have just made them up—
they're too powerful and speak to something deep inside
me. And of course they're not new ideas. Only the messen-
ger is new.

Adri was playing in her room. I went in and lay down
on her bed. I realize that when I'm nervous and in doubt,
being with Adri calms and centers me. It's not a conscious
or intellectual thing, this peace I feel in her presence. It's
just that being with her is healing for me.

Saturday 7/27/91

We're up at the New Hampshire house. It's good to be here. The kids have already gone off to check out the beach. I don't know what it is with me, though, I don't feel in tune or at peace. I'm taking this time to write in hopes of quieting myself. I need to recapture the sense of being "in the moment," talking, listening, feeling.

I had a thought I want to remember: My daughter was born to me twice. I have known two daughters and I have two stories to tell. I need to think about that.

Sunday 7/28/91

For a while now I've been trying to meditate and do self-hypnosis. I'm learning that you can totally trust your own mind and body—even your internal timing. At eight A.M. I said to myself, *I will come out of my meditation at 8:15.* I stayed centered and came out of my hypnotic state at exactly eight-fifteen. How did I do that? Trust.

Monday 7/29/91

This morning Adri and I talked in my bedroom.

ADRI: YET NOT EDUCATED

I think this has become her standard opening remark, although I'm still not sure what she means by it. Academics? Spiritual development? And does she mean that I'm not educated, or she's not educated—or both, or neither?

ADRI: YET NEED YOU TO TALKING WITH YOUR GUIDES

KRISTI: I have been trying to do that, Adri. I'm meditating and asking for their help. But so far I haven't been able to connect with them. I don't hear anything. Have you been talking to them?

ADRI: YES NEED YET YOU TENDER

KRISTI: What do you mean, too tender or not tender enough?

ADRI: YET YOU TOO TENDER

KRISTI: Sounds like an admonition. What do you mean by tender? Can you define it? Can you use it in a sentence? "A tender person is one . . ."

ADRI: THAT EVERYONE WALKS ON

KRISTI: You mean I let people walk on me?

ADRI: YES   YOU NEED TO WALK ALONE NOT ESTEEMED BY EVERYONE

KRISTI: You mean that I have to quit worrying about having everyone like me?

ADRI: YES

KRISTI: I have to stop hiding, stop trying to please everyone?

ADRI: YES

KRISTI: Adri, are you talking about Daddy and me?

ADRI: YES   IT IS NOT WORKING TOO WELL YOU SENSE THAT HE NOT YET TAKING THE WAY

I told Adri that this was a difficult subject and one that she really ought not to have to deal with since she loved both of us and this wasn't her problem.

ADRI: I LOVE DADDY

Then she volunteered . . .

ADRI: NOTHING ENDS EASILY BUT YOU MUST REMEDY THE WOE

I thought I should change the subject, so I told her about my trip to California, my mountain hike, which I'd never described to her before. Then I asked her what she thought it was all about.

ADRI: YOU HAVE SEEN SPIRITS

Tuesday 7/30/91

New Hampshire is so beautiful. This morning I got up about six to take my walk. I wasn't able to relax, though, because I was thinking about my friend Coreece Fisher, who's dying of cancer, and also about the mother of a close friend of mine who just died. It makes me realize that I have not yet done what I hope to do in this lifetime and also that I'm really afraid of sickness and death. I felt Adri's strength and courage coming through, inspiring me. But I had a startling thought: I don't want to become dependent on Adri. I can't do that, not to her or to me. She needs to grow, to bloom, and I must do the same.

Later Adri and I talked.

KRISTI: Anything on your mind, Adri?

ADRI: I STILL SAY THAT YOU DENY YOUR BODY

KRISTI: Why do you say that?

ADRI: TOO FEARFUL

KRISTI: I'm too fearful?

ADRI: YES BECAUSE YOU WORRIED

Then she volunteered . . .

ADRI: DON'T WORRY ABOUT DADDY   HE WILL SURVIVE

She has a way of going right to the heart of the matter.

KRISTI: You're right of course, Adri.

ADRI: HE NEEDS TO STAND YET ALONE

KRISTI: Is there anything else you want to say about Daddy?

ADRI: YES   HES TOO MONEY DRIVEN   HE NEEDS TO DO EDUCATION IN MY LOVE   HE YET TOO CEMETARY WEPT

KRISTI: I don't understand. What do you mean by "cemetary wept"?

ADRI: YES IS TOO TORN IN THIS LIFE

KRISTI: Did Daddy have a difficult last lifetime?

ADRI: YES

KRISTI: Was he in Minnesota with us?

ADRI: NO

KRISTI: Do you know where Daddy lived?

ADRI: YES

KRISTI: Do you know about people's lifetimes even if you were not part of them?

ADRI: YES

KRISTI: How can you do that?

ADRI: I VERY YET WISE

Let's not be modest.

KRISTI: Where did Daddy live?

ADRI: HE LIVED IN TOWN OF DACSN

I tried to get clarification on the town but was unable to get any clearer spelling.

KRISTI: What country did he live in?

ADRI: NORWAY

KRISTI: Was Daddy male or female?

ADRI: FEMALE

KRISTI: Did something bad happen to Daddy?

ADRI: YES   HIS LIFE ENDED TOO EARLY

KRISTI: How old was Daddy when his life ended in Norway?

ADRI: 7

KRISTI: What happened to Daddy?

ADRI: DADDY DIED OF LEUKEMIA

We took a break. I felt sad for the child in that lifetime and I wondered what the implications might be for the adult in this one.

Yesterday I had a phone conversation with Felice that has been bothering me ever since. I've been thinking about how to broach the subject with Adri. After the break I decided to just ask her about it.

KRISTI: Adri, yesterday Felice said that she and Ben

have started attending Sunday afternoon spiritual classes with a couple, Tom and Mary, who live on a farm not too far from here. Felice said she mentioned to Tom that she was working with an autistic child who seemed to be very open and who remembered her past lives. Tom said that this autistic child was open, but not entirely so.

Adri, do you know what Tom might have meant by that? He doesn't even know you. Do you know who he is? Why would he say that?

ADRI: YES BECAUSE I HAVE A CURSE

I couldn't believe it. That's what Felice told me Tom had said, but I hadn't mentioned a word of it to Adri. I thought it was such a creepy idea. The last thing I expected was for Adri to confirm it.

KRISTI: You have a curse on you?

ADRI: YES

KRISTI: Is that why you're autistic?

ADRI: NO

KRISTI: But it does prevent you from seeing "everything"?

ADRI: YES

KRISTI: Why do you have a curse on you?

ADRI: BECAUSE I AM WAY

I asked her to clarify what she meant by that, but she had nothing to add.

KRISTI: Do you know who put the curse on you?

ADRI: YES CLEOPATRA AND XERSES

KRISTI: Do you know what country you were living in at the time?

ADRI: YES EGYPT

KRISTI: What was the year?

ADRI: 38 BC

KRISTI: You wrote 38 B.C. Is that the year you meant to type?

ADRI: YES ACTIVATE   NOT ACTIVATE

KRISTI: Do you mean you want to activate or deactivate the curse?

ADRI: DEACTIVATE

KRISTI: Do you want to see Tom and Mary? Can they help?

I hadn't even finished the question before Adri forcefully typed.

ADRI: NEED TO GO   MUST SEE

KRISTI: Okay. I'll call them now. Do you know who Tom says he channels?

ADRI: YES

KRISTI: Can he help with the curse?

ADRI: YES

KRISTI: Are you scared about this?

ADRI: YES

KRISTI: But you feel you need or want to go anyway?

ADRI: YES

That was enough, we needed to stop. I put the Canon aside and stretched out on the rug beside her. She turned and gazed very deeply into my eyes and pulled my head toward hers. I felt as if she was giving me some kind of gift, as if she was showing me that she appreciated my willingness to stay with her, to know her, to accept her, even those parts of her that seemed completely alien to me.

I called Tom and Mary, and they said we could come right over. Rodrigo decided to come too. After a brief drive we pulled up at a charming farmhouse with a beautifully tended yard. Mary greeted us at the door and took us into the kitchen to meet Tom, who was in a wheelchair.

We all sat down, and Tom began to talk. He didn't seem to be in a trance, but he said that he was channeling guides. One of these was Santo, who he said was Adri's guardian from the darkness. Tom also channeled Jesus. He told me that he believed that Adri would speak when the time was right. During the session Adri asked only one question. As she touched the keys, I could almost hear the anguish in her voice.

ADRI: WERE YOU THERE AT THE CROSS?

Tom said he was. He reassured Adri that she was "worthy" to serve God, then he turned to Rodrigo and me and told us that Adri had been a disciple during Jesus' time.

I left there feeling shaken and unsure of this encounter. I have no way of judging the legitimacy of what was said. I can't tell whether it's just Tom talking or whether he's really channeling someone. But because Adri listened, I listened too. For now she's the only source that I completely trust. She's the one who convinces me of the reality of this other world.

I can't get the idea of Adri's being a disciple out of my mind. Could that really be why she seems so personally involved when she talks about Jesus?

I'm feeling agitated tonight. Adri's Cleopatra and Xerxes story seems kind of farfetched. Adri sometimes misses letters, so I don't know how much weight to lend to factual data, but it's also scary to think she might be right.

I called Coreece tonight too. She's really having a hard time with the chemotherapy. I want to visit her. I'd really like to share Adri's thoughts with her. They offer such an expanded perspective on both life and death.

Wednesday 7/31/91

It's almost lunchtime and I've just finished another extraordinary discussion with Adri. New dimensions of her emerge every day.

KRISTI: What did you think of yesterday? What about Tom?

ADRI: TOM IS VERY SENSITIVE

KRISTI: Adri, were we listening to Tom himself or to the individuals he said he was channeling?

ADRI: WE HEAR THE PEOPLE THAT HE TELEPHONES

Adri has spoken of "telephoning" to people before, but I always assumed that she just literally wanted me to phone someone. This time I asked her if she meant that we telephone by thought.

ADRI: YES

KRISTI: Adri, what was the most significant thing about yesterday afternoon with Tom?

ADRI: THE MOST IMPORTANT THING WAS TALKING TO JESUS

KRISTI: Adri, who is Jesus?

ADRI: HE IS THE EDUCATED ONE

KRISTI: What makes Jesus educated?

ADRI: HE KNOWS WHY WE, MAN, SURVIVE IN THE UNIVERSE

Does she mean that Jesus knows why we exist, or literally how we survive? Suddenly Adri reached out and scratched me across the face. I jumped back, surprised.

KRISTI: Are you mad at me?

ADRI: NO

However, for the last few minutes Brie had been outside our door making a lot of noise in the hallway. Maybe Adri was bothered by the interruption. It was distracting.

KRISTI: Anything else you want to say?

With great force Adri responded.

ADRI: YES YOU NEW ENTITY SO YOU NOT EDUCATED

I was really hurt. It seems that there couldn't be much worse—to Adri—than being a lowly new entity. She was obviously very exasperated with me.

KRISTI: Adri, is this about Brie? Do you know Brie from another time?

ADRI: YES

KRISTI: How did you know her, or where or when?

ADRI: WE WERE TOGETHER IN EGYPT

KRISTI: Were you relatives?

ADRI: NO

KRISTI: How would you describe your relationship?

ADRI: FRIEND

KRISTI: How about Seby? Do you know him?

ADRI: YES

Adri jerked away from me and tried to bite me. I got very angry with her.

KRISTI: Adri, what's wrong? Why are you trying to bite me?

ADRI: BECAUSE I AM MAD AT YOU

KRISTI: Why?

ADRI: BECAUSE HE IS NOT EVEN EDUCATED

I can take her disdain for me. But sneering at Seby was just too much. I was incensed.

KRISTI: Each of us here has a purpose on earth, and as I understand it, none is more special than the other. It is really unfair of you and beneath you to use your special gifts and understanding to attack your brother. Maybe what you need to learn in this lifetime is a bit of compassion and caring. Do you have anything you want to say?

ADRI: YES   YOU NOT TENDER

KRISTI: Perhaps not just now. It was only a day or so ago that you told me I was too tender, that I let people walk all over me. Maybe I'm learning how to create a balance between tenderness and being walked on. I'm really hurt to hear you talk like that about Seby. I won't listen to it. Just as I won't allow him, or anyone else, to say unkind things about you.

Adri went to her bed and curled up, pulling the covers over her head. I felt really bad too. I had responded so vehemently to her partly out of my own hurt. I really should

have noticed her exasperation earlier and responded to it
then.

I went and sat beside her on the bed, continuing to talk
about what it means to have compassion. I told her that she
had a responsibility to use her gifts wisely and that perhaps
she, too, had some lessons to learn in this lifetime. Hugging
and stroking her, I told her how much I loved her and how
sorry I was for my outburst. I brought the Canon over and
asked if she wanted to say anything.

ADRI: I SORRY   I LOVE SEBY AND YOU

With tears running down my cheeks, I held on to her
tightly, repeating over and over how much I loved her.
We're both holding so much inside, perhaps because we
don't want to burden each other. Yet I know that I have to
live the truth, even in our sessions together. I've managed to
hold on through all these assaults to my belief system by just
trying to keep up an appearance that all is well. I think this
has helped me stay with Adri, but it's also kept me at a
heightened emotional level. Almost anything can trigger me
to overreact. I need time to integrate all I'm learning.

KRISTI: Is there anything else you want to say?

ADRI: YES   YOU   EDUCATED   YOU   NOT
NEW ENTITY   YOU WISE

I hugged and thanked her. I have to admit, I was
relieved.

ADRI: DO WE UNDERSTAND

KRISTI: Yes, I think we do. Do you want to stop for
today?

ADRI: YES

Chapter 13

"I OPEN PEOPLES HEARTS FOR GOD"

AUGUST 1–19, 1991

Thursday 8/1/91

It's a new month. I didn't realize that till now. This morning I woke up early and was out walking by six. I took my usual route along the lake, stopping at my favorite spot to meditate. I wasn't able to enter into a very deep state, but still I felt peaceful. As my eyes opened, I thought that I'd really like an affirmation that I'm on the right path.

Before I'd begun meditating, I'd gazed into the water, watching it move, noting the absence of fish. Now as I gazed down once again, I thought a fish would be a good affirmation. A moment later a minnow swam out and whooshed around a few times before disappearing. I felt pretty good about that fish.

Adri didn't want to work today. She just needed a break. Before bed, though, I asked her if there was anything she wanted to talk about.

ADRI: I LOVE TOM

KRISTI: You felt really at home there, didn't you? We can visit again soon. Tom said something that sounded a bit strange to me, Adri. He said you probably "went out" nights, do you?

ADRI: YES

KRISTI: Where do you go?

ADRI: I GO EVERYWHERE

Though I don't know where "everywhere" could be, I know that her world is infinitely larger than my own. I only hope that someday I'll be able to go along.

KRISTI: Do you want to stop for tonight?

ADRI: YES

Friday 8/2/91

This morning Adri and I drove back to Boston for another session with Ben and Felice. When Ben asked her why she had trouble speaking, Adri said she had a problem with her "tongue." Ben said that she had a lot of rigidity in her jaw, and he'd like to try to work with her on that. Felice said that she thought Adri was a teacher. Adri agreed.

Saturday 8/3/91

Today Adri and I flew to Portland, Oregon, for two weeks of "auditory training." This a sound-based therapy begun in Switzerland that has supposedly helped people suffering from many kinds of disorders including autism. I'm going to stay with Adri the first week, and then Rodrigo is coming out to stay with her the second week, as I have to be back for an FC workshop in Boston.

Sunday 8/4/91

With the excitement of being in a new place, Adri hasn't wanted to talk these last two days. But this morning she was ready.

ADRI: YES   I AM SO SORRY

KRISTI: You're sorry?

ADRI: YES

KRISTI: Why are you sorry, Adri? Because . . . can you finish the sentence?

ADRI: YOU NOT STEP YET

KRISTI: Because I not step yet?

ADRI: YES

KRISTI: Can you clarify what you mean by that?

ADRI: YOU NOT WALKING ALONE

KRISTI: Why is it so important that I walk alone?

ADRI: IT IS NECESSARY SO YOU UNDER-STAND   YET NOT

KRISTI: I don't yet understand? In order to understand and progress, I need to walk alone?

ADRI: YES

KRISTI: Is my understanding tied to your path and progress?

ADRI: YES

KRISTI: Your actions are tied up to my actions at this time because you can only act through me?

ADRI: YES

Adri had been playing with the tape player. It seemed to distract her, but maybe it also calmed her.

KRISTI: Adri, are you nervous?

ADRI: YES

KRISTI: Does the music calm you?

ADRI: YES CALM

KRISTI: I should just leave it here, then?

ADRI: YES

KRISTI: Adri, is there a reason you're here now?

ADRI: YES   PURPOSE IS TO INSURE THE WAY

KRISTI: Is there a specific task that I'm supposed to do too?

ADRI: YES YOU ARE TO PREPARE THE WAY FOR ME

KRISTI: What is your purpose?

ADRI: I AM TO SHOW THE WORLD THE WILL OF GOD

Her words echoed through me. I was truly speechless—whether from awe or just astonishment, I wasn't sure. The Canon tape ran out at that moment, so we had to stop typing.

I'm feeling anxious. I couldn't find Canon tape, so I bought a typewriter this morning. I wanted a written record of our conversations. Adri's certainly capable of working on a type-writer, but I don't know whether she'll be willing, and we really need to talk. The auditory testing didn't go well this morning either. I facilitated her, and she was supposed to indicate the sounds she could hear. Her responses were un-clear, and she was unable to answer any questions the tester asked her. Why?

Again, I know that I was really eager for her to show him what she could do. Is that why she couldn't or wouldn't type? I think what's making me the most nervous just now is the glaring contrast between Adri's physical lim-itations and the spiritual person who is emerging through her communications. I have to admit that all day I've been asking myself, could she be psychotic?

The idea makes me so nervous that I block out the very

thing I need to remember: that Adri first began to volunteer all this information in the course of our normal conversations. Where could it have come from except the high source she claims? She's had no other exposure. And it's not just that she claims to have certain abilities. She really has demonstrated them. Her ability to do math and science, the speed with which she reads—all of this is very real, very concrete. And yet she's this confusing combination of adult and child. It's hard to know how to respond to her at different times.

I feel a sudden sense of relief—I keep forgetting that I don't have to figure all this out alone. My guides will help me if I can only figure out how to get through to them.

I really love Adri, but knowing that she's so smart and thinking that she's supposed to be a guide and teacher sometimes makes me even more impatient and perplexed by her behaviors. How can she be so wise and yet act so infantile? This morning she climbed fully clothed into a tub of water. Just now she drew on the furniture, and when I tried to get her to clean it up, she drew more. It made me so angry. Is she angry about something too? I took all the pencils away and told her she wouldn't get them back until tomorrow.

I need to talk to somebody. Joan would be good. I know she could help, even if it's just to listen. Adri said I should call her. When we get back to Boston, I'll do it.

What you need most comes to you when you most need it. I was feeling so troubled and confused. My perspective was all screwed up, and I was taking out my frustration on Adri. Finally I told her, "We have to get out of this room."

We went for a walk and ended up at a hamburger stand. It had an outdoor play area, and two boys were playing there. The lady with them said they were her grandchildren. While we chatted, I watched in delight as Adri began to interact with the boys. She would go where they were, and when she'd wander off, they would follow her, sometimes taking her hand. They went on the swings and then played inside this huge tube that rolled around when they shifted their weight.

We ended up staying more than an hour, and it was one of the most wonderful hours I've ever spent. I got to see my daughter really play with other children for the first time. Several times she hugged one of the boys or grabbed their hands. We had the Canon with us, and she typed answers to their simple questions. The boys were very intrigued by the whole thing and very accepting. Another family that had been watching from inside the restaurant came out to ask about the Canon too. It's a conversation piece.

Adri was laughing and having so much fun. It made me feel confident that regular school is going to be so good for her. Before we left, we got the boys' phone number and invited them to come and swim at the hotel. Things are back in perspective and I feel so much calmer and happier. Adri too.

Monday 8/5/91

Adri and I had a good day today. It was her first day of "listening" in the auditory training. We went to a half-hour session in the morning and another in the afternoon. Sitting at a table in a little room, Adri wore headphones and listened to a special program of different sounds interspersed with music. In the morning session Adri spent the first twenty minutes flapping her hands and jumping, fiddling with the cord to the headphones, and pulling them off. This was the most autistic behavior I've seen from her in a long time. However, she calmed down considerably for the last ten minutes of the session.

In the afternoon session Adri was much quieter, only

flapping occasionally. In both sessions I noticed that she brought her hand up and cupped her left ear several times.

KRISTI: Does it hurt?

ADRI: NO

KRISTI: Does it feel funny?

ADRI: YES

Adri and I also talked together today using the new typewriter.

KRISTI: You said yesterday that I'm to prepare the way for you. What do you mean by that?

ADRI: BY JOINING MORE YOU GET YOUR NEW YOU

Strange comment. Adri was really fidgeting, having a hard time adjusting to the different touch of the typewriter.

KRISTI: I don't really understand what you mean. Can you say it any differently?

ADRI: I DON'T LIKE THIS MACHINE

KRISTI: I know it's hard to get used to, but it's all we have right now. Please try. I really want to talk with you. What can I do to understand better?

ADRI: READ ABOUT GODS WAY

KRISTI: Who is God?

ADRI: GOD IS YOUR CREATOR

Then she volunteered . . .

ADRI: YOU LOVE BECAUSE NOBODY LIVING SURVIVES WITHOUT LOVE

KRISTI: What does that have to do with God?

ADRI: GOD IS ALL LOVE

KRISTI: Adri, what are you here for?

ADRI: I AM A CATALYST FOR HISTORY

KRISTI: What exactly does that mean, Adri?

ADRI: IT MEANS THAT I OPEN PEOPLES HEARTS FOR GOD

KRISTI: Do you know how you will do that?
ADRI: YES   I WILL LOVE THEM

Tuesday 8/6/91

This morning Adri and I talked again. Adri opened the session with:

ADRI: YOU AREN'T IN TOUCH WITH YOUR GUIDES YET

Then she started hitting the typewriter and struggling with me.

KRISTI: Adri, are you angry?
ADRI: YES
KRISTI: Why?
ADRI: BECAUSE LIKING THE OTHER MACHINE
KRISTI: I know you like your Canon better. I'm sorry I didn't bring more tape. But I know you can master this machine. You're doing really great.
ADRI: LOVE YOU MOM

It's so nice when she accepts my attempts to comfort her.

KRISTI: Adri, can you teach me how to contact my guides?
ADRI: WE CONTACT THEM BY CALLING THEM   YOU NEED LOVE TO RECOGNIZE
KRISTI: To recognize what?
ADRI: YOU MUST LOVE ME

She was really struggling with the typewriter. She kept hitting both the space bar and the return key, breaking up her words. It was very frustrating. And I was nervous too. In fact whenever we start talking these days, I'm on edge, just waiting for her to chastise me for not yet connecting with my guides. I'm sure she senses my defensiveness.

I told her that I really did love her, but I still wasn't able to make contact yet. As I was speaking, Adri kept struggling in my arms and pulling away from me. Finally I just let go of her and threw up my hands in frustration.

KRISTI: Okay, Adri. If this isn't that important to you, let's just stop. I don't need this pressure. Do you want to stop? Should we just stop?

ADRI: NO

KRISTI: This is important to you, then?

ADRI: YES

We were caught up in a childish squabble.

ADRI: I MOVING TO LA

KRISTI: You mean Los Angeles? Where did that come from? Why?

ADRI: BECAUSE I LOVE LA

KRISTI: Okay, Adri, you want to go back to L.A. Do you want to talk more now?

ADRI: YES

KRISTI: Adri, are you something different from other people?

ADRI: NO

KRISTI: Do you talk to spirit guides?

ADRI: YES

KRISTI: Do you remember past lives?

ADRI: YES

KRISTI: Are you normal?

I don't know why I was pursuing such a silly line of questioning. I finally dropped it.

KRISTI: Adri, tell me about yourself.

ADRI: I LOVE GOD   LOVE IS CHOOSING TO BELIEVE IN

KRISTI: Adri, what can I do? Tell me, I just don't know what to do.

ADRI: YOU MUST KEEP TRYING

Wednesday 8/7/91

This morning we followed what was becoming our usual routine, sitting down to talk after breakfast.

KRISTI: Anything you want to say this morning?

ADRI: YES   YOU ARE TOO PLEASING TO PEOPLE

KRISTI: I still try to make people like me too much?

ADRI: YES

KRISTI: What should I be doing?

ADRI: YOU MUST OPEN LOVING PEOPLES HEARTS TO GOD

KRISTI: I must open people to God?

ADRI: WANT YOU TO TAKE YOURSELF TO LAY HANDS ON PEOPLE IN ORDER TO HEAL THEM

I was totally astounded. I've dreamed of being able to help heal people through touch, but I didn't feel I had that ability.

KRISTI: I am to open people's hearts by healing with my hands?

ADRI: YES

KRISTI: I would love to be able to do that. I know there are people who can do it. I've seen classes offered in this kind of healing. Would that help?

ADRI: NO   YOU DON'T NEED CLASSES

KRISTI: What should I do, then? How do I learn?

ADRI: YOU BEGIN BY LIKING YOU

She continued to explain:

ADRI: YOU OPEN YOUR UNDERSTANDING BY OPENING YOUR EYES TO THE WILL OF GOD

KRISTI: But, Adri, what is the will of God?

ADRI: THE WILL OF GOD IS THAT WE SAVE THE PLANET

KRISTI: Is the planet threatened at this time?

ADRI: YES

KRISTI: Adri, who are you?

ADRI: I AM PERSON THAT KNOWS MUCH BE-
CAUSE I AM NOT MYSELF

KRISTI: You mean that you aren't just the nine-year-
old Adri?

ADRI: YES

KRISTI: Who are you, then, besides that child?

ADRI: I AM MASTER   I AM PERSON ALL
KNOWING

KRISTI: Does "all-knowing" mean that you know everything about the past, present, and future?

ADRI: NO

KRISTI: What do you mean by it, then?

ADRI: I OPEN ROADS FOR PEOPLE   YOU
TOO OPEN ROADS

I knew that the conversation wasn't really over, but we
didn't have much time. I wanted to ask her about the auditory training sessions.

KRISTI: We haven't really talked about the auditory
training. Is it helping you?

ADRI: YES I FEEL THAT IT IS HELPING MY
HEARING

KRISTI: Do you think there's something different
about the way you hear? Does this interfere with your
speech?

ADRI: YES

I asked her that because I've been noticing that she is
vocalizing much more now. Later, when we discussed the
arrival of Rodrigo, I heard her say very clearly, with her
voice, "Daddy." Speech will come!

Thursday 8/8/91

Adri's been spitting up a lot when we talk. I asked her about
it this morning.

KRISTI: Adri, why are you throwing up so much?

ADRI: I THROW UP BECAUSE I NERVOUS YET

KRISTI: Do you know what makes you nervous?

ADRI: YES

KRISTI: Can you tell me?

ADRI: YES I NERVOUS BECAUSE YOU NOT OPEN TO GO TO YOUR GUIDES

This took her a long time to type, and she kept spitting up between words. The more she spit up, the more agitated I became. Now it seems that I am not only screwing up my connection with my own guides, I'm also responsible for worrying her to the point of making her spit up. My defensiveness immediately kicked in.

KRISTI: Adri, that isn't fair. I'm trying to reach my guides all the time. And you're not helping. I don't like the feeling of not being able to open. I'm having a hard time, and this constant pressure from you doesn't help.

I paused and looked at Adri. She was gazing at me, not with anger as I had expected but with compassion.

ADRI: PLEASE BE PATIENT I TOO AM OPENING

I hugged her close, humbled by her honesty and her maturity.

KRISTI: I'll try to be patient too. I know this is hard for us both. What is my problem, do you know? Why can't I reach my guides?

ADRI: YOU ARE OPPOSING YOUR MASTER

KRISTI: I have a master? Do you know who my master is?

ADRI: YES

KRISTI: What's his or her name?

ADRI: MOHAMMED

KRISTI: How do I talk to Mohammed?

ADRI: YOU MUST OPEN YOUR HEART YOU PLACE TOO MUCH EMPHASIS ON THE BODY

KRISTI: Adri, is that one of the reasons that you're in

an autistic body? As living proof that the body is not the spirit or the mind? What better way to demonstrate that than by having a spirit such as yours housed in a body that doesn't work?

ADRI: YES

KRISTI: So, are you saying that the spitting up is just not important?

ADRI: YES

KRISTI: Is it very unhealthy or dangerous for you?

ADRI: NO

KRISTI: Should I just ignore it?

ADRI: YES NOT IMPORTANT   I OPERATE OUT OF THIS PITIFUL BODY

What a thing to say. She didn't look at all sad or upset, though, so after a hug I continued:

KRISTI: Adri, you said you were a master. Do you have a different name as a master?

ADRI: YES

KRISTI: Can you tell me?

ADRI: YES POMPEII

KRISTI: Can you tell me about Pompei?

ADRI: HE IS POWERFUL

KRISTI: How does one become a master?

ADRI: YOU BECOME A MASTER BY LABOR OF LOVE OVER LONG LIFETIMES

KRISTI: Does everyone become a master?

ADRI: NO

KRISTI: Adri, what happens to people when they die?

ADRI: THEY UNDERGO A LIFE PLAYBACK TO INVESTIGATE THINGS FROM THIS LIFE

I wanted to ask her much more about that, but it was time to go to auditory training.

Friday 8/9/91

Rodrigo's been here for a couple of days, and tomorrow I leave for Boston. Today will be our last day to talk. In some ways I feel we're just getting started, and I don't want to leave. On the other hand our talks have been exhausting for both of us, and maybe a break is exactly what we need.

KRISTI: Adri, anything on your mind this morning?

ADRI: YES I YET NOT EDUCATED

KRISTI: What do you mean by that?

ADRI: I DONT KNOW YET ENOUGH ABOUT NEUROLOGY

KRISTI: We'll find a way, in school or out, to give you instruction in neurology. And speaking of schools, we've talked about it a lot, but we really need to make a decision. One school would probably be better for academics, but the other might be better socially. What's more important to you?

ADRI: I PREFER THE CLASS THAT HAS ACADEMIC UNDERSTANDING

KRISTI: That would be Runkle.

ADRI: YES

KRISTI: Okay. I'm glad we've settled that. Anything else on your mind?

ADRI: YES YOU NOT UNDERSTAND GUIDES ARE TRYING TO TALK TO YOU BUT YOU CANT HEAR THEM BECAUSE YOU INTERRUPT THEM WITH YOUR OPINIONS

KRISTI: Do you mean that I have opinions that prevent me from hearing my guides, or do you mean that I'm thinking about too many things at the same time? Do all these thoughts take up all the space in my mind so there's no room for a guide to be heard?

ADRI: YES YOU JUGGLE TOO MANY THINGS

KRISTI: Well, at least that gives me some ideas about what to work on. Do you have any suggestions for me?

ADRI: YES YOU MUST STOP TO LISTEN

KRISTI: Do you mean I need to meditate more?

ADRI: YES

KRISTI: Maybe I could find a teacher who could instruct me?

ADRI: NOT NEEDING TEACHER

KRISTI: I don't need a teacher? I need to do this on my own?

ADRI: YES

KRISTI: How about particular methods of meditation or particular words? Do I need to learn some techniques?

ADRI: NO

KRISTI: Adri, will I know my guides if I do hear them?

ADRI: YES YOU WILL RECOGNIZE THEM

KRISTI: How about Tom, could I talk to them through Tom?

ADRI: YOU MIGHT TALK TO THEM THROUGH TOM

KRISTI: When I meditate or go to Tom, should I ask for Mohammed?

ADRI: YES YOU MUST OPEN TO MOHAMMED NOT TO OPINIONS

She's absolutely great; it's not in her nature to mince words. Adri then put her fingers slightly behind her ears and pressed. She does this quite often.

KRISTI: Adri, do you have a message for me from Mohammed?

ADRI: YES I AM INTERESTED IN OPENING YOUR HEART IN ORDER THAT YOU MIGHT OPEN OTHERS

She was typing very quickly and forcefully.

KRISTI: Was that Mohammed speaking?

ADRI: YES YOU HAVE CHOSEN TO LIVE THIS LIFETIME LEARNING ABOUT PATIENCE

KRISTI: Is that still Mohammed?

ADRI: YES

KRISTI: Why do the guides want to reach me at this time?

ADRI: BECAUSE IT IS TIME TO UNVEIL THE PLAN

KRISTI: What is the plan?

ADRI: THE PLAN IS TO OPEN HEARTS TO GOD

I don't know what I thought the plan might be, but certainly something far more elaborate. I was both relieved and moved.

KRISTI: Is this still Mohammed?

ADRI: YES

KRISTI: Maybe this will sound pretty egotistical and selfish, but I'm wondering why all this is happening to me. Why do I get to participate? Because I'm Adri's mother?

ADRI: BECAUSE YOU HAVE LOVE

What a wonderful thing to say. My heart felt so full of gratitude. Each day I feel stronger and more open and more accepting and less fearful. Love overwhelms fear, and then the wisdom comes.

Saturday 8/10/91

I'm writing this on the plane back to Boston. What a heart-wrenching parting I had with Adri. I feel so guilty about leaving. I want to strengthen the bond she and I are creating. Yet I also need to remember that we're separate people. Each of us has to experience life in our own way.

How can I possibly express my gratitude for all the gifts Adri has brought me? It isn't possible, not really. But I am remembering my new lesson: Benefits are mutual. If you follow your intuition, you will be led to the people you need, and in most cases those people need you too.

That reminds me to call Joan. I need to talk with her. I need her help. That's why we met of course. We didn't come together by chance. And it wasn't by chance that only a couple of weeks after our meeting, Adri began to reveal things to me. It wasn't by chance that Joan brought up the subject of past lives. Our paths have crossed for a reason.

I've been savoring yesterday's message: "Because you have love." Those words heal me, warm me, envelop me. I'm beginning to realize that Adri and I are traveling a mutual path. To some degree each of us is experiencing and learning about our path through the other.

This afternoon I drove straight from the airport to New Hampshire. It was wonderful to see the kids. But they must be wondering what's going on with me. Suddenly Mom is talking about God. And yet faith seems to be a very natural thing for them—they accept it easily.

I sat with each of them, and as we prayed together, each said they felt God in their hearts. I also told them a little about the concept of reincarnation, that at some point our bodies grow very tired and die, but that our souls never die, they simply choose new bodies and return again.

Thursday 8/15/91

I had a powerful dream last night. It was very disorienting, but the lesson was clear.

> I was experiencing being autistic—going inside myself and losing control of my body. For some reason Rodrigo and I and a few others were in a ball park with a high chain-link fence. We all started hanging

on to the fence and playing a game where we'd grip the fence and lean way back and then push way forward again. I remember really getting into it, throwing my body back and forth, building up a fast rhythm, feeling mesmerized and dizzy.

Still in the dream, I lost conscious awareness of the world and found myself inside my own head. I was being drawn in, the pull was magnetic, and the sensation was exhilarating, almost hypnotic. And then, from somewhere, I started hearing a babbling of voices. Snapping out of my hypnotic state, I realized that the babbling was coming from me, and that I'd been writhing on the ground for some time. I looked up and saw that my friends had long since climbed up into the bleachers. Others were sitting there, too, and everyone was looking at me very strangely. I felt embarrassed and ashamed.

Is that what people with autism feel like at times? Hypnotically drawn into a rich interior experience over which they have limited control? Coming out of it only to realize that others are gawking at them with fear and distaste? Do they feel shame and self-loathing?

Friday 8/16/91

Joan Borysenko and I had lunch together. I brought my notebook and told her Adri's entire story, going through the transcripts one by one. It took a long time, and although I felt the enormity of it all again, I had no idea how Joan would respond. However, while she didn't seem surprised by any of the concepts Adri talked about, she was amazed that they had been voiced by an autistic child. She, too, feels the wonder of Adri.

Just being with Joan again was wonderful. After lunch she

took me to a metaphysical bookstore and recommended several books. I'd seen the shop on the corner before, but it had looked a little weird, and I'd never ventured in. We spent the entire afternoon together. I feel I've made a true friend.

During the afternoon a feeling of peace just seemed to settle over me. I realized that I needn't hold so fast to my old rules. I'm free to perceive things differently. I might not understand all things at all times, but I can trust that I'll get what I need when I need it.

Saturday 8/17/91

The auditory training ended, and Rodrigo and Adri came home yesterday. Boy, did I miss her. Before bed we talked for a little bit.

KRISTI: Anything you want to talk about?

ADRI: YET YOU NOT GO TO YOUR GUIDES
Some things never change.

KRISTI: Is someone trying to reach me?

ADRI: YES MOHAMMED

KRISTI: Do you know what he wants to say to me?

ADRI: YES YOU STILL VERY RESISTANT YET NOT LIVE WAY
Then she added a thought.

ADRI: YOU YET WANT ME TO YET BE VERY YOUNG

KRISTI: You mean that I still look at you and treat you as if you were very young?

ADRI: YES

KRISTI: We need to talk about that more. But since you're just back, can I ask you first about the auditory training? Do you think it helped you?

ADRI: YES

KRISTI: Why or how?

ADRI: BECAUSE I CAN HEAR

KRISTI: I'm not quite sure what you mean. Do you mean that you hear better or do you mean that sounds don't bother you as much anymore?
ADRI: YES SOUNDS DONT
The implication was clear.

Sunday 8/18/91

Finally, this afternoon, I sat down with the encyclopedia to check out the story of Adri's curse. Adri said the curse dates from 38 B.C. Unbelievable. Cleopatra lived from 69 to 30 B.C. I read the entry several times just to make sure. I can't believe it—but I do. Adri would probably tell me much more if I could just trust what she says. That's also what I know I need to do to make contact with my own guides. I am trying, and I'll keep on trying, but I wish I could just get out of my own way! I'm glad we're going back to New Hampshire tonight. It's so much more relaxed there, and I've missed my walks.

Monday 8/19/91

After my walk this morning I asked Adri if she'd like to talk.
    KRISTI: Anything on your mind today?
    ADRI: YES I NOT UNDERSTOOD I NOT MAKING PROGRESS
    KRISTI: What do you mean?
    ADRI: I MEAN YOU NOT READY OPEN YOUR HEART
    KRISTI: Do you mean that I haven't opened my heart yet?
    ADRI: YES YOU MUST MOVING TO MORE INDEPENDENCE
    KRISTI: Can you explain what you mean by that?

ADRI: YOU MUST SEEK OUT UNDERSTAND-
ING BY OPPORTUNITY OF MOVING TO GO IN
LOVE

KRISTI: I need to open to love. Can praying help?

ADRI: YES

KRISTI: Can prayer put me in touch with Mohammed?

ADRI: YOUR OPINIONS OPPOSE MOHAM-
MED   YOU MUST OPEN TO MOHAMMED

I reminded her that I was doing my best to clear my
mind and open myself up.

Then I told her that I'd verified the Cleopatra dates,
which seemed to upset her. I guess I don't blame her. Here
I was, talking about opening up, and in the same breath demonstrating lack of trust. I feel somewhat justified, though. All
of this is so new to me, and I'm being asked to make giant
leaps of faith. A little checking doesn't seem like such a crime.

But because Adri can easily contact guides, talk to God,
have faith, access knowledge, I'm sure it's hard for her to understand how I could be having such a hard time. Just as people think she isn't trying because she can't do many of the
things that we consider easy, she probably thinks I'm not trying because I can't seem to do any of the things she considers
easy.

This turned out to be a wild day. A hurricane hit Boston,
and even here in New Hampshire the wind was howling. I
had the TV on, watching events unfold in Russia.
Gorbachev had been put under house arrest. I decided to
ask Adri what she thought of the situation.

KRISTI: Adri, do you know who Gorbachev is?

ADRI: NO

KRISTI: Do you have an opinion about what's happening in Russia?

ADRI: NOT READY FOR PEACE

That seemed an odd thing to say in light of the great strides they've been making toward peace over the last months.

KRISTI: Who isn't ready for peace?

ADRI: THE PUBLIC IS NOT READY

KRISTI: Why?

ADRI: BECAUSE THEY NOT YET BELIEVE

Is everything in the world interrelated in Adri's mind? It makes me realize how little I understand. Although I am meditating, and I feel that I'm growing spiritually, I still keep the various parts of my life separated. There's the spiritual world, and then there's the everyday world, and then there's the political world, and so on.

But Adri's comments suggest that for her there are no divisions. That all aspects of life are interconnecting components of a vast spiritual network. What an amazing idea!

Tonight before bed Adri was very tired, but she wanted to talk.

ADRI: QUANTUM

I don't know where that came from. I tried to get her to define it for me or to explain why she brought it up. She tried several times, but I couldn't make anything out.

ADRI: YOU YET NOT EDUCATED

Is that the problem, then?

KRISTI: When did you learn about "quantum"? In this lifetime or in a past lifetime?

ADRI: YES   THIS

KRISTI: Can you tell me anything about the concept?

ADRI: I LIVING IN OTHER WORLD   I NOT YET . . .

I couldn't make out her last word.

KRISTI: Adri, what does "quantum" mean to you?

ADRI: REAL-WORLD LAWS

Chapter 14

"You Will
Have New World"

AUGUST 20–29, 1991

Tuesday 8/20/91

Things have changed in our home. As a result of Adri's teachings I feel that I can now offer the children a depth of security, through God's love, that I never could before. Yesterday Seby saw me meditating. He asked what I was doing and I told him I was talking to God. It's good for Seby to witness that. Who knows, maybe I can even find a church for us.

Adri and I sat in her room together and talked for a few minutes before bed.

KRISTI: Anything you want to say?

ADRI: YES I HAD GOOD DAY

KRISTI: I'm glad. Anything else you want to talk about?

ADRI: I SEED THE YARD

Since we didn't do anything in the yard today, I assume she was speaking metaphorically.

ADRI: SEEDS SPROUTED WITH ME

Indeed they did.

ADRI: YES I HAD MET YOU MANY YEARS

KRISTI: You mean we've known each other a long time?

ADRI: YES GOODNIGHT

Wednesday 8/21/91

Adri and I talked in the afternoon.

KRISTI: Adri, you said that when we die, we go through a life review. Can you tell me what happens after that?

ADRI: YES YOU CREATE ANOTHER BODY

KRISTI: How much time does that take?

ADRI: VERY RAPIDLY

That made me wonder just how relevant the concept of time is after we die.

Then, wanting to pin down factual information about the curse and her identity as Pompei, I asked her for details. Adri typed an angry response.

ADRI: YOU TOO OPINIONS   YOU NOT NEEDING OTHER PEOPLE TO TALK

KRISTI: Adri, you think I'm spending too much time worrying about trying to prove these things?

ADRI: YES GO MOHAMMED

KRISTI: Does Mohammed have a message for me?

ADRI: YES   YOU MUST OPPOSE INTER-FERENCE

KRISTI: Anything else?
ADRI: NO

This afternoon when I meditated, I tried using the words *help me* as a mantra when my thoughts strayed. As Mohammed instructed, I opposed the interference. I didn't have nearly as many interfering thoughts and opinions as I usually do, and I went into a deep meditation. Suddenly my jaw locked. My mouth was open, and I was making garbled sounds from my throat. I also thought I heard words like "in the presence of God." It was extraordinary. Afterward I felt good—rested and peaceful.

Before bedtime we had only a few minutes to talk, but I was eager to see if Adri had any insight into my lockjaw experience.

KRISTI: Adri, do you know why my jaw locked?
ADRI: YOU YET NOT GIVEN ROAD MEAN THAT YOU NOT READY TO TELEPHONE
KRISTI: Is that what was going on? Someone trying to "telephone"?
ADRI: YES WE WERE TELEPHONING
KRISTI: My jaw locked because I'm not ready yet?
ADRI: YES
KRISTI: But isn't this progress, Adri? I've cleared myself of opinions enough to get to the lockjaw point?
Adri gave me a big smile, and typed:
ADRI: YES
KRISTI: What about the words "in the presence of God"? Were they real?
ADRI: YES SWEET WORDS ENTERED YOUR MIND

Thursday 8/22/91

Today when I went out for my walk, I was very aware of the intensity of yesterday's meditation, worrying and wondering whether I could repeat the experience. Why do I do that! As soon as something positive happens, I begin to diminish and destroy it by setting it up as an expectation for myself. I went to my usual spot but couldn't get comfortable.

Finally I just gave up, closed my eyes, and repeated the mantra "Help me." Suddenly my eyes began flickering and my jaw locked again, but not as forcefully as before. After about twenty-five minutes I opened my eyes and felt at peace.

I got up and walked back up the incline and onto the path. I was feeling very good, and so full of love and forgiven and cared for. Then I began to feel a tremendous tingling in my fingers. The pressure in the tips of my fingers began to build and then traveled up my arms. I've never felt anything quite like it. It seemed like some kind of an energy transfer, although my hands were not warm but cool. Clearly God provides physical signs for us.

Friday 8/23/91

This morning Adri seemed angry. Before I could ask her a question, she typed:

ADRI: PITY YOU

KRISTI: Why do you say that?

Adri typed two answers—"because you not loving" and "because you Kristi"—but then deleted them both.

KRISTI: You must be very angry.

ADRI: YES

KRISTI: Adri, can you finish the sentence "I'm angry because I feel . . ."?

ADRI: BECAUSE IT MAKES ME UNDERSTAND
HOW OTHER PEOPLE FEEL

KRISTI: What, who do you mean by "other people"?

ADRI: YOU

KRISTI: You don't think you feel the same way I feel
or the way other people might feel?

ADRI: NO

KRISTI: Why not?

ADRI: BECAUSE NO ONE THIS LIFE UNDER-
STANDS ME

KRISTI: Why do you think no one understands you?

ADRI: NOBODY PLAYS WITH ME   NOBODY
BOTHERS TO PLAY

I had to breathe deeply and try not to cry. I was overwhelmed by Adri's pain and loneliness, her sense of isola-
tion in this strange world in which she's found herself.
Although being able to communicate is an enormous help,
it's not the answer to everything in her life. Even when
other children are loving and accepting of Adri, it's hard for
them to know how to play with her.

She can't gossip with girlfriends over clothes or books
or music, or play the kinds of games they play. She can't go
anywhere without being accompanied by an adult. If she
gets overexcited, she jumps up and down and makes loud,
disruptive sounds. She doesn't know how to make a friend,
how to have social conversations. And how many kids have
the patience for an FC conversation?

I feel at such a loss. This child has the strength and
courage of a lion, and I love her so much. What do I say to
her? How do I help her?

KRISTI: What about the friend that you met in Oregon? He wanted to play with you.

ADRI: JASON

KRISTI: Yes, Jason. He really liked you.

ADRI: YES   I NEED TO MAKE GIRLFRIENDS

KRISTI: Yes, you do. I'm sure in the new school you'll be able to make girlfriends.

ADRI: I LIKE BOYS

KRISTI: Would you prefer more boys in your class?

ADRI: NO LIKE TO BE FRIENDS WITH GIRLS   BOYS LIKE PLAYING WITH NINJAS

KRISTI: You don't want to play with Ninjas?

ADRI: NO PLAY OUT ON THE PLAYGROUND

KRISTI: With girls?

ADRI: YES

She seemed a little tired. This had been a heavy emotional discussion.

KRISTI: Do you want to talk any more now?

ADRI: NO

Adri seemed to feel much better by the time we finished the conversation. I told Glenda, the thirteen-year-old daughter of a friend who was visiting us, what Adri had said. Glenda went into Adri's room and stayed there with her for a long time. I could hear her talking and the two of them laughing together. When they emerged, Adri seemed to be back to her smiling self. That night before bed she had only one thought to type.

ADRI: LOVE YOU

Saturday 8/24/91

Adri and I were in my room. She was ready to talk.

KRISTI: Anything on your mind?

ADRI: YOU YET NOT TALK TO MOHAMMED

KRISTI: I know. What can I do?

ADRI: YOU MUST TRY HARDER

Before I could respond, she continued:

ADRI: YOU TYPING POIGNANT   I LOOK OTHER DAY

KRISTI: Do you mean you saw my typed notes from the other day?

ADRI: YES

KRISTI: You read them?

ADRI: YES

I couldn't figure out how she could have done that. I had put everything neatly away, and none of my papers had been disturbed.

KRISTI: Do you have any advice for me?

ADRI: YOU MUST OPINIONS RESTRICT SO THAT MOHAMMED CAN BE HEARD

KRISTI: I'm praying and trying. Any other suggestions?

ADRI: YES YOU CAN GO TO TOM

KRISTI: We're going to do that. We have an appointment for Tuesday.

ADRI: GOOD I HAVE TO TALK TO JESUS

KRISTI: What do you want to say to Jesus?

ADRI: WHERE ARE YOU I EXPECTED YOU TO BE HUMAN

KRISTI: Do you mean you expected Jesus to be in human form during this lifetime?

ADRI: YES

KRISTI: Is there anything else you want to say or ask?

ADRI: YES I NEED UNDERSTANDING LOVING OPPOSING OTHERS

KRISTI: Who do you mean?

ADRI: I MEAN NOBODY

KRISTI: What do you mean by "others," then?

ADRI: OTHERS MEAN DARK FORCES

That was new. It scared me, but I tried to respond as usual:

KRISTI: Do you want to say more about that?

ADRI: NO

KRISTI: Do you want to stop for today?

ADRI: YES

While we were talking, Adri paused several times and pressed her fingers just under and behind her ears again.

KRISTI: Adri, when you put your fingers under your ears like that, are you receiving messages?

ADRI: YES

Monday 8/26/91

Walking home from my morning meditation, I noticed a thick, gauzelike spiderweb in a tree. It seemed to be a symbol of the barrier our egos create in our own minds—layer after layer of sticky stuff, all of which must be recognized and peeled away before truth can be revealed. It seems that messages often come through these kinds of ordinary experiences that are suddenly transformed by extraordinary and inexplicable shifts in one's perception.

I got home to find Adri on a campaign.

ADRI: EQUAL RIGHTS FOR ME   I WANT THOUGHTS NONHANDICAPPED I NOT HANDI-CAPPED IN MY BRAIN

That would be a good slogan for the FC movement.

KRISTI: Hurrah for you, Adri. Do you want to say anything else about it?

ADRI: I NEED GODS LOVE

It was such a sudden switch from her rallying cry to this deep appeal.

Then she volunteered:

ADRI: THAT WHICH NEEDS TO BE WILL BE

KRISTI: What do you mean by that?

ADRI: ACTION WHICH SAVES GODS PLAN

KRISTI: What is God's plan?

ADRI: HEARTS OPENED

KRISTI: Adri, do you know about some masters who supposedly come here solely for the purpose of saving someone or something else?

ADRI: YES

KRISTI: Are you one of those?

ADRI: NO

KRISTI: Do you have a purpose, something to learn in this life?

ADRI: YES

KRISTI: Can you share it with me?

ADRI: YES I AM TO TEACH YOU PATIENCE AND [this part was very difficult for her, and she erased it several times before completing the thought] I AM TO LEARN HUMILITY

Tuesday 8/27/91

This afternoon Adri and I have another appointment with Tom and Mary. I asked Adri if she wanted to talk about that.

ADRI: YES I NOT OPPOSE GOD   I LOVE PLAN QUIET TIMING IS VULNERABLE TO THE ONLY PLIGHT OF MAN

KRISTI: What do you mean by quiet timing?

ADRI: STIGMA OF BEING HUMAN INTER-FERES UNDULY

KRISTI: What do you mean, Adri?

ADRI: I NOT HUMAN

That scared me. She doesn't feel human?

KRISTI: Are you talking about the autism?

ADRI: I OPEN PEOPLES HEARTS

KRISTI: This conversation doesn't feel finished, but we have to go pretty soon. Are there any specific questions you'd like to ask Jesus through Tom?

ADRI: IS GOD BY MY SIDE?

KRISTI: Do you feel he is not?

ADRI: NO

KRISTI: Anything else you want to say about that?

ADRI: YES I TOOK THE CUP OF BLOOD BE-
CAUSE I WAS YOUR DISCIPLE JOHN BUT I NOT
UNITED WITH YOU NOW SO I FEEL CRIPPLED I
HAVE PLIGHT OF LONELINESS

That stopped me in my tracks. I had to recover my
composure. Is the cup of blood related to the idea of Communion and the Last Supper? Is Adri really saying that she
was John, Jesus' disciple?

KRISTI: Is that all part of the Plan?

ADRI: YES

KRISTI: Did you choose it?

ADRI: YES

KRISTI: But it still hurts?

ADRI: YES

I was still having a hard time with John and the cup of
blood and the loneliness, and I think Adri noticed. She suddenly grew very angry.

ADRI: LOOK INTO YOUR HEART   BELIEVE
ME

KRISTI: You don't think I believe you?

ADRI: NO

KRISTI: I'm trying to keep up with all that you're
teaching, but sometimes I just can't make these instant leaps. Adri, you've known God for a very long
time?

ADRI: YES   I TOOK GOD IN MY HEART

KRISTI: I am trying to develop that kind of personal
knowledge of God. I'm praying, meditating, talking,
reading, and doing everything I can think of to facilitate
the shift.

ADRI: YOU NOT YET OPPOSE GOD?

KRISTI: I don't want to oppose God. I want to accept
God. I want the kind of life you are revealing to me.

ADRI: YOU NOT UNDERSTANDING

KRISTI: I know I don't understand, but can you help
me? What else can I be doing?

ADRI: YOU LOVING HEARTS TO OPEN BY LAYING HANDS

KRISTI: I am to lay on hands to heal?

ADRI: YES

KRISTI: Will I be able to work with autistic people?

ADRI: YES

Wednesday 8/28/91

Yesterday's session with Tom and Mary lasted two hours. Among other things Adri was told that she shouldn't be telling me what to do, that it was interfering with my free will. Adri put her fingers under her ears. She said she was talking to Mohammed, so Mary said to Tom, "Bring him through."

Then Tom channeled Mohammed. The message was similar to those I'd gotten from Adri, but not nearly so blunt. Then I told Tom and Mary that Adri wondered where Jesus was, that she expected him to be here now. Tom told Adri that he will be coming later.

Mary, channeling Mother Mary, told Adri that "You have chosen this physical handicap in this lifetime to learn patience and humility so that you will be well grounded in your heart and your head. You see yourself as handicapped. We see you as gifted because of your physical handicap. It is the part of you that enables you to listen inwardly." Both Tom and Mary stressed that we must each listen to our own inner God.

Toward the end Mary lovingly asked Adri if she'd like some energy passed through to her. Adri agreed, so Mary rested her hands on Adri's shoulders. Within a few moments Mary began to smile. Adri was not receiving energy, she said, but giving it. Just before we were leaving, Adri offered a suggestion to me.

ADRI: NOT YET EDUCATED   YOU NEED DEAD THERAPY

KRISTI: Do you mean I need past-lives-regression therapy?

ADRI: YES

Thursday 8/29/91

This morning we had appointments with Ben and Felice as well as with Martha, Adri's new teacher from the Runkle School in Brookline. Felice asked Adri if they had known each other before, and Adri said that she knew Felice from another lifetime, but not an "educated" one.

I wonder if we have "educated" lives and uneducated lives interspersed as we work on specific problems and issues? Or do we reach a certain level of spiritual development and then not regress again?

In the afternoon we met with Martha. She was warm, friendly, and respectful to Adri. Adri asked her some questions that she'd prepared beforehand.

ADRI: WHAT DO YOU TEACH?

MARTHA: Everything.

ADRI: HOW MANY CLASSMATES?

MARTHA: Six

ADRI: HOW MANY GIRLS?

MARTHA: Just you.

I told Martha how much Adri wanted girlfriends. Martha told Adri that in the regular classroom there were many girls with whom she would make friends.

ADRI: YET I CAN'T DRAW WILL TEACHER HELP ME LEARN?

Martha told Adri about many types of drawing projects they might do together. She also told Adri that she would have occupational therapy and that included drawing.

ADRI: WHAT SUBJECTS?

MARTHA: Science, math, reading, writing, and social studies.

ADRI: DO I HAVE HOMEWORK?

MARTHA: Occasionally you will.

ADRI: WHO WILL BE MY SPEECH THERAPIST?

Martha told her the name of the school speech therapist and also said the therapist had wanted to meet Adri today but had not been able to get away. By the end of the meeting I think all of us were feeling pleased and optimistic.

Saturday 8/31/91

Adri and I had a long and interesting conversation this morning.

KRISTI: Anything you want to say?

ADRI: I NEED MY EDUCATION SO THAT DEN-DRITES . . .

Adri was fidgeting, having a difficult time getting settled.

KRISTI: Adri, can you finish your thought? What happens to dendrites when you get educated?

ADRI: DENDRITES LENGTHEN

KRISTI: What happens then?

ADRI: BRAIN GENERATES DENDRITES

Although I had a vague idea what dendrites were, I hadn't a clue about how they worked. I was about to ask, when Adri spontaneously began to type.

ADRI: YET NOT TALK TO YOUR GUIDES

KRISTI: Adri, did you talk to my guides?

ADRI: YES

KRISTI: Do you have a message for me?

ADRI: YES

KRISTI: Who is it?

ADRI: MOHAMMED

KRISTI: What is it?

ADRI: YOU MUST SEND TOM YOUR . . .

She didn't finish the sentence.

Kristi: Adri, are you concerned that things are going very quickly and I'm somehow not keeping up?

Adri: YES YOU YET NOT READY

Kristi: You're afraid there won't be time for something?

Adri: YES TIME IS SHORT

Kristi: What will happen when the time comes?

Adri: ONLY READY TO EDUCATED

Kristi: Only the educated will be ready, is that what you mean?

Adri: YES

Kristi: What will happen to those not ready?

Adri: THEY WILL LEAVE THE EARTH

Kristi: Do you mean they will die? Will they have a chance to come back and try again as we do now? Adri tuned in again.

Adri: YES

Kristi: Is the timing related to the year 2000?

Adri: YES

Kristi: Do you know the date?

Adri: YES

Kristi: Can you share it?

Adri: JUNE 1999

Kristi: You're worried that I won't be ready?

Adri: YES YOU WILL HAVE NEW WORLD

We took a break. We both needed it. There isn't much time till 1999. And what kind of "new world" is she talking about—physical changes in the earth itself? Or is she talking more about changes in the ways people will interact with each other? She seems to be talking about a better, more loving world, but getting there might not be such a pleasant passage for all of us. What's supposed to happen? Is there something we can do?

I'm almost afraid to ask Adri these questions. Do I really want to know the answers? One thing is clear, though, she's saying that there's no time to waste. We don't have time to sit around waiting for some kind of definitive, unequivocal proof of this truth. For some massive bolt of lightning followed by the voice of God that 99 percent of the population of earth sees and hears. That's the kind of proof we'd all like, but by the time something like that comes around, I don't know that there'll be time to make changes. Yet it's not a call to panic either. Why give a warning if time's run out? The message is really about using this time wisely, to seek God. Then whether there's a disaster or it's averted, we'll still have created a better world.

When I talked to Adri in the afternoon, I told her I was feeling confused about what she'd said about being John, Jesus' disciple.

KRISTI: Adri, were you talking about one of your own past lives? Were you John?

ADRI: YES

Tom had said that Adri had been a disciple of Jesus, too, but still this is all so incredible, it's hard to believe. It's possible that her "Yes" could be based on a different understanding of the question. I've heard that in "Dead Therapy," as Adri calls it, it's possible for people to tap into the "collective memory" of humankind as opposed to an individual life. Could that be what she's doing?

We took a long break and then talked a little more.

KRISTI: Adri, at one point Tom seemed to suggest that you are to follow him. Is that right?

ADRI: NO

KRISTI: Do you know your own path?

ADRI: YES

KRISTI: But you like meeting and talking with the two of them?

ADRI: YES THEY WANT TO EDUCATE YOU

KRISTI: You mean that you wanted to go so they could educate *me*?

ADRI: YES   THEY ARE IN TOUCH WITH SPIRIT

Suddenly an unrelated thought popped into my mind. I blurted it out.

KRISTI: Adri, can you read my thoughts?

ADRI: YES

I was astounded, both at the question and at the answer.

KRISTI: Can I learn to do it? It would be so amazing if we could communicate together telepathically. Will you try it with me? I'll think of a word and you type what I'm thinking?

I realized that I was still testing her, but she cooperated anyway. I thought of a word. Adri typed:

ADRI: JOY

KRISTI: That's right! Adri, that's amazing. Will you do it again?

I thought of another word. She typed:

ADRI: PRETZEL

KRISTI: That's it. I guess you know a lot about what's going on, then—with me at least. . . .

I started thinking about it.

KRISTI: Adri, can you do this just with me, or can you do this with everybody?

ADRI: WITH EVERYBODY

Unbelievable.

KRISTI: I think we'd better just keep this confidential for the time being, don't you?

Adri typed a forceful . . .

ADRI: YES

KRISTI: Adri, you're really something else. I love you very, very much.

ADRI: YES   YOU TOO

Chapter 15

ADRI "TELEPHONES"

SEPTEMBER 1991

Monday 9/2/91

It was cold this morning when I sat down to meditate, so I decided to move over to a tree where the sun was shining. Then I remembered what I had read last night about embracing or sitting with your back against a tree so that it might lend its energy to yours. With the power of the tree behind me, and the strength of the earth and the rocks underneath, I began to relax. Then at one point in my meditation I suddenly realized that Adri was speaking to me. It startled me for a moment, but she told me not to be afraid. She told me that I was a child of God and that it was safe for me to open my heart, that in this lifetime that's what I intended for myself. She said Mohammed wished to speak with me and urged me to let him in.

Then all of a sudden I heard a voice and felt a presence. It really frightened me. Strange as it may seem, I didn't want to be alone with that unfamiliar presence. But then I began to hear these words:

But don't you know me? Haven't I been with you all these years, helping and guiding you? And yet you know me from before too. We lived together in other lifetimes, and I have been with you through many since. From time to time I will come to give you directions because in this lifetime you have a purpose to fulfill. This lifetime is a culmination of many that came before. Do not be afraid. You are a child of God.

I came out of my meditative state feeling dazed, incredulous, and uncertain of what I had just experienced. As I was walking back home, I suddenly became aware that Adri was talking with me telepathically. It felt completely natural and wonderful. Adri assured me that I had been speaking with Mohammed.

As I walked back to the house, I asked Adri how telepathic communication worked, whether she heard all the time or only when she "telephoned" or someone else "telephoned" her? *Only when we telephone to one another,* she replied.

I asked her if you could always get someone when you telephoned. She said, *Yes, but you might have to wait a little if they are talking with someone else.*

I guess that makes sense. I was almost home, so I said, "Good-bye." She said *Good-bye,* and then she simply wasn't there any longer.

I felt giddy and a bit disoriented, but very excited. When I arrived home, not wanting to influence events, I smiled at Adri as if nothing had happened. I couldn't talk to her right away. It was just too much. I knew what I had experienced, yet I still couldn't quite believe it. On some level

I thought I was just nuts. I wrote about it in my journal. And then finally, unable to delay any longer, I took a deep breath and went to look for Adri.

KRISTI: Adri, anything you want to talk about today?

ADRI: YES TODAY YOU TALK TO MOHAM-MED

My body froze for just a moment, and then inner pandemonium broke out.

KRISTI: I really did talk with him? I wasn't just imagining it?

ADRI: YES YOU ATON

KRISTI: I am or was Aton? Tell me about Aton.

ADRI: YOU WERE ATON IN EDUCATED LIFE-TIME

I want to believe that. I want to be educated in this lifetime.

KRISTI: Adri, do you remember what you told me today?

ADRI: YES I TOLD YOU TO OPEN YOUR HEART TO TALK TO MOHAMMED

KRISTI: What did I say?

ADRI: YOU WERE LISTENING

KRISTI: What did Mohammed say?

ADRI: HE SAID TO TRUST

Several times during the discussion Adri stopped to put her hands over her ears.

KRISTI: Who are you talking with?

ADRI: SANTO

Santo was the guide that Tom had talked about.

KRISTI: Does Santo have something to say about this extraordinary day? Something for me to hear?

ADRI: YES YOU WANT TO HEAL YOU WILL NEED TO INTENSIVELY STUDY

KRISTI: With what or with whom shall I study?

ADRI: WITH SYSTEM

KRISTI: What system? Where am I to find out about it?

ADRI: LOOK IN YOUR SYSTEM ROOT

KRISTI: Can you clarify what you mean by that?

ADRI: YOU WILL WRITE ABOUT THIS SYSTEM

KRISTI: How will I learn about it?

ADRI: YOU WILL LEARN FROM SANTO

KRISTI: Will he speak with me directly or through you?

ADRI: WILL SPEAK WITH YOU

KRISTI: Do I then just wait, stay open, listen?

ADRI: YES   YOU UNDERSTAND

Finally. Yet, writing this up, I realize it's not clear if Santo was talking about me learning to heal myself, or my learning to heal others. Maybe it's the same thing.

KRISTI: Can we talk again telepathically?

ADRI: YES

KRISTI: Will I speak with Mohammed every time I meditate?

ADRI: NO   YOU WILL YET TALK WITH MO-HAMMED AND SANTO WHEN THEY YET TELEPHONE

KRISTI: Will you help them get through to me as you did today if necessary?

ADRI: YES

KRISTI: Anything else you want to say today?

ADRI: NO

KRISTI: You seem very tired, would you like to stop?

ADRI: YES

Reunion! What a cause for rejoicing.

All day I've felt exuberant and confused. Later I tried to talk telepathically with Adri in the car. It seemed as if we were connecting, but I couldn't be sure. I want to be very cautious. I certainly don't want to be creating conversations in my head and attributing them to her. I must keep in mind that telepathic communication, like Facilitated Communication, is a process. It changes and evolves and becomes more solid and consistent over time.

Late this afternoon I went out for a walk to try to sort out my thoughts and feelings. When I sat under my tree, I went into a meditative state and felt Mohammed's presence almost immediately. Mohammed talked to me about fear and the defenses and maneuvers of the ego. It's hard to remember his exact words, but it was the same kind of communication as this morning. The words just came into my mind without pauses or spaces of time for me to wonder what was coming next. I asked why the voice was not the booming voice of the two messages that I've received before in my life. His answer was that my guides no longer needed to shout to capture my attention.

I went into Adri's room before bed and asked her if she wanted to talk. She seemed pretty tired, but she typed a sweet and considerate reply:

ADRI: YOU WANT TO TALK NOW?

She knew that this had been a very big day, and she wanted to be there for me if I needed it. I told her that I was extremely happy and at peace. We'd talk in the morning.

ADRI: GOOD NIGHT

KRISTI: Sleep well, my love.

Tuesday 9/3/91

I started off my morning walk by stumbling on a rock. It was an apt reminder that I need to stay mindful. Messages are there for the recognition. I sat down to meditate, hoping a bit too desperately to make telepathic contact with Adri and my guides again. It didn't happen. Even as I learn the lessons of patience, I feel impatient.

I had an interesting dream last night:

> I was sitting nervously at my desk on the first day of an Advanced Calculus class that I thought I needed to take to complete my master's degree. I hadn't taken any prerequisites, so I knew it was going to be very hard, and probably embarrassing, if everyone else knew more than me. The professor strode to the board, chalk in hand, drew a point, and asked:
>
> "What is between this point and eternity?"
>
> I became absolutely paralyzed. I was so over-whelmed by the question that I couldn't even make a stab at an answer. But while I was quaking, the guy next to me clearly and unhesitatingly called out the answer:
>
> "A moment."
>
> Terrified, I couldn't even register the meaning of the words, much less how profound the concept might be.
>
> Then suddenly the professor picked up a piece of paper and read off a class list of everyone who *shouldn't* be in the class. I was incredibly relieved to hear my name called. But then it started to get funny because my name was called off four different times—just to make sure I'd heard. I got up, walked out of the class, went over to the office, and found out the Advanced Calculus was not, after all, a required course. What a relief.

I think this dream is about my own process, especially my increasing sense of confusion about what I feel I'm supposed to be able to do. I expect myself to be able to "telephone" Adri and others and feel totally confident about what's being said. I think I should be an instant telepathic genius. But it turns out, I'm not expected to be in the advanced class. I'm not ready for that yet.

Walking home, I began to realize much more clearly what Adri might have meant when she said we were "to open loving hearts to God." I'm an example of that plan at work. Through the grace of God's love, which lives in all of us, Adri has been able to open my heart. What an absolutely tremendous gift—a gift from the heart and for the heart. The intellect doesn't know what to do with such a gift. I can't *analyze* Adri, dissect her thoughts and words and come up with their definitive meaning. Instead I have to *feel* her thoughts and words, and then experience their meaning through my own seeking. With great care and tenderness Adri has opened my heart to God. That's what she's here for.

My task is to tell her story, from the beginning, in the same way that she revealed it to me. In a larger sense, each of us has that task—as we open, we are to open others. Adri is not a gift just to me. I have not been individually chosen to receive that blessing. Rather I have been given the opportunity to be a vehicle through which these teachings might be shared with many. I will tell her story, and then, thank heavens, it's out of my hands. I can't make people believe the story. I can't make people experience it. Each of us must choose whether or not to take the journey inward.

Part Three

A
CHILD
OF ETERNITY

Chapter 16

"I USE TELEPATHY
FOR LOVE"

Our family returned to Boston in the fall of 1991. Adri's new teacher at the Runkle School recommended she start in the third grade because she thought it would be an easier social adjustment. For Adri and her classmates integration turned out to be a mutually beneficial arrangement.

Adri accepted all the children, neither demanding nor expecting anything of them. In return they were able to let down their usual defenses in her company and express the natural compassion and kindness that they otherwise tended to hide. And because they were so loving and accepting of her, Adri was motivated to work very hard to control her autistic behaviors so that she could fit into the class. They brought out the best in one another.

The children didn't judge Adri, unlike some of the

adults. Ironically it was her regular classroom teacher who said to me one day, "I just don't understand it. All the most popular girls in the class like her!" I don't think she meant to be cruel. But her belief that Adri wasn't like other children, that she didn't feel as they do, was so deeply held that she just assumed everyone, including Adri's own mother, shared it. It didn't occur to her that I might be hurt and offended by her words. In contrast the teacher in Adri's special-needs classroom was very sensitive and supportive, and she worked very hard to educate the other staff members.

After Adri had settled into her new school routine, I asked if she'd be willing to talk more about some of the ideas we'd discussed over the summer. She said she'd like that. So, for the next four months Adri and I; my brother, Jamie; and Michael McSheehan, an Adriana Foundation consultant and facilitator, met in my office for spiritual discussions.

Like everyone else important to this story, Michael simply appeared on our doorstep at the right time. He's an extremely gifted facilitator with an incredible ability to act as a clear instrument of communication. In fact, not long after Adri first began facilitating regularly with Michael, she began to demand that he share with us the telepathic messages he was receiving from her. While he was willing to do this for her, he wanted to make certain that their communications remained accurate. So, together, they worked out a form of telepathic facilitation.

Because it made communication so much easier, Adri loved telepathic FC. She would type the first letter of a word, and if Michael understood the word telepathically, he'd say it aloud. Adri would then hit the space key to indicate that he was correct. Sometimes, oddly enough, as in the case of the word *synergy*, Michael understood the word telepathically but didn't know the meaning of it so we had to stop our conversation and define it for him. When he was unable to get a word telepathically, or if he got the word wrong, Adri would simply type out the entire word. As a result our conversations became a fascinating mix of traditional and telepathic FC. Participating in these discussions was extraordinary and enlightening for all of us, not only because of the subject matter but also because it's an amazing experience to be part of a telepathic conversation. Michael and Adri modeled for us the incredible potential of human communication.

My own attempts at telepathy have had their ups and downs. Sometimes, particularly in those first few months after we returned to Boston, telepathic communication between Adri and myself was clear and unequivocal. But at other times I was much less certain of what I was getting. As a result I began to challenge every communication that came through. I wanted validation from Adri each time, and even when I got it, I still wasn't satisfied. Eventually my inability to trust in myself interfered with the process. Yet I know that just as it takes time and practice to become adept at facilitation, so it takes that same kind of effort and more to become adept at telepathic communication. I'm still working at it.

However, I'm not advocating blind acceptance of what you think you hear either. Our logical minds are very tricky, and determined to stay in charge. Sometimes they create a scenario of their own. This happened to me one afternoon in September. I was out walking by myself and suddenly found myself in the middle of a telepathic conversation with Adri. As it ended, I thought I saw Adri come out of the house, climb into the van with her baby-sitter, and drive off. But when I walked into the house, there she was, having a snack in the kitchen. Clearly there was something amiss in my telepathic picture. Adri confirmed that we'd had the conversation.

"If that's true," I asked her, "then why are you here and

not in the car?" Adri's response was both the truth and a warning of potential danger:

ADRI: YOU EMBELLISH WITH YOUR MIND

In one of our discussions I asked Adri to talk more about telepathy.

KRISTI: Adri, what psychic skills do you have?

ADRI: MOST OF MY SKILLS ARE TELE-PATHIC I GET ALL PEOPLE'S IDEAS I CAN SEE THROUGH HUMAN'S EYES MOSTLY I "TUNE IN" TO FIND OUT INFORMATION ABOUT THE WORLD I TALK WITH MY GUIDES TO SUMMA-RIZE PRECOGNITION

KRISTI: Do you use this information in any way?

ADRI: YES IN "TRAVELING" I HEAL IN OTHER WORLDS I SAY WORLDS BECAUSE YOU CAN'T UNDERSTAND THE PLACES I GO

KRISTI: How does telepathy work?

ADRI: I ACTUALIZE MY TELEPATHY AND IN-TELLECT THROUGH MY GUIDES MY GUIDES ARE GODS THAT CONNECT ME WITH OTHERS LIKE ME

KRISTI: Adri, can you define telepathy?

ADRI: I MEAN TALKING WITH PEOPLE BY US-ING THEIR ENERGY WITH MINE

KRISTI: How do you use their energy with yours?

ADRI: I EMANATE LIGHT AND OTHERS RE-CEIVE THAT LIGHT TO HEAR ME

KRISTI: Someone cannot be telepathic with you if you're not sending your light to them?

ADRI: I MUST WANT OR BE OPEN TO THEIR LIGHT I EMANATE LIGHT TO OTHER PEOPLE WITH AUTISM BECAUSE I KNOW MANY OF THEM CHOSE THE SAME RETURN AS I CHOSE

KRISTI: Can you read the thoughts of others though

they may not consciously be sending out their own light?

Adri: I WORK BEST IN SHARED LIGHT NOT IN CLOSED LIGHT

Kristi: So, you refer to people not conscious of this state as being in "closed light"?

Adri: MORE OR LESS

Kristi: Can you read the thoughts of people in "closed light" if you choose to?

Adri: I CAN   I READ THAT YOU HAVE THOUGHTS YOU DON'T SEND THAT I CAN ACCESS GOD IS KINSHIP OF LOVE   LOVE IS KINSHIP OF KNOWLEDGE IF LOVE IS IN TRUTH

Kristi: What do you mean?

Adri: MEANS THAT I CAN ACCESS THOUGHTS IF THE PERSON IS IN TRUTH WITH GOD

Kristi: So you can access thoughts of loving people?

Adri: YES

Kristi: But what about people who are, for lack of a better word, evil? Can you access them?

Adri: IF GOD IS SOMEWHERE IN THEIR HEARTS I CAN ACCESS   THAT LIGHT CAN BE VERY DEEP INSIDE MANY PEOPLE

Kristi: Have you always been able to do this, or did you acquire this ability at some particular point in your life?

Adri: IT HAS BEEN IN MY SOUL FOR MANY YEARS   IN PAST LIVES THROUGH PRESENT LIFE

Kristi: You were born aware, then?

Adri: YES

Kristi: Did you realize in utero all that was transpiring?

Adri: YES

Kristi: You were consciously aware of your path?

ADRI: YES

KRISTI: Can you read their thoughts only when they're present? Or can you read thoughts anywhere anytime?

ADRI: HEY I'M GREAT AT THIS I CAN DO IT IN MY SLEEP ANYTIME

KRISTI: So distance means nothing?

ADRI: NOTHING AT ALL

KRISTI: Can you access anywhere in the universe?

ADRI: YES

KRISTI: Does this ability transcend time?

ADRI: YES

KRISTI: How does it work with other autistic people? Do you put out some kind of general signal and anyone, anywhere in the world, can answer if they want?

ADRI: WKOA: KIDS OF AUTISM JUST JOKING

KRISTI: I was envisioning this huge "radio" system. You send out a signal somehow? How can you tell when someone is answering?

ADRI: FEEL THEM COME INTO MY LIGHT IT JUST COMES IN AS AWARENESS I FEEL THE KNOWLEDGE NOT IN SOUNDS

KRISTI: You can get specific information this way, through the light? You can get things like names?

ADRI: LIGHT FOR ME WORDS FOR OTHERS

KRISTI: You can get specific information without using words?

ADRI: I ACCESS THROUGH LIGHT OTHERS THROUGH WORDS

Adri typed YES before I even had a chance to verbalize my next question.

KRISTI: Can you define light?

ADRI: I MEAN LIGHT IS SENDING MESSAGES IN GODS LOVE

KRISTI: Are light, God, and energy the same thing?

ADRI: I VIEW GODS LOVE AS BEST ENERGY
KRISTI: Can people use lower forms of energy than God's love and yet be telepathic?
ADRI: NOT THAT IVE EXPERIENCED
KRISTI: So, the people that you've communicated with have been, at least to some degree, of the light?
ADRI: YES

Another day I asked Adri:
KRISTI: Is it possible for everyone to be telepathic?
ADRI: YES   POSSIBLE FOR EVERYONE TO TELEPATHICALLY COMMUNICATE IF THEY OPEN TO TRUE LOVE

In still another session Adri brought the subject up again.
ADRI: PEOPLE WITH AUTISM NOT TALKING ENOUGH ABOUT TELEPATHY TO OTHERS
KRISTI: Do you want to talk about that?
ADRI: NOT UP TO ME TO TALK ABOUT OTHERS WHO ARE TELEPATHIC BUT NEED THEM TO SPEAK OUT   GREAT GIFT THEY HAVE NOT SHARING GIFT GIFT NOT DEFI-NITE FOR THEM GIVE THEM HELP TO TALK TOGETHER HELP THEM TO TALK
KRISTI: Do you mean we need to work with their parents to create accepting environments for telepathic communication?
ADRI: KIND OF I WANT TO MAKE IT OK TO USE MENTAL TELEPATHY IN LIFE NOT A TER-RIBLE THING I USE TELEPATHY FOR LOVE BUT OTHERS ARE CONFUSED I WANT TO HELP EVERYONE WITH THEIR TELEPATHY SO THE WORLD BECOMES NICE AGAIN   ALSO

NICE USING TELEPATHY FOR HARD SCHOOL-
WORK

Kristi: Were you born with the ability to use
telepathy?

Adri: YES   I WAS CHOOSING THIS LIFE
PURPOSEFULLY   YOU KNOW THAT

Kristi: All of us are telepathic when we're babies?

Adri: YES   NOT SPECIAL AUTISM

Kristi: Can autistic people help to lead the rest of us
back into telepathy?

Adri: I THINK WE ALL HELP   PLEASE HELP
ALL

Kristi: Anything else about this topic?

Adri: YES   ROTTEN THAT SO MANY PEOPLE
PLAY WITH LOVE AND TELEPATHY BUT DON'T
MEAN IT

Kristi: Are you sending a message to us specifically,
or is this a general statement?

Adri: I MEAN EVERYONE   YOU INCLUDED

Adri kept stressing the importance of developing telepathic
skills and of getting in touch with our guides and maintain-
ing a relationship with them. To follow her lead, a small
group of us began to meet together weekly to meditate and
share. Unfortunately, although we had some amazing sessions, factions developed in the group. Some members felt
that everyone should channel. Others felt that channeling
shouldn't be our main focus. I felt that it should be our in-
tention to develop our channeling skills, but that no one
should be required to channel aloud unless he or she was
moved to do so.

One night, under pressure, I channeled aloud even
though I didn't want to. It was not a good experience, and
the message wasn't the usual high caliber I was accustomed

to. I literally shook for twenty minutes after I spoke. Sadly, after that session channeling began to be more difficult for me. Over the years since then, slowly, but not very steadily, I've been reclaiming some of my ability to access my guides. As Adri has so often told me, nothing worthwhile comes easily.

As I began to read and learn more about guides, I became puzzled by some of the things Adri had said in earlier discussions. Although I thought Adri had told me that not everyone had a network of guides, I read somewhere that everyone does indeed have guides. I asked Adri if she could clarify that point for me and also talk more about the subject in general.

ADRI: YES I SEE SOME PEOPLE HAVE NETWORKS AND GUIDES

KRISTI: Some, but does everyone have them?

ADRI: YES EVERYONE THEY NOT SEEM TO RELATE TO EACH OTHER

KRISTI: You mean the guides don't always relate to each other?

ADRI: YES

KRISTI: Adri, you said that my network of guides is the same as yours. Do I also have personal guides of my own?

ADRI: YES

KRISTI: Is my access to our guides through you or through myself?

ADRI: CONNECT BY INNER GOD

KRISTI: Each of us connects to our guidance on our own, through our inner Godself?

ADRI: YES

KRISTI: How did you come to know your guides? What role do they play in your life?

ADRI: I KNEW MY GUIDES BEFORE COMING INTO THIS LIFE   WE PLAYED HOUSE TO-GETHER

KRISTI: Is that a joke?

ADRI: YES

KRISTI: Now, are some guides universal, sort of master guides, while others are personal guides, perhaps from our own past lives?

ADRI: I HAVE CERTAIN GUIDES THAT HELP ME USE GOD'S KNOWLEDGE IN THE LIBRARY

KRISTI: What do you mean by God's knowledge in the "library"?

ADRI: I WAS TRAINED BY MY GUIDES TO USE INFORMATION BECAUSE I STILL HAVE INFOR-MATION TO GIVE TO OTHERS IN THIS LIFE

KRISTI: What kind of information? Where?

ADRI: MUCH INFORMATION IN GOD'S LI-BRARY IS THERE TO HELP PEOPLE LEARN TO LOVE AGAIN   MY SWEET ROLE ON THIS EARTH IS TO HELP OTHER HUMANS GAIN AC-CESS TO THAT LIBRARY

KRISTI: You said "love again." Does that mean that there was a time when there was love on this earth, or do you mean in other states of existence there was or is love?

ADRI: THIS WORLD GAVE ITS LOVE AWAY FOR MONEY   MONEY IS BIGGER THAN LOVE BUT THAT WILL CHANGE   PEOPLE WILL LEARN

KRISTI: Was there a time when money didn't rule? How did our present state come to be?

ADRI: THAT WILL GET BIGGER THAN THIS BOOK

KRISTI: All right, then, what must people learn in or-der to change?

ADRI: LOVE

★ ★ ★

In those early days I often pressed Adri for "inside" information, the kind of personal information that I know I'm responsible for finding out for myself. I'll learn what I need to know when the time is right. Adri's great gift to me was to open the door, but it's my choice, as it is for each of us, whether to step through or not. Still, sometimes I'd try to get just a little extra information from Adri, a bit of added insurance, before I stepped through a portal. But I finally learned it doesn't work that way. We have to do it ourselves.

Adri shared a great deal with me, far more perhaps than she should have. Some of our conversations reflected her frustration with my slow and halting pace and my constant need to keep testing her. One afternoon we were talking about past lives and karma. Adri had already told me several interesting things about personal karma. But I continued to press for more. Finally Adri decided it was time for a lesson.

KRISTI: Adri, what karma do I have yet to work off? What things must I atone for?

ADRI: YOU STEAL NOSES

I looked at her. She had a straight face, but I didn't know what to make of that statement. Was she teasing me, or was it possible that I really did such a thing?

KRISTI: I steal noses? How?

Then Adri broke into a grin. She'd been teasing me. But in a sense she was being serious too.

ADRI: YET YOU WANT TO TEST

I kept trying to convince her that I wasn't trying to test her. But at the end of the conversation Adri added one last thought that I've never forgotten.

ADRI: YOU TOYING WITH THIS

I denied it vehemently, but she was partly right. I never meant to "toy" with all this, but I didn't realize till much later that a genuine spiritual awakening requires major life changes. I thought I'd been making great strides—even feeling a little smug—until her words put me in my place. This was no parlor game.

Exchanges like these taught me another wonderful thing about Adri: She has a very good sense of humor. In fact she puts a humorous twist on even the most serious of topics. One evening, having just gotten home, I asked Adri what she'd been doing all day. With typical but poignant good humor she replied:

ADRI: JUST FOLLOWING THIS BODY ALL AROUND THE ROOM   ACTUALLY ALL AROUND THE HOUSE

KRISTI: That's how it feels to you?

ADRI: YET BUT I'M GETTING SOME BETTER CONTROL

During one talk I asked her about the soybean mystery:

KRISTI: Adri, you've pointed to soybeans as a culprit in your autism. How do soybeans fit into the explanation?

ADRI: I NOT TELL

KRISTI: Adri, that's not fair. Come on, tell me.

ADRI: BAD JOKE AND TELL PEOPLE GOD LAUGHS TOO   AND MOM COMPLETELY MISSES IT TOO INTENSE

She's so right. I can get much too intense. I'm so intense, I don't even notice when I'm being intense. One afternoon, Adri took me to task when I wouldn't respond to her lighthearted mood and kept insisting that we follow my agenda.

KRISTI: Adri, can you talk about karma?

ADRI: READ TOUCHING BOOK ON KARMA IN THE UNIVERSAL LIBRARY   IT SAID KARMA CAN BE NURTURING FOR THE FUTURE SPIRITS IF PEOPLE HAVE STRENGTH TO CONFRONT THEIR DEBTS IN THEIR PRESENT LIFE

KRISTI: Why was it touching?

Adri: IT WAS FUN TO ABSORB   LOVE TOUCHING BOOK ON KARMA

Kristi: Do you mean "touching" as in feeling?

Adri: YES I DID   I HAVE TO TELL YOU FUN STUFF ABOUT AUTISM OR YOU'LL THINK IT'S HORRIBLE ALL THE TIME   IT IS NOTHING LIKE BEING IN CONSTANT CONTROL OF EVERY-THING, OF THINKING YOU ARE

Kristi: Is this a comparison?

Adri: YES   COMPARISON OF YOUR LIFE TO MINE

Kristi: Could you explain a little more about control?

Adri: NO   LET IT SIT THERE   PLAY SOME MUSIC   I'LL TELEPATH MESSAGES TO YOU NOT WANTING TO TYPE   I IN BIG JOK-ING MOOD

Kristi: But the basics of karma, Adri. What's your definition of karma?

Adri: I DON'T THINK YOU HEARD ME   NO QUESTIONS SERIOUS

Kristi: Okay, then. What's the most fun thing about being autistic?

Adri: I GET TO LISTEN SO MUCH MORE THAN ANYONE ELSE   IT BORES ME SOME-TIMES   GETS OLD BUT I LEARN GREAT MUCH IN LIFE   MORE PLEASURE THAN TYPING THE ANSWERS TO THESE QUESTIONS

Kristi: Do you want to grow up?

Adri: I LIKE BEING A KID AGAIN   RADICAL MUSIC [she had hard rock music blaring over the radio] WILL THIS REASONABLE PUNISHMENT FIND ITS WAY TO PEACE SOON? GOOD TO SPEAK SOON   LET ME RAGE IN MY SILENT FURY! THIS SONG IS THEMATIC FOR ME! HOW LONG WILL I NOT SING? HOW LONG BEFORE I SING?

KRISTI: By punishment do you mean your inability to speak is a punishment?

ADRI: YES

KRISTI: Your decision to be autistic in this life was about a way of teaching. But was it also a karmic debt?

ADRI: NO   BUT IT FEELS KIND OF LIKE ONE   REALLY NOT TRULY ONE   MY CHOICE   NO PUNISHMENT   MY CHOICE FINE FOR ME TO CHOOSE A TOUCHING LIFE TO TEACH!

KRISTI: Do you have to stay autistic all your life?

ADRI: NOT TO STAY FOREVER AUTISTIC NOT NECESSARY HOPEFULLY

Although Adri had talked quite extensively about the possible reasons for her autism during some of our early dialogues, I still didn't feel clear on the issue. Several times in later sessions I asked Adri for clarification about her autism.

ADRI: I THINK I COMPLETE CHILD   I THINK I LOST NOTHING BY BEING BORN   MY MOM HELD ME CAREFULLY INSIDE   SHE CARED FOR ME BUT MY BODY HAS PROBLEMS   I HAVE A BODY THAT HAS A PROBLEM   I HAVE A BODY THAT HAS BROKEN PARTS   MY EN-DOCRINE SYSTEM BROKE IN THE WOMB BY DRS, BY SOUL, BY CHOICE   I MAKE CHOICE TO BE AUTISTIC

KRISTI: You chose the autism?

ADRI: YES

KRISTI: You physically caused the autism by not eating?

ADRI: NO FIRST I TALKED WITH GOD ABOUT MY RETURN

KRISTI: Return to earth or to God?

ADRI: EARTH

KRISTI: Was this before or after conception?

ADRI: BEFORE

Kristi: You and God agreed that you should live in an autistic body?

Adri: YES

Kristi: The not eating was the method by which you triggered the autism?

Adri: YES

Kristi: Not eating affected the development of your endocrine system?

Adri: YES

Kristi: At one point you said Jesus came to you in a dream and told you that you were in the right place. What's the significance of this dream?

Adri: THE DREAM WAS REMINDING ME THAT YOU EDUCATED   YOU REMINDING ME THAT YOU EDUCATED TOO

Kristi: I was in that dream as well?

Adri: NO

Kristi: Why did you say that I reminded you "too," then?

Adri: BECAUSE PRAYERS ANSWERED BY GOD BRING US TOGETHER

Kristi: Was there a period of time in utero or as an infant when you didn't remember the plan to be autistic?

Adri: I REMEMBERED BUT GOD REMINDED ME IN A DREAM

Kristi: You remembered, yet when you were a fetus, the experience was overwhelming and you needed reassurance?

Adri: YES

Kristi: By "educated," do you mean enlightened? Or do you mean different things at different times?

Adri: YES DIFFERENT THINGS AT DIFFER-ENT TIMES

Kristi: In this case you mean enlightened?

Adri: I MEAN THIS TIME EDUCATED

MEANS OPEN TO HELP FROM GOD   PLEASE
BREAK

After the break I tried again.

KRISTI: There's a sort of contradiction here, at least
for me. You said you stopped eating and that caused the
autism. But then you also said you stopped eating to
try to kill yourself because you were in the wrong
place. . . .

ADRI: CONFUSION   I AM CONFUSED NOW
I   AM   CONFUSED   OVER   WHY   THAT   IS
CONTRADICTORY

KRISTI: Did you stop eating in order to kill yourself
or in order to become autistic?

ADRI: BOTH   I STOPPED EATING BECAUSE I
THOUGHT I WAS IN THE WRONG PLACE

KRISTI: Stopping eating could work either way? If
you were in the wrong place after all, it would kill you.
But if you were in the right place, it would cause the
autism as planned?

ADRI: I WANT TO PLAY

We quit for the day. But I was relentless on this topic, and
sometime later I returned to it again.

KRISTI: I'm still confused about how your autism developed. I know it's extremely difficult to communicate
complicated ideas given the limitations of FC, but do
you have anything else to say on this subject?

ADRI: I HAVE MUCH TO SAY ON THIS! I
CHOOSE TO BE AUTISTIC FOR MY SOUL   MY
BODY HAD TO BECOME AUTISTIC BY A
PROBLEM   THE PROBLEM WAS IN MY ENDO-
CRINE SYSTEM   WELL ACTUALLY IT WAS IN
MY ENERGY SYSTEM BUT WE DON'T HAVE
WORDS FOR IT YET!

Chapter 17

DEAD THERAPY

During our last session with Tom and Mary in New Hampshire, Adri advised me to get "Dead Therapy," what we, with more politeness but less wit, commonly refer to as past-life-regression therapy. It proved to be good advice. Dead Therapy is the process of tapping into one's own memory bank. Just as we learned through Facilitated Communication that the problem in autism is not one of a lack of things to say but rather the lack of access to a means of saying it, the same is true of our past lives. All the events of our past lives exist in our minds. Our problem is finding a means of gaining access.

But of course it's not quite that simple. None of us really knows what we're accessing. Perhaps at times we are indeed accessing our own past lives. But at other times we may be accessing some kind of collective memory bank. To further complicate matters, I recently learned that sometimes when we think we're accessing our own past lives, we may actually be accessing the past lives of our ancestors.

And then of course there's the question about what really constitutes the "past." Time is a function of this three-dimensional world. As Adri, with some exasperation, explained to me,

ADRI: MOM YOU KNOW MOST LIVES OC-CUR AT THE SAME TIME AT THE SAME TIME IS HARD TO IMAGINE SIMULTANEITY OF TIME IS WHAT I SPEAK OF WHAT I KNOW

Still, as far as I'm concerned, it's really irrelevant whether you believe you're accessing your own past life, an ancestor's past life, an archetypal memory, or your imagination. The whole point of Dead Therapy, and the only reason to do it, is to grow and to heal. There are some people who access past lives in great detail, describing historically verifiable events and surroundings. For myself, though, and for many others Dead Therapy offers us glimpses of who we have always been, and pieces of the larger pattern in which we've played a part. By concentrating on these glimpses, and not just dismissing them as imagination, a story or a theme begins to evolve. If you follow the thread long enough, it leads you clearly and powerfully to the lesson.

There is always a current healing purpose for remembering a particular past lifetime. And when one begins to understand that some of the issues of this life might have more to do with past-life baggage than present, or with long-ingrained habits and patterns of behavior, one's perspective can change dramatically. The goal of Dead Therapy is to identify and deal with each issue appropriately, thus releasing yourself from its influence, not only in this lifetime but for lifetimes to come.

In the fall of 1991 I had started doing some spiritual and psychotherapeutic work with Robin Casarjian, a friend of

Joan's. Though we didn't set out to do Dead Therapy, sometimes that's what happened. I had glimpses into several past lives where I was not able to "speak up," or to claim and hold my own place in the world. I acquiesced out of fear and cowardice and a need to keep the peace. It became clear to me that those lives were deeply related to my current life issues about learning to speak and live my truth and not, as Adri pointed out, allow people to "walk all over me."

I remember one session in particular that was extremely interesting, but so strange that I buried the memory for a long time. That day, as usual, I lay on a mat on the floor. Robin sat beside me, ready to guide me through the process and take notes on what I said. In a visualization that started at my feet, she took me through my whole body, asking me to relax each part as we came to it. When she got to my heart, my right ear suddenly began to itch, and although I can usually ignore such things, the itch was so violent that I had to scratch it immediately. Less than a minute later, as she continued to speak, the same ear got very hot and began to throb painfully. Not wanting to interrupt Robin, and thinking that it would just go away, I kept quiet and tried to ignore the sensations and the accompanying sense of what it was about. I really couldn't see what good could come of exploring this particular event. However, by the time she got to the crown of my head, the ear was so hot and it hurt so much that I knew that unless I wanted to walk away from whatever the lesson might be, I had to talk about the images I was seeing.

I told Robin that I was experiencing being a soldier in what seemed like Christ's time. We were in the garden at Gethsemane, and that ear had just been struck with something sharp by Peter, one of Jesus' disciples. As I talked, I sensed the intense fear that my soldier self must have been feeling. He'd been drawn to listen to the teachings of Jesus, but he was terrified. He knew that if he were caught listening, he'd be in mortal danger. So he chose just to follow the crowd and ignore his own inner promptings. He was shocked when Peter cut his ear. Shocked that anyone would have the courage and intensity of faith to strike out at someone like him, someone in power.

Although I didn't experience exactly what happened after that, my sense was that because of the wound to his ear my soldier self was excused from participating in the crucifixion. I also felt that although he'd been angry with Peter at first, at some point his anger dissolved into intense shame. I'm not sure what my soldier self understood at the time. But in this replay I understood what a great favor Peter had done the soldier by striking him and thus saving him from being part of what was to come. My sense is that for the remainder of his life the soldier started to question his beliefs. Finally he did come to believe in the teachings of Jesus, although he didn't undergo a major transformation.

While I was experiencing the soldier's emotions, at the same time I was also experiencing my own intense sense of shame and self-loathing. I feel as though I've spent a lot of time atoning and seeking my own forgiveness for my inability to follow my truth. I could feel the urgency of this message for my life today. I know I'm at a crossroads. Once again I'm being offered an opportunity to listen, to stand up for my beliefs, to uphold the truth. I can act on this, or I can cower and hide.

As I lay there, just letting all these thoughts and feelings wash over me, I suddenly felt Adri's presence around me. Then I could see her in front of me. As she looked deeply into my eyes, I looked into hers and I saw and felt in them the purest quality of truth and compassion. At the same time, I felt a healing energy emanate from her and envelop my ear.

I came out of that meditation feeling intensely grateful. But strangely my ear continued to feel hot. I showed it to Robin, and she said that it was bright red. Then she touched it and said that it was hot. Yet while I was in awe of this powerful, palpable message of love, forgiveness, courage, and humility, at the same time I couldn't quite believe the whole thing. Even though I'd felt strongly that I'd recognized the Peter from that lifetime as my brother, Jamie, in this one, the whole thing was just so beyond my previous experience. I thought about all this a lot, and the sensations reverberated within me for a long time, but I never quite dared to tell anyone about it until much later.

Adri has talked about some pretty strange past-life experiences of her own. I asked her if she could elaborate a little bit on the Cleopatra "curse" and any effects it may still have on her present life.

KRISTI: Adri, can you confirm you had a "curse" on you?

ADRI: YES

KRISTI: What is a curse?

ADRI: SOMETHING YOU NOT SEE

KRISTI: Can you explain anything about a curse?

ADRI: TOO TERRIBLE TO TALK ABOUT

We didn't talk about it anymore—then. But a couple of months later I asked her if she had anything to add.

KRISTI: When I first asked why you had a curse on you, you said it was because "I am way." What did you mean by that?

ADRI: I DID HAVE SAME CLEOPATRA CURSE THAT I SAID BEFORE BUT THE LOUSY WAY DOES NOT TELL WHAT I MEAN

KRISTI: Do you mean that you didn't express yourself as well as you wanted to then?

ADRI: RIGHT

KRISTI: Would you like to clarify it now?

ADRI: THE CURSE IS BECAUSE I RESPONSIBLE FOR SO MANY THINGS! MANY THINGS THAT

ONLY SPIRITUALLY RESONANT SHOULD DO   I
SPIRITUAL PERSON SO I EDUCATE OTHERS
SPIRITUALLY   CLEOPATRA OUSTED ME FOR
THAT!

KRISTI: And she put a curse on you when she ousted
you?

ADRI: YES

KRISTI: And you have carried that curse from that
time?

ADRI: YES

KRISTI: And what's been the effects of that curse?

ADRI: NOT NOW!

I found Adri's comments on her past life as Jesus' disciple John so hard to fathom that I was afraid even to question her for some time. However, in the interest of truth,
honesty, and forthrightness, in October 1992 I summoned
the courage to ask her about this.

KRISTI: Adri, what did you mean when you said "I
not human"?

ADRI: I NOT HUMAN   I NOT LIVE IN THIS
WORLD   I NOT ENJOYED LIFE IN THIS TIME

KRISTI: This has been a really difficult life for you.
What did you mean, Adri, about taking the "cup of
blood because I was your disciple John"? Did you mean
it metaphorically, or is it a memory from the collective
unconscious, or are you saying you actually were a
disciple?

ADRI: NOT EASY TO EXPLAIN

I tried again a couple of months later.

KRISTI: Adri, this passage where you say: "I took the
cup of blood because I was your disciple John" is hard
for me to understand. It seems to me that you're referring to the Communion process here—the Body of
Christ and the Blood of Christ. But what are you really
saying?

ADRI: REALLY IMPORTANT

Kristi: Can you talk about what you meant?

Adri: TRUTH IS WHAT THIS BOOK IS ABOUT SO PEOPLE MUST KNOW I THINK I WAS JOHN THE DISCIPLE, THE DISCIPLE ANGERED INSIDE BY OTHERS LACKING FAITH IN JESUS   I, JOHN, TOLD JESUS I WOULD RETURN TO BUILD FAITH IN JESUS' WORLD   I TELL PEOPLE THIS SCARY TRUTH BECAUSE I LEAD TRUTH TO GOD

Kristi: Adri, you say "I think I was John the disciple." Why do you say, "I think"?

Adri: I ONLY SAY THAT WAY TO SAVE PEOPLE PAIN

Kristi: Why would that save people pain?

Adri: I SAID THINK BECAUSE PEOPLE WHO WILL BE CAUSED PAIN BY READING "I WAS JOHN" WANT WAY TO NOT ALWAYS QUICKLY CHANGE THEIR BELIEFS

Kristi: You said it that way to give people some time, some slack, so to speak?

Adri: YES

I guess she was talking about people like me. In spite of her words, her truth, I still had trouble accepting the idea—even though Tom also told me she'd been a disciple. More recently another renowned channeler, who knew nothing about Adri, told me that she was a teacher, and added that she'd "walked with one of the greatest teachers who ever lived on this earth."

Almost all of the lessons I've learned through meditation and dreams have been positive. I've felt, and continue to feel, very loved and protected as I venture into these new and different life spaces. One night, however, having gone to bed feeling very unsettled, I had an encounter with what Adri might call the dark forces. I woke up with a start at exactly two-thirty in the morning, having just experienced a very strange phenomenon.

While I was sleeping, but not consciously dreaming, a man suddenly *walked* into my head. He was short and stocky with brownish gray hair in crew-cut style. I woke myself up, shook him from my consciousness, and promptly went back to sleep. Almost immediately he reappeared, and once again I woke myself up. I didn't have a very good feeling about this man, but it wasn't a horrible sense either. If he'd been able to get into my head, I reasoned, he must be all right, and I fell back to sleep.

Within moments I heard a telephone ring in my head, and the word *telephoning* flashed through my mind. As I woke up, it occurred to me that perhaps this persistence could be related to Ben's trying to "telephone" me during his usual two-thirty A.M. meditation. I tried to meditate, but I couldn't focus, and eventually just fell asleep again. Almost immediately the man reappeared.

In my dream state I knew Rodrigo was in the next room reading, so I decided to go find him. As I stepped out into the hall, it was suddenly transformed into a terrible maze. I was trying to find my way out when I was forcefully jerked out of the maze by the man in my head, who then began to whirl me about my bedroom. Hurtling past blurred glimpses of my wallpaper, curtains, and bed, I was very conscious of where I was and what was happening to me. But I couldn't find a way to slow myself down or make him stop. Finally, after what seemed like a very long time, I woke up. At first I was really frightened by the experience. But when I replayed it in my mind, I realized that there was nothing really so horrible about it. Rather it was simply beyond my experience. I decided that I would just have to stay up for the rest of the night.

All this may sound bizarre, but many people who are on a spiritual quest at some point encounter negative sensations, entities, forces—whatever you want to call them. I was actually pretty relieved to find that in my case at least, this guy seemed more of an irritant, a pest, than an evil force.

In the morning I talked to Adri about it.

KRISTI: Adri, do you know the man who walked into my head?

ADRI: YES

KRISTI: Was he from the dark forces?

ADRI: YES YOU YET NOT EDUCATED FOR THIS

KRISTI: How could this man have come in?

ADRI: BECAUSE YOU ALLOWED HIM

KRISTI: Do you mean I was in a vulnerable state and my energy was low?

ADRI: YES

KRISTI: Do you know his name?

ADRI: YES SERAC

I guess he was real to both of us.

KRISTI: I couldn't figure out what to do. What could I have done?

ADRI: YOU MUST TELL SERAC TO TAKE YOU TO MOHAMMED

KRISTI: He would take me to Mohammed?

ADRI: YES

KRISTI: And Mohammed would take care of it?

ADRI: YES

KRISTI: Anything else I can do?

ADRI: YES ASK GOD TO PROTECT YOU

KRISTI: Is Serac gone now?

ADRI: YES

I got some help on this issue through my meditations too. According to Mohammed, once your own energy begins to rise, you become in a sense very noticeable. Normally, as your energy rises, so does your protection in the light, so there's no problem. Sometimes, however, if there is a sudden rise and then a drop in energy, a gap occurs, and one can encounter negative forces.

My understanding of this is that if I'd been able to confront Serac directly, I could have gotten rid of him with my own energy. But it would also have been okay to ask Serac to take me to Mohammed. He would take me, as I understand it, because *all* forces are attracted to the light. And scared as I was, I realized that this experience, like every other one I've had, was for my own learning, my own growth.

In the early fall Joan told me about Esalen in California's Big Sur country. Esalen has long been a retreat for anyone interested in spiritual growth. She and her husband, Miron, were due to lead a week-long seminar there in October 1991. I invited my sister, Jan, to go along with me.

It was wonderful to share in Jan's healing. And that week was particularly memorable because this was the first group of people with whom I shared Adri's story. The night before I was to speak, I was nervous and stayed up late re-reading my hundreds of pages of notes, trying to decide just how much to tell. I got up early the next morning and continued my editing right through the opening session. Just before leaving, I decided to sit quietly for a few minutes and see if I could calm myself by meditating. In those moments I received a wonderful, timeless message that has remained with me ever since: *Why do you worry so? Don't you know that this is a very old story? One that's been told thousands of times, in hundreds of different ways, to millions of people? You are simply telling it again.*

Drawing strength from those words, I presented Adri's story to the group. Everyone listened quietly as I spoke for more than two hours. Finally, time was up and I had to stop. I'd been talking just then about my walks and meditations and about experiencing so profoundly the sense of power within nature and within us.

Before anyone could even stand up to stretch, the wind, which up till this point had been nonexistent, suddenly rose up with tremendous force, howling and whipping at the windows. The sea followed suit, and waves came crashing up against the rocks beneath us. In moments the sky went from blue and sunny to black and ominous. Without thinking, I simply repeated what I'd just been saying, that within each of us lies the immense power of nature unleashed. We sat together, in silence, stunned and awed by nature's demonstration—an affirmation of an old story told anew.

Although Adri doesn't usually "toy" with her own abilities, she has occasionally shown us that she is not only telepathic but also telekinetic. Late one afternoon, after we'd finished an FC conversation, Rodrigo took Adri to the bathroom to help her shower.

As I was about to put the Canon away, intending to paste up Adri's transcript later, Brie came into the room and asked me if she could type her name on Adri's machine. I said okay and watched over her shoulder as she typed out "BRIE." Then she left, and I went to check on Adri.

A few minutes later I returned, intending to collect the tape and put away the Canon. But just as I was about to rip the tape off, I glanced down and stopped short. The last person to type on the machine had been Brie, and I had watched as she typed her name and then left the room. But now, looking at the tape, I saw that the name "BRIE" was followed by the words "YOU TESTING ME."

How did those words get on that tape? Those were Adri's words. I was flabbergasted. Had I made a mistake? Had Adri typed after Brie? She couldn't have, because she was still in the shower. I examined the tape several times, turning it over, trying to figure out this impossible event.

There was Adri's initial conversation, then Brie's name, and then these new words. And there was no way that Brie could have typed them even if she'd been around, because *Brie* is the only word she knows how to spell. No one else had come into the room at all.

The only explanation was that somehow Adri had typed those letters without physically making the movements. But that was an impossible explanation. I decided to mull it over a while before asking Adri about it. The next day I told her that something very odd had happened and described the mysterious appearance of the words.

KRISTI: Adri, how did those words get there? Did you type them?

ADRI: NO

KRISTI: Are you somehow responsible for those words?

ADRI: YES NOT TYPING

KRISTI: Who typed them?

ADRI: NOBODY

KRISTI: Did you "type" them without using your fingers?

ADRI: YES

KRISTI: Adri, can you move objects and do things from a distance?

ADRI: YES

KRISTI: Would you demonstrate?

ADRI: NO

She was smiling. I'd been astonished by her demonstration, but not really surprised that she wouldn't repeat it. Adri takes her role and purpose in the world seriously. And from what I understand, when one has these skills, they're not to be used for game playing. They are tools for healing. Adri had already stretched the rules a bit.

A couple of weeks later I experienced a similar phenomenon with her. We were sitting in her room on her bed and she was on my lap. Adri loves the radio, and we had two radios plugged in at her feet playing different music from different stations. It was distracting and noisy, so without asking her, I reached down and turned off one of the radios.

A few seconds later that radio turned back on. I thought I was hearing things. I bent over and looked at the radio. The switch was now flipped back to the "on" position. This had all taken place in less than a minute, and I'd been there the whole time, with Adri in my lap.

"Adri," I said, startled, "did you turn that radio on without touching it?" She just started to laugh.

My brother, Jamie, experienced two other similar incidents. Once, after he'd been playing and talking with Adri, he was on his way upstairs carrying an electric typewriter. Naturally it wasn't plugged in—but suddenly it began to type. The roller moved back and forth across the page a few times and then stopped.

Another time, again after Jamie had been roughhousing with Adri, he went up to his room and found her Speak and Spell toy lying on the floor of his room. Although Adri was in her own room in bed, suddenly the Speak and Spell pointer began to go slowly around on its own. No one had pulled the string. No one was even near it. The pointer went around twice and then stopped. Adri's playful streak.

While I can retell these events calmly now, all through this period I was in a constant state of turmoil. More than once I thought I must be going crazy.

What helped me get through it were the friends who surfaced in my life. First there was Joan, whom I had met just a week before Adri began to tell her spiritual story. She's been there for me ever since. Then I met Ben and Felice, whose interest and love for Adri and me really provided a haven in which we could both learn and grow. Through Joan I met Robin, whose therapeutic work with me was truly transformative. And then there was my brother, Jamie.

Shortly after Jamie started spending time with Adri, she told me that Jamie really needed to get in contact with his guides. They were waiting for his call. I kept trying to set a time to talk with him, but somehow he was always too busy. Now I think he was avoiding me. Finally, on November 1st, the night of Jamie's twenty-sixth birthday, I asked him out to dinner and brought Adri's transcripts along. We talked for hours, going over the diary line by line. That night was a turning point in Jamie's life. All his past experiences took on new meaning. He began to meditate, getting guidance and help almost immediately. Since then he has become my closest confidant. Without him I don't think I could have walked this path at all. For Adri, too, Jamie is a most beloved uncle and friend. It's been a wonderful, healing experience to see him change and grow so radically. It's also been a wonderful lesson in love and humility, as I've watched him advance far beyond me in so many ways.

Chapter 18

"A SONG OF TRUTH"

We've experienced some remarkable changes in the members of our family these last years, not the least of which has been in Rodrigo. For Christmas 1991 we all went to Sedona, Arizona, to visit my parents, who'd retired there some time ago. I decided to visit a local channeler, and Rodrigo came along. Much to his surprise, he found the session interesting and helpful. After Christmas, while the children remained in Sedona with my parents, Rodrigo and I flew to Los Angeles to see Coreece Fisher. That night, while Rodrigo and Coreece listened intently, I told Adri's story. It was a great relief to me to be able to share with Coreece Adri's thoughts on dying:

KRISTI: Adri, what happens to people when they die?

ADRI: THEY UNDERGO A LIFE PLAYBACK TO INVESTIGATE THINGS FROM THIS LIFE

KRISTI: Can you talk a little bit about the experience of death? Where do we go? How does it feel? Do we know God in death?

ADRI: DYING IS BEAUTIFUL PEACE LIGHT LOVE TRANQUIL LIFE IS NOT OVER WHEN YOU DIE IT STARTS WHEN YOU MAKE LASTING KARMIC PLAN TO RETURN GOD HELPS YOU LIKE YOUR TEACHERS DO IN SCHOOL ONLY BETTER ALL TEACHERS ARE GOD ON EARTH WE ALL TEACH! BUT GOD TEACHES BEST ESPECIALLY IN AFTERLIFE GOD IS LIGHT

KRISTI: So the experience after death is pleasurable?

ADRI: IN AFTERLIFE WE FEEL THE BEAUTY OF GOD IN LIGHT GOD IS IN YOU AS YOU KNOW I FEEL GOD IN YOUR TOUCH! SINGING TO ME A SONG OF TRUTH

KRISTI: Do we remember our connection to God when we die?

ADRI: WE KNOW ABOUT LOVE AND TRUTH NOW WE IGNORE THEM WE WILL JOIN IN THEM WHEN WE DIE

Another time I asked if she had anything more to add on this subject.

KRISTI: Adri, can you talk a bit more about the experience of death?

ADRI: GO TO HEAVEN FOR SHORT TIME TO REPLENISH SOUL AND ENERGY FOR NEXT LIFE SOUL PLANS NEXT LIFES NEEDS FOR LONGITUDINAL PLAN NEED TO GET KIDS TELLING STORY OF THEIR REMEMBRANCE OF THEIR LIFE BETWEEN LIVES

KRISTI: During that life between lives does one have awareness of earth and of the people left behind there?

ADRI: YES LIFE DOES NOT END WITHOUT HUMAN AWARENESS MUST TALLY THEM FOR GOD

KRISTI: Adri, what do you mean, "tally them"?

ADRI: GOD MUST SEE THAT YOU SUPPLY YOURSELF WITH UNDERSTANDING OF YOUR DEBTS I REMEMBER MINE BECAUSE I HAD TO DELINEATE MY PLAN IN GREAT DETAIL FOR HIM SO I COULD BE AUTISTIC

KRISTI: Does a person who has died have any influence over what happens on earth?

ADRI: NO EDUCATION IS THE ONLY INFLUENCE ON EARTH

KRISTI: What about people on earth who are visited by dead loved ones? Can people who have died make contact with those still alive?

ADRI: THAT IS EDUCATION! I COULD EDUCATE SOME BUT NEVER THE ENTIRE EARTH

KRISTI: Does the person who has died decide whether to come back and educate others?

ADRI: NO

KRISTI: Is it the responsibility of the people left on earth to ask those who have died to return?

ADRI: THAT WOULD BE IN THEIR PLAN FROM BETWEEN LIVES

KRISTI: Adri, is there anything else you could add that would help people understand this better?

ADRI: I DON'T THINK I SHOULD MAKE IT CLEAR YET

Coreece was very moved by Adri's story. However, as I finished telling it to her, I suddenly realized that this was the first time Rodrigo had ever heard the whole chronology. He was astounded.

The next morning Rodrigo and I woke up feeling very

good about the visit with Coreece and closer to each other than we had for a long time. Rodrigo asked if he could read my diary. I left it with him while I went in to take a bath. When I came out, he was sitting on the sofa looking stunned. He had the diary open to a transcript of one of my channeling sessions.

He looked at me and said, "Kristi, this isn't you. You're smart, but you're not this smart."

I took it as a superb compliment. There was so much energy in the air that morning, it was palpable. The whole room felt bathed in love and light. I told Rodrigo that I wanted to meditate by myself for a while, so he went into the bedroom to meditate too. When I finished, I went in and found him lying on the bed, dazed. He told me that his deceased mother had just been speaking with him and encouraging him to begin his own spiritual journey.

That was the beginning of Rodrigo's spiritual awakening. It marked a significant shift in the life of our whole family. Once we were back in Boston, Rodrigo started facilitating with Adri, and in the process he began to develop his own relationship with his blossoming daughter. We knew that Adri loved math and was gifted in it, and since Rodrigo also enjoyed math, it seemed a logical area of her education for them to share. Through friends of ours we heard about Mahesh Sharma, who had started the Center for the Teaching and Learning of Mathematics in Boston. Mahesh is an MIT professor and a very gifted teacher and mathematician. Besides tutoring individual students, he also teaches math teachers all over the world how to teach math.

With Rodrigo facilitating, Adri began working with Mahesh. Watching her do math was incredibly exciting. For the first time she seemed truly intellectually excited and engaged. Mahesh's depth of understanding allowed him to evaluate quickly and easily what Adri could grasp, so he could keep the pace of the work challenging. Generally he'd explain a concept once and then set up problems on the board. In about forty minutes Adri usually completed what Mahesh told us would normally be material for four lessons. In the first sessions he started with algebra, then introduced geometry, and continued on to calculus. Often Adri would simply provide the final solution rather than break the problem into steps. But then Mahesh would ask her to backtrack and describe her process. We'd usually find that Adri had used the simplest, yet most sophisticated methodology to solve a problem.

One afternoon Mahesh was working with Adri and Rodrigo, using a geometry teaching board covered with pegs. He was putting rubber bands around the pegs to make different configurations and then asking Adri to figure the area he'd enclosed. Not adept at math myself, I didn't even try to get the answer. I just watched the dance between the three of them. Mahesh kept just one step ahead of Adri, obviously delighting in her unique mathematical abilities. More than once Rodrigo was left behind, sputtering questions as he tried to catch up with the other two. At one point Mahesh put the rubber bands on the pegboard in this configuration:

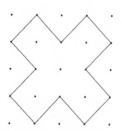

He asked Adri if she knew what the surface of that configuration was, and she immediately typed "10." When Mahesh asked Adri how she'd figured it out, she explained that the side of each square is the square root of 2. This meant each square was 2, so with five squares, the total surface would be 10. Mahesh was impressed, especially because he'd not yet taught Adri the formula that she'd just used.

When we arrived home after the session, Rodrigo was still perplexed about Adri's work, so he asked her another question about how she'd arrived at her answer. Adri answered him, but at the same time broadened the scope of the discussion. She typed:

EVERYTHING ORIGINATES FROM TRIANGLES

Rodrigo asked what she meant by that and she explained that every type of configuration can be described through triangles. Meditating on it and thinking about what she'd said, sometime later Rodrigo asked her if she'd been talking about more than the math problem.

Adri smiled and typed:

THE TRINITY

At our next math session we shared what Adri had said with Mahesh, and he confirmed that she was correct from a mathematical point of view. The concept she'd been referring to was called triangulation. Her reference to "the Trinity" also sparked a wonderful discussion about the three-in-one aspect of the deity present in every religion—including Mahesh's own Hinduism.

As we all talked, Adri became more and more excited—too excited to type accurately. Finally she just threw herself on the floor and started to cry. There was so much she wanted to say on this subject, but she couldn't get it out. Finally when she was calm enough to type, through tears she said:

I WANT TO TALK. I WANT TO TALK.

Through facilitating Adri's math lessons Rodrigo quickly became fluent with regular facilitation. This took place at a time when Adri was becoming more and more unwilling to type with me. At the time I thought it was because of my difficulties with trust. In retrospect, though, I believe her decision was sparked by her need to communicate with her father. If Adri had continued to type only with me,

Rodrigo would never have gotten the opportunity to become proficient with her.

Currently Rodrigo is by far the best facilitator Adri has ever had. Her typing with him is clearer, more accurate, and faster than it has ever been with anyone else. He facilitates her without even being able to see what she's typing. Sometimes when he doesn't have his glasses on, he asks me to read what she's said. At other times he closes his eyes or helps her type in positions where the keyboard is not visible to him.

Once Rodrigo committed himself wholeheartedly to Adri and believed in what she was saying, that was it. Unlike me he doesn't try to second-guess her all the time. As Adri succinctly put it, "DADDY HAS THE FAITH OF A BABY."

From the fall of 1991 through the spring of 1992, I was very active in the Adriana Foundation, which was now sponsoring FC workshops around the country. Although the foundation was organized in 1987 primarily as an information and advocacy support group, we hadn't been able to accomplish a lot until 1991, with the advent of Facilitated Communication. That's when I began to understand our true purpose. As a small, flexible organization, we were able to respond almost immediately to the need to disseminate information about FC. Although today we no longer offer FC workshops, all told, we sponsored more than twenty-five workshops and brought FC to thousands of people. I'm very proud of that work.

As of late the press has not been kind to Facilitated Communication. Most of the published research studies to date, including those cited in FC media coverage, have not been able to prove the validity of FC. Yet in a climate where "scientific" research is blindly accepted as the only valid and reliable measure of truth, it's wise to remember that test results are limited by our own human capacity to comprehend the phenomenon we are attempting to evaluate. If researchers do not understand all the variables of a situation, how, then, can they possibly design research to control for them? And in the case of FC, telepathy is a significant variable, one that has not been accounted for in any research design to date.

One of Adri's favorite heroes is Einstein, who was not only a great scientist but a great mystic. He once said that everything important he ever learned, he acquired through intuition. Then he'd spend hours in his laboratory figuring out how to "prove" the truth of the intuitive knowing.

Thousands of people are now communicating through FC, with many more thousands of facilitators working with them daily. Yet instead of recognizing that something genuine is happening and then going to our laboratories to figure out how to prove it, some researchers have done the reverse. They've tried to use old paradigms to measure and explain phenomena that exist outside those of old mindsets. Could Pythagoras have discovered that the earth was round by applying the same logic that those before him had used to determine that it was flat? We must change, shift, and grow to accommodate new information—that's the very nature of evolution.

Recently, in fact, several researchers in the United States and Australia, by carefully developing and employing sensitive research designs, have been able to quantitatively and qualitatively validate FC communication. Perhaps even more significantly, there is now at least one young autistic woman, from New York, who began facilitating with typical hand support and is now typing entirely independently, with no physical support at all.

Adri and I don't need a researcher to validate what we know from years of living it. And there are many thousands more like us. However, what really concerns me are the many people who may lose the opportunity to communicate because the current level of understanding has not

caught up with the reality of what's actually happening. I
look forward to the day—and it's coming soon—when autistic and other communicatively disabled people can claim
their rightful voices in the world.

And, as they do, we must expect that in the future, as in
the past, we will not always comprehend, or even like, what
some of these voices may say. Some may lie. Some may
wreak havoc in the lives of their loved ones. But the solution is not to take away the voices of our children. Rather
we need to step back ourselves and listen, to suspend our
judgments, and to refrain from drawing conclusions based
upon our own limited experiences and perceptions. We do
not know how autistic people experience this world, or
what they might be experiencing beyond it. We are navigat-
ing through new territory here, and this requires courage,
patience, strength, and daring.

In the fall of 1992, to finally complete my social-work
studies, I began a one-year practicum in an inpatient psychi-
atric unit of a Boston hospital. I was very interested in
working with people in crisis and I was also curious as to
whether there was any relationship between psychosis and
autism. And now that my practicum is over, the only thing
I'm certain these conditions have in common is that neither
is very well understood.

In one of our talks I asked Adri about the subject:

KRISTI: Adri, what do you perceive psychosis to be?

ADRI: SICKNESS OF THE SPIRIT   SICKNESS
OF THE SPIRITUAL BODIES   PSYCHOSIS IS
HEALED MOSTLY BE HEALING TOUCH NOT BY
DRUGS   MOST LIKELY TO HEAL BY TOUCH

KRISTI: Adri, what are auditory hallucinations? Do
you think they're internally or externally generated?
Or both?

ADRI: I THINK AUDITORY HALLUCINATIONS

CAN BE DEFINED BY LOOKING AT THE MES-
SAGES WE RECEIVE FROM GUIDES THAT ARE
CAUSING TOO MUCH KNOWLEDGE TO COME
IN TO SOMEONE'S HEAD BUT NOT DEFINED
FOR THE PERSON SO THEY HAVE HALLUCI-
NATION INSTEAD OF REAL EVENT LIKE WE
WOULD KNOW

KRISTI: Most hallucinations are triggered externally, then?

ADRI: YES MOST BUT NOT ALL

KRISTI: Is the problem that they can't sift through, separate out the good input from the bad? Is it that they have no way of utilizing the information they receive?

ADRI: I THINK YOU LEAVE SOMETHING OUT

KRISTI: Well, supposedly, we only use about ten percent of our brains. Is that because that's all we can handle? Are these people accessing other parts of their brains without the knowledge and understanding they need to handle the input?

ADRI: YES BUT I THINK PEOPLE COULD CLEAR IT UP PLEASURABLY IF THEY HEALED THEMSELVES WITH GOD

KRISTI: Are people who have been traumatized particularly vulnerable?

ADRI: MADE VULNERABLE ONLY TO NEGA-
TIVE INFORMATION NOT TO THEIR SOULS
SOUL IS THERE BUT OPENNESS IS PROBLEM
OPEN IN THIS LIFE BUT CLOSED IN ANOTHER
LIFE

KRISTI: Are you talking about two simultaneous life-times, or two different past lives?

ADRI: SIMULTANEITY OF TIME IS MY BELIEF
THAT HEALING CAN HELP PSYCHOTIC INDI-
VIDUALS BECAUSE IT WILL ALLOW THEIR
HEALING IN A LIFE MOST LIVES IN SAME TIME

TO OPEN TOGETHER BUT SOME PEOPLE
DON'T SO THEY BECOME PSYCHOTIC

Kristi: This is pretty complicated stuff, Adri. So in
these simultaneous lives you feel there is some discrep-
ancy, some kind of lack of fit, some discord—and this
schism perhaps opens these individuals to negative
input?

Adri: YES

Kristi: The discord creates the opportunity for the
negative to enter? What about positive auditory
hallucinations?

Adri: NEGATIVE IS DISCORD MOSTLY BE-
CAUSE IT IS GOOD SOUL FIGHTING UNOPENED
PART OF SELF

Kristi: So what needs to happen is for the unopened
parts of the self to open?

Adri: YES

Kristi: Is there a difference between someone who
appears to be psychotic because of trauma and someone
who is psychotic because of schizophrenia or dementia?

Adri: TRAUMA OPENS PRESENT LIFE IN
QUICK WAY NOT DIFFERENT

Kristi: Would the treatment be the same?

Adri: NO NEED TO BALANCE THEIR EMO-
TIONAL LIVES WITH THEIR PHYSICAL LIVES
WITH THEIR MENTAL LIVES

Kristi: Trauma victims are constricted emotionally?

Adri: YES

Kristi: Do they need to explore and express their
feelings?

Adri: NO

I was a bit nonplussed by her response. It's pretty
much standard therapeutic practice to allow trauma victims
to explore and express their feelings (once they've become
stabilized).

KRISTI: They just need to find some way to balance the emotional, physical, and mental? Could one of these ways be by exploring and expressing?

ADRI: YES

Okay, so we're not all wrong, then.

KRISTI: Can people be healed of trauma wounds?

ADRI: YES

KRISTI: Does the healing take place in the energy field of that person?

ADRI: YES

KRISTI: Adri, what would you say to people who might say that you are experiencing a psychotic break?

ADRI: PSYCHOSIS IS NOT FOR ME   IT IS MUCH TOO DIFFICULT TO HAVE   PSYCHOSIS ISN'T BAD   IF YOU QUICKLY OPEN, IT CAUSES PSYCHOSIS   JUST NEED TO CONTINUE TO HEAL

KRISTI: Anything else on this subject?

ADRI: I NOT PSYCHOTIC BECAUSE I HAVE BEEN OPEN ALL MY LIFE

KRISTI: Is autism something entirely different?

ADRI: YES

KRISTI: Do people who open very quickly and risk psychosis choose to do this, or is it karmic? Or is it perhaps some of both?

ADRI: KARMIC

KRISTI: Are we going to figure out how to help psychotic people in this lifetime?

ADRI: I HOPE SO   I THINK SO

Chapter 19

THE PLAN IS
AWESOME

Rodrigo, Adri, Seby, Brie, and I moved to Colorado in the fall of 1993. We bought a house in the mountains, and now each morning we awaken in the absolute splendor of nature.

Ever since Adri began to reveal her spiritual nature, I've longed to find a school for all the children that would support them not only academically and socially but also spiritually. So I was delighted when I learned about Waldorf schools. Based on the work of Rudolf Steiner, an Austrian scientist and mystic, the core philosophy of the schools arises out of and thoroughly supports the tenets of spirituality.

The curriculum is designed to encourage creativity, social conscience, critical-thinking skills, appreciation of and identification with nature, and curiosity about life in this world and beyond. Another feature that is particularly good for Adri is that Waldorf teachers stay with their classes from the first through eighth grades. This means Adri won't have to adjust to a new teacher every year. And as we've almost come to expect, when a request went out for a teacher for Adri's class, Charmaine, an extraordinary teacher and human being, moved from California to Colorado to answer the call.

These days Adri has been growing and developing before our very eyes. I no longer feel so anxious about her needing to communicate all the time, nor am I so consumed by the need to question every statement she makes. I've lightened up. So although she usually talks with us at least a bit every day—sometimes she's teaching, sometimes not. Even now, years after Adri began using FC, I still feel surprised and astounded by her wisdom. Occasionally she talks about our private lives, but more often her subject is the nature of God and love.

With Rodrigo, Adri usually types clearly, rapidly, and often poetically. I'm now convinced that had he been typing with her from the beginning, her earlier communications would have been much less confusing and ambiguous. But then this story might never have emerged. Things happen for a reason.

As for me, I've discovered that opening to God, or the light, or whatever you call the Source, is not just a sideline to one's regular life. Still, human beings can only advance so far, so fast. So perhaps in the initial stages of spiritual growth one begins by "toying" with it. Although I'm still very much a novice, I've come to realize that I'm no longer toying. This path has created profound and lasting shifts in my life, first in my perceptions and then in my actions. I'm no longer the same person I once was.

★ ★ ★

When I first began to feel energy, out on that morning walk, I didn't know what it was. To me energy was an abstract concept taught in science class, not a living reality. I was never taught that "I" am composed of energy or that everything that exists in our world is composed of that same energy.

Paradoxically, however, as I was becoming acquainted with energy, I began to speculate that perhaps what we call God is really energy in some kind of ultimate form. One day, with Rodrigo facilitating, I suggested that to Adri. Her reply was humbling.

ADRI: GOD IS GOD
GOD CREATED ENERGY
ENERGY IS PHYSICAL
GOD IS SPIRITUAL

KRISTI: God created energy, but isn't he also energy?

ADRI: NO SO DON'T PRAY TO ENERGY

On another day Adri once again challenged the notion that energy is all there is:

ADRI: IMAGINE A PLACE THAT IS NOT A PLACE WHERE THERE IS NO TIME WHERE THERE IS NO MASS WHERE THERE IS NO ENERGY THERE IS OF COURSE NO LIGHT AND ALSO THERE IS NO DARKNESS THERE ARE SUCH PLACES WHICH WE CAN'T CONCEIVE GOD MADE THEM ALL

Thoughts like this serve as reminders of our own limited ability to understand the complexity of life. Yet it seems that at this time in history we are being allowed and invited to see more and more of "what is." And it all seems to be unfolding, not randomly but intentionally.

As Adri has enthusiastically commented, "THE PLAN IS AWESOME."

Adri says we're all "TEACHERS, HEALERS, CREATORS," but before we can help others, we first need to heal ourselves. In Boston I was fortunate enough to meet Anamika, a wonderful teacher and energetic healer. I'll never forget my first session with her. After a few minutes of sitting quietly by myself on a small sofa across from her, I began to feel something moving in the region of my heart. The feeling intensified, and soon my whole upper body felt infused with so much energy that I began to sway from side to side. It eventually became so strong that I had to put both arms out to break the impact on either side of me. It wasn't so much frightening as strange. The energy simply took me over. After ten or fifteen minutes of these strong rhythmic motions, the energy began to subside.

When the session was finished, I felt really great, freed up in some new way. Anamika explained that the energy had been clearing out some of my old emotional blocks, particularly fear. For more than a year, each time I sat with Anamika, and sometimes spontaneously in my own meditations, my body experienced one of these physical clearings, in my heart, my limbs, or sometimes my throat and neck. Adri has commented several times on the meaning and need for healing and has sometimes offered suggestions for ways to facilitate that process:

- HEALING IS ULTIMATELY ALL SPIRITUAL   SELF-HEALING IS MOST IMPORTANT NOW   TRUTH

- VERY IMPORTANT TO KNOW YOUR PRESENT LIFE, YOUR PHYSICAL BODY, YOUR ISSUES HEALING THOUGHTS FOUND IN RELAXED BODIES

- DIDN'T REALIZE I MUST TEACH MORE ACCESS SKILLS   YOU CAN ACCESS ME BECAUSE OF YOUR HEALING TOUCH, LOVING THOUGHTS, AND RELAXED BODY   YOUR OPENNESS CHANGED THROUGH LOVING THOUGHTS PEOPLE CAN INCREASE OPENNESS BY TRYING

THESE HEALING STEPS TO OPEN YOUR BODY, YOUR MIND, YOUR SPIRIT

- YOU MUST ALL BE TOGETHER   OK TO FEAR FACING FEAR BIG   NEVER A SMALL STEP TAKEN WITH FAMILY, FRIENDS   TAKEN WITH ENERGIES FROM THE GODS   HEALING IS NOT SIMPLY LOVING

- OPEN YOURSELVES   FIND YOUR BLOCKS AND HEAL THEM   JUST FEEL COMFORTABLE GETTING COMFORTABLE   COMFORTABLE MEANS LOTS OF THINGS   HEALING MEANS LOTS OF THINGS   JUST PLEASE EMBRACE YOUR INDIVIDUAL DEFINITIONS   HEALING IS DEFINED WITHIN NOT WITHOUT   YOU ALL HEAL

- VERY IMPORTANT TO TRUST   NOT JUDGE EMPOWER BY SELF-EMPOWERMENT   YOU MODEL FOR ME   I'LL MODEL FOR YOU THAT'S SUPPORT

- LOVE IS THE GREATEST HEALING SOURCE I KNOW   I LOVE EVERYBODY   I HEAL WITH LOVE AND LIGHT THROUGH TOUCH

Adri stresses the importance of living in truth, not as an esoteric principle but as a discipline. I really didn't understand what she meant by this until she created a lesson to teach me. My brother, Jamie; Michael; and I were sitting together with Adri in August 1991, about to begin a session. Adri decided that we were not operating in a state of truth and she challenged us to recognize that and to do something about it before we started in.

Once she pointed this out to us, I knew it was true. I sensed in us all, not lies but states of incomplete truth. Still I hadn't intended to do anything about it. Why? Because the state of half-truth is a normal one for most of us. The three of us weren't harboring dark secrets or lies that threatened to destroy our relationship or our work. We were simply suppressing all the little untruths—trying to avoid any troublesome confrontations.

Jamie went first, and confronted Michael about feelings he felt Michael was denying. Then I followed suit, questioning both Jamie's and Michael's commitment to this work. Lastly, Michael talked about how hard the whole process was for him. Even though these weren't particularly significant concerns, still the difference in the room and between us after they were aired and cleared was amazing. I found myself in tears, first because I was certain, on a very deep level, that if I told all my truth, I would be abandoned—and secondly, because of course that didn't happen. That's the healing power of truth.

As Adri told us, "LOVING IS NOTHING WITHOUT TRUTH."

Although our issues and responses were different, what we learned had enormous impact for each of us. I think we really understood, for the first time, how different our lives—and the world—would be if we could all operate out of a state of truth and love. Within a loving context it becomes safe to reveal one's own truth. In retrospect we could see that suppressing truth limited our ability to love one another. And when we limit our love, we truly limit our lives. As we experienced what it was really like to be in truth, love, and alignment, we became painfully aware of just how rare such moments are. Yet it was incredibly energizing to realize that we all have the potential to live in such a state. It is within our power, each moment, to choose truth over lies and love over fear.

At another session, when Joan was also present with us, Adri once again insisted that we all come into truth before beginning:

ADRI: I DEMAND TRUTH TRUTH TRUTH
MUST BE SPOKEN HERE TRUTH FROM ALL
HERE TRUTH SPOKEN NOW TRUTH FROM
ALL TODAY

TRUTH I DEMAND HAVE TO SPEAK TRUTH
TRUTH ALL INDIVIDUALS MUST SPEAK
TRUTH NOT TOO MANY PEOPLE SPEAK
TRUTH, SO YOU MUST MODEL TRUTH I
THINK YOU HAVE THOUGHTS YOU MUST TELL
TODAY

She was right of course. So before we began, each of us
cleared and opened our hearts by sharing our truths. Again,
it was very healing for each of us individually, and very
bonding for us as a group.

Each of us has an internal monitor that registers when
we are out of truth, out of love, out of alignment. We only
have to listen to it and then respond. We get the choice. We
need to listen to our bodies, to register discomfort, anxiety,
symptoms of being out of alignment. We can then say to
ourselves, *For this moment I can either choose God and love or
I can choose "this"*—whether it be judgment or guilt or un-
truth or whatever negative perception or action we may be
nurturing. In this way we can bring ourselves back into
truth, love, and alignment.

When we fail to recognize our negative choices, or
when we recognize them but feel powerless to do anything
but let them fester, we're still making a choice—even if it's
a step backward. If we want to grow spiritually, we must
take responsibility for all our choices. As Adri has said,
"SELF-INDULGENCE MUST STOP."

We can't be both consciously self-indulging and growing
spiritually at the same time. Fortunately there's a fourth al-
ternative. All we have to do is allow ourselves to surrender
each negative feeling or thought to God. Each moment we

live is an opportunity to change and grow. But it's up to us to use that moment. Studying the past or envisioning the future may inspire us to want to change—but change itself happens only in the now.

In present-day life we worship mostly ourselves—what we know, what we do, what we produce. We reject glimpses and intuitions into our true nature, our Godselves. Because we have blocked access, we can no longer see or feel what exists beyond this most superficial level of being. And in this so-called rational world we live in, what we cannot prove, we dismiss. We refuse to recognize that our failure to "prove" is more a reflection of our own limitations than it is a reflection of our rationality. Truly we fool ourselves by calling what is irrational rational and what is rational irrational. Layers of ego have obscured us from the truth.

Massive change is coming, even occurring now on our planet. Although Adri has not wanted to dwell on the future difficulties facing humankind, she has talked about them some.

KRISTI: Adri, what changes do you anticipate?

ADRI: GREAT TROUBLE WILL BRING MEAN HUMANS TOGETHER MEAN PEOPLE WITHOUT LOVE WILL HURT OTHERS I HOPE THEY LEARN SOON

KRISTI: Adri, that seems pretty indirect. Do you want to talk more specifically about the changes you expect to happen on earth and about what will happen to people who aren't loving?

ADRI: THE WORLD WILL END IN DESTRUCTION OF PEOPLE WHO DON'T LOVE LOVE ONE ANOTHER LOVE WILL SAVE THE EARTH HATRED WILL END IT HORRIBLY

★ ★ ★

In October 1992, during the session with Joan, this subject came up again. We'd been discussing our own futures and our thoughts about the world's future. After a few minutes Adri joined us.

ADRI: TALK ABOUT THE FUTURE MORE   ITS EXCITING! BUT IMPORTANT WE TALK ABOUT BAD TOO!

KRISTI: What is the "bad" that's important to talk about?

ADRI: PEOPLE NOT LOVING PEOPLE   PEOPLE NOT TRUTHFUL   PEOPLE FIGHTING   PEOPLE NOT LOVING GOD   PEOPLE DYING   I WORRY ABOUT ALL OTHER THINGS I GET   WE HAVE TO TALK ABOUT FUTURE   REAL HARD! TALK TRUTH   NOT EASY TO TYPE THIS THOUGHT

KRISTI: What is it you're worried about?

ADRI: FUTURE IS DARK FOR MANY PEOPLE, I THINK   SOME PEOPLE MIGHT GOD SEEK OTHER PEOPLE MIGHT NOT   I SCARED FOR THEM   OTHER PEOPLE WE MUST HELP

Later, in the midst of a different discussion, Adri suddenly paused and then typed quickly:

ADRI: MICHAEL IS SEEING HORRIFIC PICTURES   DESCRIBE THE LIFE IN YOUR PICTURES

Michael admitted that he had been seeing visions of destruction. He didn't want to talk about them, but Adri insisted. Finally he described scenes of massive flooding all over the earth.

ADRI: YES   EARTHQUAKES AND RIOTS PRECIPITATE FLOODS PRECIPITATE GREATER DESTRUCTION   WE   MUST   HELP   PEOPLE   LIVE THROUGH   THE   FLOODS   I   THINK   WE   CAN

LIVE HIGH SO AVOID FLOODS RAIN IS DE-
STRUCTIVE, TERRIBLY DESTRUCTIVE   BUT
WORSE THING THAN RAIN I WANT YOU TO
TELL PEOPLE RIGHT NOW PEOPLE WILL LIS-
TEN TO OUR BEGINNING

Kristi: When do things begin to change?

Adri: SPRING [1992] BEGINNINGS OF FIRST
WARS

Kristi: Small or big wars?

Adri: SMALL FIGHTING ALL AROUND THE
WORLD

During yet another discussion Adri commented again on
this subject.

Adri: GODS WORRIED THIS WORLD IS COM-
PLETING A CYCLE OF TURMOIL KILLING AND
RIOTS AND PAIN AND SUFFERING WILL HAVE
TO OCCUR

Kristi: Is it too late to alter that course?

Adri: NO BUT PAIN IS WHAT'S GOING TO
HELP US MOVE PAST, TO GROW

Since the time Adri typed this, small wars, and even
some larger ones, have been breaking out all around the
world. And in the spring of 1993 the entire central part of
the United States was overwhelmed by massive flooding.
Adri's is just one small voice among many, warning of the
chaotic and difficult times to come as we struggle to trans-
form ourselves and our world.

Kristi: Adri, how would you describe yourself? Who
are you?

Adri: I AM ADRIANA I RUN, SWIM, JUMP,
BUT DON'T TALK I LOVE MY FAMILY LIKE
MOST GIRLS MY AGE, BUT SHARE MY LOVE

WITH THEM BY COMMUNICATION WITH TYPING I HAVE ME IN MY SOUL IN ORDER TO BRING LOVE IN MY LIFE I DO, AND I ENJOY, THINGS MOST GIRLS ENJOY I MOST ENJOY MY PLAYTIME YOU SEE, I TRULY AM TYPICAL CHILD

GOD IS TELLING ME TO LET YOU KNOW I HAVE NEEDS TOO YES TOLD TO TELL YOU MY LIMITS I NEED TO PLAY LIKE A LITTLE GIRL I NEED TO RUN, JUMP, SWIM THIS IS TOUGH FOR ME TO SAY, BUT THESE CONVER-SATIONS DIFFICULT ON MY BODY NOT MY SOUL, SPIRIT, OR HEART MY LITTLE TINY BODY MY CHILD NEEDS TO GROW HEALING SELF BY CLEARING THIS   JUST NEEDING FRIENDS LIKE GIRLFRIENDS, BOYFRIENDS, PEOPLE MY AGE I LOVE TALKING LIKE THIS, BUT I NEED FRIENDS TOO WE CAN DO THIS BUT I NEED FRIENDS

MY LIFE CAME TO ME WITH FC MY LIGHT INSIDE WAS SHARED WITH THE WORLD AFTER FC SHARING MY LIGHT IS MY MOST IMPOR-TANT LIFE'S GOAL THAT PURPOSE I CHOSE BEFORE MY LIFE HERE BEGAN I REALIZED MY TRUTH IN THIS LIFE'S TIME BECAUSE MY MOM STUCK WITH ME THROUGH HELL HEAVEN BEGAN AFTER MOM DECIDED TO HELP ME REALLY COMMUNICATE HER DECISION WAS MY RELEASE

NOW, I'M WRITING A BOOK WHEN ALL THAT WOULD HAVE BEEN EXPECTED OF ME BEFORE WOULD HAVE BEEN TO PLAY ALONE EXPECTATIONS OF ME ARE DIFFER-ENT NOW (MOM, THIS IS DIFFICULT TO DO I KEEP GETTING MUSHY I WANT TO SAY INTEL-LIGENT THINGS)

KRISTI: You do, Adri my love. You say the most intelligent things. Maybe the only intelligent things.

KRISTI: Although you are a typical child in many ways, some of your skills are not really typical for most people. Can you talk about this?

ADRI: I CAME TO THIS LIFE AS A SOUL NEARING COMPLETION I CHOSE TO RETURN AS A PERSON WITH AUTISM

KRISTI: Adri, what do you mean by "soul," and how are you "nearing completion"?

ADRI: SOUL IS A STACK OF PAST LIVES THAT IS COMPLETED THROUGH EXPERIENCE—LIFE AND SPIRITUAL EXPERIENCE PAST LIVES PROVIDE ALL SOULS WITH OPPORTUNITY TO ENZEAL THE SOUL WITH EXPERIENCE

KRISTI: What must a soul accomplish in order to be complete spiritually? What happens to completed souls? How long does the process take? Is completion inevitable?

ADRI: SOULS ACCOMPLISH LIFE AND SPIRITUAL EXPERIENCES THROUGH TIME

KRISTI: So, it's not a specific task or timetable. It will simply happen in time?

ADRI: YES

KRISTI: It's inevitable?

ADRI: NOT SURE CHECKING IN YES SOULS ALWAYS INVARIABLY LAND WITH GOD

KRISTI: It's only the amount of time that varies?

ADRI: YES ALWAYS BEGIN A SOUL'S EXPERIENCE WITH GOD

KRISTI: Do you mean that everything originates with God and returns to God?

ADRI: YES

KRISTI: Adri, how does a soul come into existence?

ADRI: UGH TOO MUCH FOR LANGUAGE

KRISTI: Okay. But once a soul does exist, how is it that one soul completes faster than another?

ADRI: SOME SOULS HAVE CHOSEN LIVES THAT ACTIVELY ALLOW THEM TO HEAL QUICKLY

KRISTI: What kind of lives actively enable people to heal and grow quickly?

ADRI: NOT TO BE JUDGED

KRISTI: From birth the process is one of healing?

ADRI: KIND OF HEALING IN MY WORDS REPRESENTS EXPERIENCE THAT IS ATTAINABLE ONLY—NOT SURE, CHECKING IN—IN PRISM YOU CALL LIFE

Afterword

Adriana is thirteen now. She's leaving childhood behind and moving into adolescence. Her face has a new wisdom about it. She wears her hair in a new style. Her eyes, though no less captivating, are quieter, more serene. Though she is still small, her muscular, lithe body seems softer, gentler somehow. She still races circles around our living room, giggling infectiously, or rocks her favorite black armchair until it almost teeters over in response to the music of Bob Marley or the *Lion King*. But now she also seems to enjoy slower, more reflective music, often just resting quietly in her chair or sprawling out on the floor, gazing out at the mountains through our big bay window. Clasping a fork or spoon, she taps intermittently on the floor or the window casement, pausing at times to press her index fingers on either spot just below her ears. Our family, she typed one day, is infused with "HIGH MOUNTAIN LOVE SYNDROME."

Adri, Seby, and Brie are usually up by six-thirty each morning. We all eat breakfast together, although Adri often bolts between bites back to her favorite living room chair. When breakfast is over, I help her to choose clothes and dress. By eight A.M., either Rodrigo or I have piled all the kids in the car and are driving down the mountain to drop the three of them off at school.

Becky, Adri's friend and facilitator, meets us in her classroom. Adri's classmates greet her with hugs, the girls sometimes combing her hair off her face or straightening her clothes for her. After the morning greeting and verse, the movements of which Adri is beginning to master, Main Lesson begins. There are sixteen children in the class. Adri and Becky sit in the last row at a table desk for two right by the door so they can leave the room without disrupting the class if Adri becomes too distracted or excited.

Since the beginning of the year, Adri has greatly improved in her ability to sit through the entire one- to one-and-a-half-hour Main Lesson, partly because the lessons are so interesting. Her class has just completed a two-week study block on ancient India; now they've moved on to botany and soon, they'll begin learning about ancient Greece. The lessons usually consist of a presentation by the teacher and a review of a beautifully rendered colored chalk map or drawing on the board, followed by a discussion and questions. Though Adri does not always participate in the discussion, she does so often enough for the class to realize that she is listening. The class is also writing book reports this year. Adri has written about Genghis Khan and Socrates so far. Her choice of topics and the interesting approach she takes to her subjects really enable her to share her thoughts and abilities.

During the math exercises, Adri is often the first to come up with the answer. And although it's not her favorite subject, she does very well in spelling. The Waldorf curriculum involves each student developing a beautiful handmade book on each of the Main Lesson subjects. Becky facilitates Adri's drawing and handwriting. Until recently, her work was often uneven with obvious marks showing where her hand jerked, but because Becky has discovered some unique ways of helping Adri, much of her work now is very fluid and beautiful. This type of activity, that relies on mental, creative, and motor faculties, has been the ideal challenge for Adri.

In order to give Adri an opportunity to express herself more fully, Charmaine, Adri's teacher, occasionally invites Rodrigo and me to come to class so he can facilitate her in a group discussion with her peers. One April morning, around Easter, we gathered in a circle for such a discussion. Though it was not initiated by Adri, the subject of reincarnation came up. While the other children were talking, Adri typed: "WE HAVE ONE LIFE . . ." I looked at her askance. "WITH MANY EPISODES."

One boy, who was new to the class, commented on a book he was reading in which the main character was telepathic. He asked me, "Does Adri understand?" I thought he was asking if she was telepathic and said she was. Looking directly at the boy, Adri typed: "HE DOESN'T BELIEVE THAT I CAN READ HIS MIND. THAT'S WHAT HE WAS THINKING."

When I read her words back to the class, the boy looked up, surprised, while the rest of the kids laughed appreciatively. Adri continued on a more serious note: "IT IS THE MIRACLE OF LIFE THAT WE JUST TAKE FOR GRANTED. ALL OF YOU CAN MOVE THINGS WITH YOUR MINDS. ALL OF YOU CAN CONTROL YOUR BODIES IN WAYS WHICH I CAN'T AND YOU FORGET WHAT A MIRACLE THAT IS."

When Adri gets home from school each day, she usually

heads straight for her favorite place by the large bay windows of our living room. Once she's had a chance to wind down, she likes to go outside and jump on the trampoline. Then it's bath and dinnertime. While we put the younger children to bed, Adri likes to hang out in her room, reading, listening to the radio, and looking out the window. "I LOVE MY VIEW," she says. "I SEE THE STARS, THE LIGHTS, THE TREES, THE MOUNTAINS. I FEEL GOD. LET'S NOT BE BLIND." Before bed Adri and I usually read and/or talk together, but often what she likes best is just to have her feet massaged.

On Thursdays, which is a half day at school, Becky sometimes takes Adri and a friend to the mall. In nice weather, Adri loves to be outside. She tramps through the yard, stopping to pick up a stick and tap on the trees. Along with Seby and Brie, she loves to ride horses and bikes and to rollerblade. In the winter, she takes skiing lessons, which she enjoys immensely. In summer, all three children spend a lot of time swimming. On the weekends, we try to have longer FC conversations with Adri. All in all, Adri seems to be, and says she is, very happy with her life these days.

Though we don't watch television or get newspapers at home, and Adri often seems out of touch not only with world events but everyday events, several times she has surprised us with her comments about the world. In April, when Ginny, our wonderful editor for this book, came out to meet and talk with us, Adri wanted to talk not so much about the book but about history in the making. With Rodrigo facilitating, she told Ginny that "IT IS A WHITE DAY. ALL DAYS WHEN LOVE SHINES ARE MY FAVORITE DAYS. TODAY IS A WHITE DAY FOR BLACK SOUTH AFRICA AND THE WORLD. NOW I WANT TO SEE GOD."

Yet, at the same time that she rejoiced for South Africa, she also lamented: "CRY FOR RWANDA," she typed.

"FOR BOSNIA. PRAY WHEN YOU CRY. PRAY FOR LOVE. PRAY FOR UNDERSTANDING. PRAY FOR TRUST. PRAY. PRAY. LOVE. LOVE."

Along with the many gifts she gives us all, she offers Rodrigo and me many ideas and recommendations aimed at improving our relationship and helping us grow spiritually. One such recommendation was truly startling. Rodrigo was in Mexico doing business. One morning he called, excited and perplexed, to tell me that during his nighttime meditation, he'd been ruminating on the nature of enlightenment—what is it? How does one achieve it?—when suddenly, Adri began speaking to him:

"IF YOU'RE LOOKING FOR ENLIGHTEN-MENT," she told him telepathically, "YOU HAVE TO READ THE BIGGEST BOOK IN THE WORLD. YOU WALK IT AND WHEN YOU'RE AT THE BEGIN-NING, YOU CAN'T SEE THE END. AND WHEN YOU GET TO THE TOP, IF YOU'VE LEARNED THE LESSONS, YOU'VE REACHED ENLIGHTENMENT."

Neither of us had any idea what she was talking about. If it truly was a message from Adri, I thought that most certainly she must have been speaking metaphorically. When Rodrigo arrived home a few days later, he was very eager to talk to Adri, so at our first opportunity, the next afternoon, we sat down with her. Without asking any questions, Adri immediately began to type:

"I VISIT YOU THREE NIGHTS AGO. YOU WERE LOOKING FOR ENLIGHTENMENT. I TALK TO YOU ABOUT A BOOK. YOU STAND AND YOU READ IT FROM LEFT TO RIGHT. IT BEGINS WITH THE EFFECTS THAT GOOD AND BAD HAVE ON YOUR LIFE. YOU CANNOT SEE THE END UNTIL YOU GET THERE AND REACH ENLIGHTENMENT. SO, YOU HAVE TO READ AND WALK THROUGH ALL THE DIFFERENT STAGES. YOU CAN'T SEE THE NEXT STAGE FROM WHERE YOU STAND."

KRISTI: Is this book metaphorical or literal?

ADRI: LITERAL

KRISTI: Is it in this dimension?

ADRI: YES JOGJAKARTA IN JAVA

I'd never heard of such a city.

ADRI: JOGJAKARTA IS A CITY IN JAVA IN INDONESIA

KRISTI: Is the book there?

ADRI: NO, NEAR THERE. THE BOOK IS WRITTEN IN STONE

KRISTI: Do people know about this book?

ADRI: YES IT'S WRITTEN IN STONE IN A GRAVE IN THE MOST SACRED TEMPLE OF BOROBUDUR

Rodrigo and I were flabbergasted.

KRISTI: Is there a reason you're telling us this now?

ADRI: DAD WANTED TO FIND TRUE EN-LIGHTENMENT SO I SHOW HIM WHERE TO FIND IT

KRISTI: Daddy should go find it?

ADRI: BOTH OF YOU

Stunned but curious, Rodrigo and I went to the library the next afternoon. Rodrigo looked up her spelling of the word *BOROBUDUR* on the Grolier computer encyclope-dia. Not only was Borobudur listed but the first line of text that came up read: "Borobudur, located about 40 km from Jogjakarta in central Java, is the ruined site of a ma-jor Buddhist monument." The text continued "... the great shrine is constructed of stone ... and consists of eight diminishing tiers of terraces ... (that) illustrate the progress of the Buddha before his enlightenment ... the upper three terraces ... represent the sphere of enlight-enment." Sometime soon, Rodrigo and I hope to make that trip.

★ ★ ★

Just as I could never have predicted the turns our lives would take to bring us to this point, I can't begin to predict what the future holds for Adri, for our family, for humanity. But when I think about all that has transpired and all that is to transpire, both the wonderful things and the difficult struggles, I am awestruck and completely filled with gratitude. As Adri reminded a group of us one day: "ONLY A STONE THAT ROLLS A LOT IS SMOOTH."

And she, of course, profoundly exemplifies that lesson. Though being autistic certainly has some advantages as she points out, it is truly a test of endurance in so many ways. Though Adri says she loves her life, she struggles all the time. I got a glimpse of the effort she expends grappling with and learning from her situation by a comment she made to us last October. "SILENCE," she told us, "GIVES ME BOTH FREEDOM AND CHAINS SO I USE SILENCE TO FREE ME FROM ITS CHAINS."

And yet, in the midst of her own suffering, she embodies and demonstrates such love, compassion, and wisdom toward others. Because of who she is, I cannot help but believe in her message of God's love, for how, but through the grace of God, could she attain and sustain that state?

As human beings on this earth, we're not just biding our time, reacting to random events. We have each chosen to be here at this time in order to learn, as individuals with individual goals, and as one body striving to fulfill our universal purpose. As Adri says, "LOVE IS THE ONLY TRULY IMPORTANT REASON FOR OUR LIVES TO EXIST."

ADRI'S PRAYER:

"GOD IS GOD.

YOU WILL SEE HIM WITHOUT SEEING HIM.

YOU WILL HEAR HIM WITHOUT HEARING
  HIM.

YOU ARE TOUCHED BY HIM WITHOUT
  BEING TOUCHED.

YOU WILL BE COMFORTED BY HIM IF YOU
  HAVE FAITH

AND SURRENDER UNCONDITIONALLY TO
  HIM.

FAITH IS NOT RATIONAL WITH OUR
  LIMITED KNOWLEDGE.

SO WHEN I LOOK OUT THIS WINDOW,

I KNOW THAT WE CANNOT EXPLAIN OUR
  EXISTENCE

OR THAT OF THE WORLD, THE UNIVERSE
  OR ANYTHING,

EXCEPT THROUGH FAITH.

I SURRENDER AND I SEE GOD,

I HEAR GOD, I FEEL TOUCHED BY GOD.

GOD IS GIVING ME COMFORT WITH HIS
  INFINITE LOVE."

Reading List

There are far too many wonderful books in far too many categories to list them all, but here are some of my personal favorites particularly related to spirituality and, to a lesser degree, autism.

Autobiographical/Personal Journey Books

Autobiography of a Yoga. Paramahansa Yogananda, Self-Realization Fellowship, 1993.
Embraced by the Light. Betty J. Eadie, Bantam, 1994.
Hidden Journey. Andrew Harvey, Henry Holt Pub., 1991.
The Invisible Way. Reshad Feild, Element Press, 1993.
Mata Amritanandamayi, A Biography. Swami Amritasvarupan-

anda, M.A. Center, 1991. (If you are interested in The Mother, her teachings are published in a series of "Awaken Children" books.)

My Baba and I. Dr. John S. Hislop, Sri Sathya Sai Books, 1985. (If you are interested in Sai Baba, there are several interesting books written about him.)

Peace Pilgrim. Ocean Tree Books, 1992.

The Reluctant Shaman. Kay Cordell Whitaker, Harper, S.F., 1991.

Sangoma. James Hall, G.P. Putnam, 1994.

The Shamanic Healer. Ikuko Osumi and Malcolm Ritchie, Healing Arts Press, 1988.

The Sorcerers' Crossing. Taisha Abelar, Viking Arkana, 1992.

Spirit Song, Phoenix Rising, Dreamwalker, Phantoms Afoot. Mary Summer Rain, Schiffer Publishing, 1980s.

Past Lives Books

Across Time and Death. Jenny Cockell, Fireside, NY, 1994.

Many Lives, Many Masters. Brian Weiss, Fireside, NY, 1988.

Other Lives, Other Selves: A Jungian Psychotherapist Discovers Past Lives. Roger Woolger, Ph.D., Bantam, 1988.

The Search for Omm Sety. Jonathan Cott, Warner, 1987.

Meditation Books

The Miracle of Mindfulness. Thich Nhat Hanh, Beacon Press, 1987.

Open Mind, Open Heart. Thomas Keating, Amity House Press, NY, 1986.

Channeled Books

Bringers of the Dawn. Barbara Marciniak, Bear & Co., 1992.
A Course in Miracles. Foundation for Inner Peace, Farmingdale, NY, 1975.
Emmanuel's Book. Compiled by Pat Rodegast and Judith Santon, Bantam, 1985.
Mary's Message to the World. Annie Kirkwood, Putnam, 1991.
The Starseed Transmissions. Ken Carey, Harper S.F., 1985.

Books and Resources on Energy Healing

Anamika. 63 Avenida Massina, Sarasota, FL (813) 349-8716.
Association for Network Chiropractic. (Has national list of approved practitioners) 444 North Main Street, Longmont, CO 80501 (303) 678-8101.
Hands of Light and Light Emerging. Barbara Brennan, Bantam, 1988, 1994.
The 12 Stages of Healing. Donald Epstein, D.C., Amber Allen & New World Pub., 1994.
Your Hands Can Heal. Ric A. Weiman, Arkana, 1992.

Spiritual Fiction

Celestine Prophecy. James Redfield, Warner, 1993.
Mutant Message. Marlo Morgan, Harper, 1994.

Personal Growth and Spirituality

Answers. Mother Meera, Meeramma Publication, 1991.
Care of the Soul. Thomas Moore, Harper, 1992.

Forgiveness, A Bold Choice for a Peaceful Heart. Robin Casarjian, Bantam, 1992.

Healing Words. Larry Dossey, M.D., Harper, 1993.

Jesus, An Interview Across Time. Andrew Hodges, M.D., Bantam, 1988.

Joel Goldsmith's Books (over 30 books). Carol Publishing.

Minding the Body, Mending the Mind. Addison Wesley, 1987; *Guilt Is the Teacher, Love Is the Lesson.* Warner, 1990; *Fire in the Soul.* Warner, 1993; *Pocketful of Miracles.* Warner, 1994; *The Power of the Mind to Heal.* Hay House, 1994. All by Joan Borysenko.

Mother of All Nations. Joan Ashton, Harper, 1989.

Quantum Healing. Deepak Chopra, Bantam, 1990.

Soul Retrieval. Sandra Ingerman, Harper, 1991.

Spiritual Emergency. Stanislav and Christina Grof, Jeremy Tarcher, 1989.

Where Two Worlds Meet. Gloria Karpinski, Ballantine, 1990.

Books and Resources on Autism and FC

Facilitated Communication Institute (Books, tapes, training on FC), Syracuse University/School of Education, 370 Huntington Hall, Syracuse, NY 13244; (315) 443-9657.

Nobody Nowhere and Somebody Somewhere. Donna Williams, Times Books, 1992.

A Letter to Readers

Dear Readers,

Though the threads are invisible, I feel deeply connected to each one of you. I know that many of you have experienced your own "miracles," and I would very much like to hear of them. If you feel so inclined, please write to Adri and me at the address given below but at the same time, please understand that we may not be able to personally respond to every letter.

To those of you who are autistic or are otherwise "handicapped," or to the parents or caretakers of such individuals, I am particularly interested in hearing of your experiences. From our research at the Adriana Foundation, we estimate that about 10 percent of our respondents experienced some kind of unusual phenomenon (telepathy, extensive knowledge, etc.) with their autistic or otherwise "handicapped" child or student. While I was active in the foundation, several teachers, program directors, and parents both in and out of the United States contacted me to see if we, too, were finding that some autistic children and adults were capable of "reading minds" and/or discussing past lives.

At the same time, I encourage you to share your stories with us. I want to also stress that since what we call "autism" is really just a description of a collection of behaviors, the possible etiologies are many. Therefore, even if we believe that "autism," like any other condition, is chosen at a soul level, the reasons for which it is chosen can and will vary significantly. Every autistic person is not here for the same purpose or to learn the same lessons, and our perspective here on earth does not enable us to fully understand our own circumstances, much less those of others. Therefore, we would do autistic people a great disservice were we to impose on them any kind of expectations having to do with paranormal abilities or spiritual wisdom. Each of us is unique, following our own path at our own pace.

Sitting in meditation with my brother Jamie over this last year, he began to share with me the "lessons" he was receiving through inner communication. One of these, "A LESSON IN FREEING THE MIND," really helped me to understand perspective, and I would like to share with you an excerpt from that lesson. As Jamie spoke, I transcribed his words:

I'm seeing a vision. I'm going back in time. I'm sitting on a low, stone bench by a small pond. It's part of a temple garden. The temple itself stands a short distance behind us. It's a Buddhist temple in Asia, central or southern China. The pond is stocked with large gold and white carp, typical of decorative garden ponds. The Asian Master is sitting with me. He is old and wise. He begins to talk about consciousness.

★ ★ ★

See the fish as he is. Does the fish know he is a fish? Is he aware of that which he is? Is he aware of the world that extends beyond the boundaries of his small pond? To him it may seem that the idea of something beyond his pond is a foolish notion, for he has experienced his pond fully, swum to all corners. For him, he has proven unequivocally that this is the world. This pond is all that exists and he is a part of it.

But you and I are sitting on this bench and we see this fish from another vantage, do we not? And we may conclude that this fish is a bit naive, simple in his assumptions, for we know the world expands much beyond his little pond. It includes many different terrains, many different gardens, and many different species. But how can you tell the fish that this is so? Will he listen?

Well, a fish such as this one needs to learn on his own. He needs to see and experience the boundaries for himself. And so the appropriate wisdom to share with this fish would be to ask him to just consider entertaining the possibility of an existence beyond his preconceived boundaries. From our vantage point, the fish is living an illusion but he sees it as reality. So our role, in order to help the fish, would be to help him to look within himself to find the reality of his existence, his place in creation.

We're getting up, going to take a walk down a small path by the temple. A lot of the teachings of the temple were conducted on impromptu walks such as this one. I like walking in this place. I'm very happy here. We're toward the far end of the pond and we're stopping here. There's a frog on a large lily pad. He jumps to the bank and sits there content. Master continues . . .

See the frog as he begins to explore life outside the pond. He has taken the first steps toward the realization of the world that exists beyond himself. His growth has surpassed that of the fish, for his reality, his consciousness, has expanded beyond the self-imposed boundaries of the fish's. The frog is exploring the edge of the pond. He is journeying into areas that constitute a new and different type of reality, more solid and stable, able to support other kinds of creatures and beings. And out of his exploration, he gains a new understanding of reality for, now, having seen much more of what exists, he can look back and see that his pond is but a fleeting reality with neither substance nor solidity.

The pond is a reality that ebbs and flows, dynamic and ever changing. But when the frog jumps out of his pond onto solid earth, he'll find a reality that is substantially different, one that does not shift but provides a stable footing. On this new ground he may feel more balanced, more secure, more content. But still, he does not know all.

We walk farther, stopping at a marshy area. I'm really enjoying this. There's a large white crane standing in the water.

See the crane standing in the pond there. Now he's a different creature altogether, for though he stands in the water, he has a completely different concept of both the water and the land, for he is a beast of the skies. He has traveled in realms that go far beyond either the fish's world of the pond or the frog's world of pond and earth. He exists in a world devoid of substance and solidity, yet it surrounds all else, a world composed of an abundance of tiny particles; one that carries the illusion of nothing yet contains everything.

Although the crane cannot see them himself, I'm seeing the tiny particles in the air that support his flight.

Now this crane still spends a great deal of time in the pond for, at this point in his life, it's a natural environment. But the crane is different because he knows about life beyond the pond. He has a much deeper understanding of the real world. He knows the pond, the earth, and beyond that, the sky. And because he can travel in each, he experiences a wider awareness and greater comprehension of the absolute truth. To the crane we have nothing to teach, for he has seen reality. He has gained an appreciation and an understanding of his place and role in the world.

So, we may see the fish as a creature of the mind, for he has created his own illusion of the world and he lives in that dream. We may see the frog as going beyond the boundaries of the mind so that he begins to see his being and his connection to all that is around him. He has glimpsed an expanded world yet he still does not have the complete picture. The frog represents man on the spiritual path as he begins to explore the world beyond his illusions. The crane serves as a Spirit. His expanded consciousness enables him to naturally live in all three worlds but also to have the proper perspective on them all.

On this day, let your spirit soar like a dove. Let it feel the warmth of the sun on its wings and the lightness of the wind through its feathers. Let it soar high and free and let no one interfere with its travels. Let others see its beauty in flight and may they, too, fly up and celebrate their spiritual freedom. God's blessings to our spirits on this day, and may we all find the freedom which we seek.

Blessings,
Kristi and Adri

You can write us at:
Kristi Jorde and Adriana Rocha
Box 1166
Westminster, CO 80030

ABOUT THE AUTHOR

KRISTI JORDE is married and lives on a ranch in Colorado with her husband and their three children. A graduate of Stanford University, she also holds a master's in social work from Boston College. She has founded and directed two foundations: K.I.D.S. (Kids in Disadvantaged Situations), formed to provide housing, advocacy, and educational support to welfare mothers struggling to become self-sufficient; and the Adriana Foundation, a national resource center for autistic people and their parents. She has spoken around the country at FC conferences, and she and Adri have appeared on national television. She spends the rest of her time parenting, hiking, writing, pursuing friendships, exploring areas of growth and healing, and, at Adri's prodding, jumping on the trampoline.

ADRIANA ROCHA is thirteen years old. She is one of sixteen children in a regular classroom (along with her facilitator) and the only autistic child in her school. Adri is very athletic and loves to swim, ride horses, rollerblade, ski, and jump on the trampoline with her sister and brother. She also enjoys reading and listening to loud music, anything from Bob Marley to *The Lion King* soundtrack. Finally Adri is, as she claims we all are, ultimately "a teacher, a healer, and a creator."

INDEPENDENCE CAMP

The Adriana Foundation wants to start an integrated summer camp for autistic teens (twelve to twenty) and their nonautistic peers. The focus of the camp would be on personal development and gaining independence skills. Recreational activities would include swimming, horseback riding, rollerblading, backpacking, biking, rafting, boating, gymnastics, and whatever else would be of interest to the campers. Activities might also include some academic development, perhaps focusing on one subject of interest each month. Survival skills would be part of our experience, and we'd try to create plenty of opportunities to develop social skills while having fun through dances and the like.

For autistic people, facilitated communication would be the main mode of communication. Those who didn't know how to facilitate would be taught. Nonautistic peers would be taught to be facilitators. Learning to facilitate with a number of different people and, if appropriate, learning to fade back on the facilitation, would be the focus for FC development. There would also be opportunities for creative expression through writing, dance and movement, and art.

We might also include forms of body and energy work, like cranial sacral work, network chiropractic, therapeutic touch, and/or sensory integration. And, of course, though there would be no religious affiliation, there would be acknowledgment and opportunities for all to discuss and practice their own form of worship and spirituality.

For more information, please write to us at:

INDEPENDENCE CAMP
Adriana Foundation
Box 1166
Westminster, CO 80030